*O*berlin
*H*istory

This drawing depicts the Oberlin Stone Age, which lasted for a quarter-century after 1885. Included in the montage are the towers of the College Chapel, Council Hall, and Talcott Hall; the entry of Spear Library (later Spear Laboratory); the tower and entry of Baldwin Cottage; the tower of Warner Hall; and the tower and entry of Peters Hall. Courtesy of Oberlin College Archives.

*O*berlin *H*istory

ESSAYS AND IMPRESSIONS

GEOFFREY BLODGETT

Oberlin College
Oberlin, Ohio

© 2006 by The Kent State University Press, Kent, Ohio 44242
All rights reserved
Manufactured in the United States of America

10 09 08 07 06   5 4 3 2 1

Library of Congress Cataloging-in-Publication Data

Blodgett, Geoffrey.
Oberlin history : essays and impressions/Geoffrey Blodgett.
    v. cm.
Contents: Early years (1833–1860)—Myth and reality in Oberlin history (1971)—
Asa Mahan at Oberlin : the pitfalls of perfection (1984)—Father Finney's church
(1997)—Finney's Oberlin (1975)—Oberlin and Harpers Ferry (1972)—Oberlin
starts the Civil War (1990)—Spiced wine : an Oberlin scandal of 1862 (1968)—
Warfare between science and religion (1999)—Oberlin College architecture : a
short history (1992)—President King and Cass Gilbert: the grand collaboration
(1982)—Saving Peters Hall (1997)—A century of football, 1891–1991 (1991)—The
day Oberlin beat Michigan—or did we? (1999)—Tobacco at Oberlin : a backward
glance at moral reform (1999)—Professor Geiser's heresies (1992)—Campus life
at Oberlin, 1930–1945 (1998)—Oberlin and the G.I. Bill (1987)—Observations
on governance at Oberlin : another look at its history (1992)—Memorial minute
for Ellsworth Carlson (2000)—An apology for the 1950s (1982)—Memorial
minute for William E. Stevenson (1986)—Student opinion at Oberlin, 1936–1976
(1976)—Spreading the calm (1984)—College and commitment (1969)—The
Oberlin mock convention tradition (1992)—Recollections of the 1960s—and beyond (1992)—Oberlin and the Kent State murders (1998)—He held his ground :
memorial minute for Robert K. Carr (1979)—The grand march of Oberlin campus plans (1995)—Memorial minute for Robert E. Neil (1991)—Memorial minute
for Barry McGill (1997)—A liberal education : how it can work (1999)—
Reflections upon retirement (2000).

Library of Congress Catalog Card Number 2006012688
British Library Cataloging-in-Publication data are available.

ISBN-13: 978-0-87338-887-0 (pbk. : alk. paper) 338.4/337
ISBN-10: 0-87338-887-9 (pbk. : alk. paper)

1. Oberlin College—History. 2. Oberlin (Ohio)—History. I. Title.
LD4168.B56   2006
378.771′23—dc22   2006012688

Contents

Later Years (1950-1990)

Foreword

Geoffrey Blodgett was a much-loved professor and a distinguished scholar of American history who dedicated his entire academic career to Oberlin College and its students. This anthology, which he compiled near the end of his life, pulls together more than thirty of the many articles and essays he published on the subject of Oberlin's history.

Professor Blodgett produced these works for an Oberlin audience. Although several pieces included here were originally published in scholarly journals, most appeared in the *Oberlin Alumni Magazine,* the *Oberlin College Observer* (for many years the college's faculty and staff newspaper), or the local town newspaper, the *Oberlin News-Tribune.* These works of history are far more sophisticated, however, than most local and institutional history; they are grounded in wide-ranging historical scholarship, and they offer nuanced interpretations of the college's history. They are also elegantly written. Taken together, they reveal a master historian at work.

Geoffrey Blodgett's relationship to Oberlin and its history was at once highly professional and deeply personal. He arrived at Oberlin as a freshman in the fall of 1949, joining the class of 1953, which was a remarkable assembly of young men and women. Many of them went on to realize careers of considerable distinction, including four (a record number) who became Oberlin professors: Norman Craig, Biggs Professor of Chemistry; Herbert Henke, Professor of Eurhythmics and Music Education; Robert Neil, Professor of History and a distinguished historian of modern European history; and Geoffrey Blodgett, Danforth Professor of History.

As an Oberlin student Jeff excelled at both academics and athletics. Although he had never played football before, he decided within days of his arrival on campus to go out for the Oberlin team. Jeff's undergraduate years were the glory days of Oberlin football, and there were so many young men who signed up for the sport in the fall of 1949 that there were not enough game jerseys for them. His Oberlin football experience resulted in a lifelong love of the game, and for the rest of his life he was the most stalwart defender of the Oberlin football program.

Jeff came to Oberlin expecting to prepare for a career in journalism or law. These plans may well explain why he chose history as his major. As an undergraduate, however, he discovered the joys of reading and writing history. His Oberlin faculty mentor was Robert Fletcher, a member of the Oberlin class of 1921, a great teacher, and a highly accomplished scholar. Professor Fletcher no doubt encouraged his unusually gifted student to consider a doctorate in history and an academic career.

Following a short stint in the United States navy, Jeff and his wife, Jane Taggart Blodgett, who graduated from Oberlin in 1954, settled in Cambridge, Massachusetts, where Jeff matriculated in Harvard's doctoral program in history. There he studied with Frank Freidel, one of the great scholars of American political history.

In the 1950s most historians of the United States studied American politics, but several members of Harvard's history faculty, most notably Arthur Schlesinger, Jr., were pioneering ways to integrate an understanding of American politics with American social, cultural, and intellectual life. This new emphasis on American culture and ideas, broadly considered, helped shape Jeff Blodgett's career and thinking as a historian. His doctoral dissertation on the Massachusetts Mugwumps marks his first and highly successful attempt to put American politics into a larger social, economic, and intellectual context. Mugwumps were men who had deserted the Republican Party to become independent voters who would support the best candidate rather than a political party. They saw themselves as men who were committed to civic duty, clean politics, and efficient, honest government. In late-nineteenth-century America, political party membership was extremely important in defining American male identity, and Mugwumps were brutally ridiculed as hopelessly ineffectual and effeminate. Jeff Blodgett was the first historian to take the Mugwumps seriously and to situate their political convictions within the framework of Mugwumps' elite class status during a time of transformative social and economic change. His dissertation turned into the beautifully written book *The Gentle Reformers*, which stands as a model of late-nineteenth-century political history and which established his reputation as an excellent historian of the Gilded Age.

In 1960, Oberlin invited Jeff Blodgett to join its history faculty. Although he would receive many offers from colleges and universities elsewhere, Professor Blodgett remained a member of the Oberlin history department for forty years. Many generations of Oberlin students remember him as a learned and engaging teacher who inspired in them a lifelong love of history. Many also credit him with inspiring them to become historians themselves. Among Oberlin faculty, Jeff was one of the first to stress the importance of independent research projects for students as a way to allow them to learn directly about researching, interpreting, and writing history. He was also a pioneer in introducing American social and cultural history to the Oberlin curriculum.

As a scholar, Jeff Blodgett continued to be interested in conservative American political reformers. He also developed a serious interest in American architecture, which culminated in his major work on Cass Gilbert, the great American architect who was responsible for many of the most distinguished and distinctive buildings on Oberlin's campus.

It was during the tumultuous years of the late 1960s and early 1970s that Jeff Blodgett turned his attention to the history of Oberlin College and its surrounding community. These years, of course, were turbulent and often difficult ones for the United States and for American campuses. Like every good historian, Jeff insisted that the past must always be understood on its own terms, but he also knew that well-researched and thoughtfully interpreted history can help a community better understand its mission and values and address its current dilemmas. One reason why Oberlinians enjoy Professor Blodgett's Oberlin essays so much is that they help us put current campus crises and conflicts into historical context.

Like his undergraduate mentor, Robert Fletcher, who wrote a magisterial two-volume history of Oberlin from its founding through the Civil War, Geoffrey Blodgett was initially drawn to Oberlin's formative years before the Civil War. Early Oberlin, especially under the leadership of Charles Finney, was the Oberlin dedicated to freeing slaves, saving souls, and perfecting human nature and institutions. But Jeff Blodgett, unlike many Oberlinians, never idealized this Oberlin.

Jeff Blodgett's first foray into Oberlin history, in 1968, was to write the first serious and extended account of the trial of Mary Edmonia Lewis, the African American and Native American student who, in 1862, was accused of poisoning two of her roommates. This article, originally published in *The Journal of Negro History*, makes clear that racial prejudice and conflict existed in early Oberlin, although Oberlinians were often silent about it.

Jeff Blodgett's work on early Oberlin suggests strongly that its first decades were no "Golden Age," despite—or perhaps because of—the first Oberlinians' faith in the possibility of human perfection and their strenuous attempts to achieve it. Early Oberlin, he makes clear, could be a very difficult and sometimes narrow-minded community, even as it worked to be inclusive of people regardless of race.

The second part of this volume covers the period from last three decades of the nineteenth century through World War II. Here, Jeff Blodgett broke ground in conceptualizing the still relatively neglected "middle years" of Oberlin's history. The tendency to focus upon the institution's early years, he believed, inclined Oberlinians to understand their college more as a "cause" than as a "college." His first aim in studying the neglected last decades of the nineteenth century was to tell the story of Oberlin's transformation from an evangelical institution into an unusually strong and ambitious secular academic institution. Not surprisingly, this transformation began with Oberlin's efforts to come to terms with Darwin and the theory of evolution. Oberlin managed to make the transition more smoothly than most American colleges. During the decades around the beginning of the twentieth century, Oberlin managed to become a secular institution without losing its social values. Jeff's essays on science and religion and on Oberlin architecture enlarge Oberlin's historical narrative and do justice to Oberlin's history as a great academic institution.

A second major theme that Jeff Blodgett explores in the "middle years" is the ways in which student values, interests, politics, and activities changed throughout the college's modern history. I believe that this topic was particularly dear to Jeff because, like all professors, he witnessed dramatic changes, particularly in the 1960s and 1970s, in student political and cultural values.

The third and last section of this anthology includes Jeff Blodgett's writings on the "later years" from the 1950s through the 1990s. These writings, by and large, are more explicitly personal. They include many eloquent and heartfelt "memorial minutes" for deceased colleagues that he originally read to Oberlin's general faculty, and they culminate with reflections upon his own retirement in 2000. These writings, too, make manifest Professor Blodgett's historical imagination, his great affection for Oberlin and its faculty and students, and his fundamental humanity.

Had Jeff lived long enough to do so, he would have produced a major interpretative essay that reflected his mature thinking about Oberlin's mission, character, and values from the 1830s to the present. Indeed, his colleagues in the history department and at least three Oberlin presidents, including myself, urged him to produce a new book-length history of the college. When it became clear that his illness would not allow him to complete such a work, he organized this compendium of subtle and sophisticated work that illuminates the history of a great college, the intellect of a gifted historian, and the character of an extraordinarily humane and gentle man.

Nancy S. Dye
Oberlin, Ohio
August 2005

Acknowledgments

Several years ago Geoffrey Blodgett gathered articles about Oberlin and its history, written during his forty-year career at Oberlin College. While college alumni and friends enjoyed reading these articles over the years in the alumni magazine and elsewhere, he wanted them preserved in book form for future generations.

I want to thank the following friends for their support and effort in bringing this collection to publication: Nancy Schrom Dye, Clayton Koppes, Al MacKay, Carol Ganzel, Molly Johnson, Roland Baumann, and Tammy Martin

Jane Blodgett

Oberlin History

Early Years (1833–1862)

CHAPTER I

Myth and Reality in Oberlin History (1971)

*H*istorians worry a lot about the difference between history and science.[1] The main difference between the two fields of study is that historians deal with phenomena of which they themselves are a part—the behavior of human beings. They find it harder therefore to achieve even an illusion of objectivity and detachment from their subject. Values, loyalties, memories, and traditions are always getting in the way. And if the historian takes a particularly tough-minded attitude toward the values and traditions of his own people or tries to clear them away to get at the hard underlying reality of things, he runs the risk of being called a debunker, a cynic, a killer of the dream. This is all the more true of historians who take on the special past of the college community of which they are a part. One finds plenty of local traditions to disturb, lots of old rocks to lift and look beneath.

There are two tempting ways to go about it. Each way has certain intellectual advantages and psychological satisfactions. Each organizes the stuff of the past so as to make it relevant to the present. And for people who are trying to prove something about the present Oberlin, both have a functional convenience, depending on what one is trying to prove. One way is the "onward and upward" approach. This approach defines the whole past of a college community as a long uphill progressive preparation for the present and the future. It sees the past as a record of successive problems that people had to solve to get closer to the present. Scattered along the way are a series of mistakes and unsolved problems that people couldn't cope with because they weren't quite as enlightened as we are now. Here and there one discovers a happy precedent (a foothill on the slope) when people seemed *almost* as enlightened as we are. In the case of Oberlin, this use of the past is especially appealing to those who want to prove their point about the local record of *in loco parentis,* or the long-standing prohibition on hard liquor, or local behavior with regard to institutional racism. For people who want to make things better than they have been, the past is mainly interesting as a record to be transcended: onward and upward.

The rival tactic is to conjure up a "Golden Age." The trick here is to discover some point in the local past when things were better than they ever were before or have been since—when the quality of life was fine; when problems were met and solved the way they always ought to be but never are anymore; when respect among all members of the community was mutual; when arrogance and deceit and evasion and other human frailties were absent from the scene. The Golden Age usually occurred quite some time ago, and it is usually beyond recapture. I suppose we all have some private version of the Golden Age to dwell on. For student radicals it might be as recent as the spring of 1970, when for a fleeting moment following the killings at Kent State, education at Oberlin achieved almost total relevance with the Liberation School. For alumni of my vintage (the Silent Fifties), it might be the time before students started growing hair, knocking the system, and treating sex as if it were legal; for the older town folk who lunch at the Inn, it might be the days when "coeds" wore shoes and the president of the college looked like Woodrow Wilson.

For those who are expected to keep track of the longer past of the college, as custodians of the local memory, the temptation is always strong to go back to the first thirty years of Oberlin's existence for a Golden Age. The advantages of this tactic are obvious. For one thing, those were the years when the twig was bent, when decisions were made that fixed the purpose and the image of the college for a century to come. For another, they were authentically exciting times—when Father Shipherd dreamed his dreams, and Charles Finney preached to packed crowds in First Church. Abolition was the cause, and to be in Oberlin was to be in the thick of great efforts to improve the human condition. Moreover, we have a magnificent record of those years in Robert Fletcher's *History of Oberlin College From Its Foundation Through the Civil War*. Fletcher spent the better part of twenty years writing about the early Oberlin, and the result is, by common consent, one of the finest college histories ever written. It is a masterpiece. Among his many other virtues, Fletcher was a splendid storyteller.

In saying something about those years myself, I'll be relying in part on Fletcher, but for the most part I've tapped other sources. While seeking my own perspective, I want to try to avoid the fallacies of both the "onward and upward" approach and the Golden Age approach. In the process I hope to cast some new light on some old myths. I am not out to destroy the myths, however. I think that local legend is a valuable part of local history. Often the myths and legends are more "real," more important, than the record of what actually happened. What people remember and believe about the past is often more crucial to their behavior than the past they don't remember. I define "myth" not as something intrinsically false, but rather as that which people believe about the past whether it is true or not.

When people rely on myth, it can sometimes seem a little cruel to expose the facts. I have recently been working on a social history of Oberlin architecture. This has involved tracing the exact history of the construction and use of certain old houses in which famous people once lived or where important events took place. Now among the more celebrated events in the local legend are the tales of the Underground Railroad and Oberlin's exploits in helping fugitive slaves to freedom. And scattered all over this town are old houses and barns that, according to the local legend, were used to hide fugitives from the prying eyes of federal authorities. Secret staircases, false walls, and hidden tunnels are in remarkable abundance. The legends are real in the sense that people believe in them, and that belief is valuable. Set back from South Professor Street behind the Conservatory parking lot is an old brick house with a wooden cupola. It once belonged to Professor James Monroe, a leader among Oberlin antislavery men in the 1850s. I have been told by people in a position to know that the narrow staircase that winds up into the cupola was used by Monroe and his friends to hide escaping slaves who were en route to Canada. The trouble is, the Monroe house was not built until the fall of 1866, a year and a half after the Civil War ended. It was built for someone else, and Monroe didn't buy it until

1870. Which is more important, legend or the facts? There are other examples of this sort of thing. During the 1971 winter term, when I was running a group project on Oberlin architecture, I thought of offering a prize for the newest house in town that was said to have harbored fugitive slaves before the Civil War. So far the prize goes to Johnson House down by Plum Creek, which was built in 1885.

The question of which is more important, legend or facts, can also be asked when the facts support the legend. Take what is perhaps the central myth of Oberlin abolitionist tradition, the Wellington Rescue of 1858. The important facts about the rescue of fugitive John Price from federal marshals and the trial of the rescuers that followed are well known and beyond dispute. The Wellington Rescue undoubtedly took place. What is interesting is the way it has been taking place ever since. The rescue was not only historically important in the 1850s—it helped humorist Petroleum V. Nasby, in considering the reasons why the Civil War broke out, to decide that "Oberlin wuz the prime cause uv all the trouble"—but it acquired enormous psychological value to later generations. The Wellington Rescue took on a glow of local legend as important in fixing Oberlin's peculiar style and self-imagery as Lexington and Concord were for New England's minuteman tradition; as the Chicago Pullman Strike of 1894 and the jailing of Eugene Debs were for the mythology of American socialism; as the refusal of Rosa Parks to give up her seat on a crowded bus in Montgomery, Alabama, was to the mystique of the civil rights movement in the late 1950s; and for that matter, as Governor George Wallace's stand at the schoolhouse door a few years later was to inspiring grass-roots resistance to racial integration.

Anyone who lived in Oberlin through the 1960s is familiar with the uses to which the Wellington Rescue was put in justifying local resistance to federal authority in connection with the antiwar movement, especially during such episodes as the capture of the navy recruiter on North Main Street in October 1967. In many ways it was the Wellington Rescue all over again, and no one was more alert to the analogy than the student resistance leaders who planned the capture. Meanwhile, over the same years the Wellington Rescue was repeatedly invoked by local civil rights leaders as a precedent for coming to the aid of American blacks. In fact the rescue was invoked so frequently that Oberlin blacks began to get a little tired of the myth—tired of white Oberlin constantly coming to their rescue. Right now the Wellington Rescue seems to be out of style with both black and white students. A few weeks ago I suggested to a white student, a disenchanted radical history major (who, incidentally, had never heard of the rescue) that she read Fletcher's chapter on it, and she came back a couple of days later and asked why those silly people thought they could accomplish anything by running all the way to Wellington—why did they think it was such a big thing? The myth is momentarily in eclipse, but I think it will survive.

The main long-term significance of the rescue—the reason why the myth has resonated as long as it has—is that it reinforced Oberlin's sense of separation from the world of orthodoxy, from official outside authority, from the accepted norms of conventional society, from the arrangements of the establishment. This has been a central theme in Oberlin's history from its beginnings to the present. Oberlin has been not merely different (every place is different); it has been *separate.* In part this view is based on the simple physical fact that Oberlin, Ohio, has always been a village—eight miles from everywhere, eight miles from conventional society, eight miles from sin. But of course it is more than that. There are lots of villages, and many of them have colleges. Oberlin's sense of separation is historically important because, paradoxically, it connects the college with one of the most vital impulses in all of American history. The founding of the Oberlin colony in 1833 was typical of a pattern that recurred among the settlers of the American continent. From the outset of settlement in the seventeenth century, groups of inspired men and women had repeatedly tried to achieve their special group aims by moving off away from the crowd. The vast continent and its receding frontier were a standing invitation to the dissatisfied, and salvation by separation became a tested tactic for those who wanted to make a better world. The first Oberlinians had something important in common with the English Puritans and Pilgrim Separatists who had settled Massachusetts Bay back in the 1620s. Their effort to launch an errand into the wilderness of the New World, to provide their fellow Englishmen with a model of pure society, was only the first in a myriad of experiments by later Americans in what might be called pilot plant reform, or reform by separate example. By the same token, the Puritan decision to found Harvard College in order to generate a supply of ministers and teachers to advance the faith would provide a model for later projects in missionary education.

Over the next two centuries the drift of population westward out of New England and across upstate New York into the Midwest was repeatedly punctuated by the efforts of small bands of dreamers and dissenters to found small, detached colonies, where they might work out their special version of the good life free from the compromises of more conventional settlements. The early decades of the nineteenth century witnessed a vivid outburst of such projects. Little utopias sprang up all over the map—socialist communes like Zoar, Ohio; millennial perfectionist communities like John Humphrey Noyes's Oneida Community in upstate New York; and transcendentalist communities like Brook Farm and Fruitlands in Massachusetts. The founding of The Church of Jesus Christ of Latter-Day Saints (Mormons) was part of this general enthusiasm. And so was the founding of Oberlin, Ohio.

Despite important differences among them, these new communities shared a common belief of the day in human perfectibility—the notion that a decisive improvement in the human condition must occur, if only the conventional standing relationships among men and women and children were changed in certain specific ways. It might be communal ownership of property; it might be a change in the sexual relation between husbands and wives; it might lie in the education of the young. Each community tried to discover the right way. Somehow the latchkey to perfection could be discovered.

Those were heady days—an exciting time for radicals and heretics and offbeat reformers to be alive. Of course there were those who watched the show with a certain skepticism, unconvinced that mankind was capable of perfection or that the millennium was at hand. The following quotation from one such sideline observer not only samples the flavor of those days, but also may remind us of comparable attitudes today toward the counterculture and the imminent greening of America:

> Foolish enough were some of the amateur philosophers who now began to paddle about infinitely in their cock-boats, and cast out their plummets to sound the bottom of things. Earnest triflers they were on subjects too vast for them: atheists on the edge of showing off their bravado, talkers but not doers; social chatters, each critical of his fellows, and all inclined to patronize the in-

comprehensible, as a visitor pats the chained house-dog. . . . A few bold thinkers were tied up into the same bundle with shallow imitators, cranks, odd sticks and originals, having one crazy notion or another. Against organized society these asserted individualism; each demanded a pedestal of his own to stand upon. Here were men, unable to make a living, who preached that taxation was a grievance, spinsters inveterate who glowed with the wrongs that women endured in wedlock, sentimental friends of humanity who at home were the hardest of all persons to live with. The cracked bell, that listened to its own tongue, was not the unfit symbol of such a reformer. He affected some striking conceit; he lived in the woods to escape society; he wore green spectacles, or a white hat, or strange garments, or long hair, or a beard untrimmed for conscience sake, or he would part his hair in the middle so as to resemble the humanized Saviour.[2]

I might add parenthetically that as far as I can tell the history of the beard in America closely follows the life cycle of nineteenth-century reform enthusiasm. Beards came into style at just about the time of Oberlin's founding. They were a highly self-conscious statement of radical rebellion among those who grew them and especially among young abolitionists. Jesus was the model; and, as expected, they caused raised eyebrows and drew expressions of distaste from bankers and merchants and other proper folks. Twenty years later beards were respectable enough that President-elect Lincoln grew one as part of his preparations for coming east to live in the White House. And twenty years after that no banker or merchant would be seen in public without a proper beard. At about this point, in the early 1880s, among bolder and more experimental young men, shaving began to be the thing to do.

But to return to early Oberlin. The college was very much a part of the Utopian perfectionist enthusiasm that swept the country in the 1830s. Oberlin's cofounder, John Jay Shipherd, came close to being a Christian communist, and as he traveled about the country signing up recruits for the Oberlin colony, he carried with him a copy of the Oberlin covenant, which each colonist was required to sign. The Oberlin covenant is a fascinating document. It has strong communal overtones, though, in the end, private property is allowed. It is very keen on plain, straight living—no smoking, no chewing, no coffee or tea; jewelry and tight dresses are explicitly renounced, as are fancy houses, furniture, and carriages. But the main thrust of the covenant is clearly toward missionary education to save a perishing world. It is primarily in the realm of educational innovation that the Oberlin colony tried to find the latchkey to perfection.

The first innovation was to make manual labor an integral part of the learning experience. In the minds of the founders this loomed larger than any other single innovation. Yet it proved to be the least successful and failed to survive more than a few years. "The manual labor department is considered indispensable to a complete education," read the first annual college report. "It meets the wants of man as a compound being, and prevents the common and amazing waste of money, time, health and life." Thus, four hours of the day of every student were to be devoted to physical labor. In the first years the experiment thrived mainly because there was so much sheer physical work to do—clearing the forest, building the houses and college halls, growing and gathering food. Students were attracted to the scheme because it helped them work their way through college. But the system fell apart sooner than anyone anticipated or desired. It proved unworkable in both economic and educational terms. Student labor was simply too expensive and inefficient. It cost more to raise crops on the college manual labor farm than it did to buy produce from local farmers. Furthermore, however beautiful in theory the idea of integrating learning and labor, in practice the two did not reinforce each other, but rather competed, to their mutual disadvantage. At the worst they were incompatible; at best, irrelevant. As President Fairchild put it, looking back on the experiment a few years later, the students simply lost interest: "To discuss first principles became their pastime. They rested on their hoes in the cornfield to look into their inner consciousness, and the manual labor cause suffered in the interests of philosophy." Little was heard from manual labor as an educational reform at Oberlin after the early 1840s.

The second major innovation at Oberlin was the idea of educating women along with men. In light of the fame and controversy that long swirled around the college for being a pioneer in coeducation, it is remarkable to discover how little discussion or debate was devoted to the subject at the outset. Although the idea is there from the beginning, it did not loom large among Oberlin's original priorities. Female education was evidently more a means to the end of producing as many Christian teachers and missionaries as possible, than a goal in itself. On the other hand, it is clear that the founders felt it very important to train the minds of those who were going to make first impressions on small children as mothers and teachers. And beyond that they felt that coeducation would reduce the follies and frivolities common to youth. When females were placed alongside males as fellow students, they were less likely to be regarded primarily as sex objects. As the *Oberlin Evangelist* put it, "The idea that the young lady is a toy or a plaything is very thoroughly exploded by the practical working of intellectual competition."[3] (That could be a sentence out of the latest *Review*, the college's student newspaper.)

What is most interesting to me about coeducation in nineteenth-century Oberlin is the odd atmosphere of conservatism that surrounded the experiment for decades. Having embarked in somewhat ad hoc fashion upon authentically radical arrangements for bringing large numbers of men and women together for educational purposes, college authorities spent the rest of the century trying to curb the most feared consequences of what they had done. One can find very little evidence of feminist militance at Oberlin before the Civil War, and when it emerged it was slapped down. After the war, when the women's suffrage movement flourished elsewhere around the country, Oberlin was strangely passive and even hostile on the subject, Lucy Stone, 1847, to the contrary notwithstanding. Moreover, recent studies in women's history have shown that when emancipated, college-educated women began to be a coherent force in American society in the late nineteenth century, providing large numbers of recruits for suffragist agitation, settlement house projects, and other reforms. They were recruited mainly out of women's colleges—Smith, Holyoke, Vassar, Bryn Mawr, and the like—rather than Oberlin. Oberlin women characteristically went into teaching and missionary work in large numbers, or in even larger numbers became the wives of teachers, preachers, and missionaries.

Perhaps part of the reason for this is that Oberlin women in their formative college years learned stern daily lessons in how to behave in the presence of men. They learned that they were expected to behave like ladies. Modesty, deference, and propriety were the lessons taught. One detects a high degree of cautious self-consciousness on the subject on all sides, and especially among college authorities in charge of the coeducational experiment. They were determined to be as respectable about it as humanly possible in order to prove the critics and skeptics wrong. When, in the early 1870s Cornell's president, Andrew Dixon White, took a deep breath and prepared to try coeducation at Cornell, he wrote to Oberlin to find out what precautions were necessary, in the way of housing, and in the teaching of certain touchy subjects like physiology and the heathen classics. Oberlin's acting president replied: "In reference to separate lodgings and special classroom arrangements for young women we should say that both are of the gravest importance. Our rule and practice has been very strict on this point." Although Oberlin wanted to avoid damaging young female minds, it seems clear that the main concern was to avoid any chance of sexual scandal breaking out to damage the college's reputation. And so throughout the first century of Oberlin's existence the college imposed on its women a comprehensive and elaborate machinery of sexual segregation that encompassed almost every part of their lives. The two exceptions were their right to sit in classrooms with men and eat at the same tables with men, the two most visible and closely supervised aspects of the academic routine. (As late as the 1890s, even the library was used on a segregated basis, with separate hours for men and women.) And although I cannot prove it, I would speculate that this great emphasis on governing the special needs of women and organizing the social life of the campus around those needs is one of the reasons why, beginning in the 1890s and continuing down to the present day, Oberlin has had much greater difficulty recruiting male students than women. The problem of male recruitment has largely transcended its historical origins, but over the past seventy years it has proved to be recurrent and durable.

The third big decision of the early years was to open college doors to blacks, a nineteenth-century open admissions policy as daring and radical for its day as any modern counterpart—possibly more so. The reasons for this decision and its consequences have been thoroughly studied and await further study. It is worth a book itself, and what follows will scarcely exhaust the subject.

The decision on blacks was only one part of the biggest and most crucial package deals in Oberlin's history. It was made by men who obviously put their pants on one leg at a time, and the deal deserves scrutiny in that

light. In 1835, two years after the founding of the college, when it was still
very hungry for students and money, had no president and few notable
teachers, and seemed on the brink of collapse, interesting things began to
happen. A rebellion broke out among the students at Lane Seminary, a
hotbed of abolitionism in Cincinnati. Their rebellion was a protest against
efforts by the Lane trustees to squelch their abolitionist activities, and they
threatened to leave the seminary. The protest was not confined to the students. Asa Mahan, a prominent and lonely antislavery voice among the
Lane trustees, had loudly dissented from the trustee action, and Professor
John Morgan, who was also opposed to slavery, had been dismissed from the
Lane faculty. At this point, Father Shipherd, Oberlin's beleaguered founder,
saw a chance to save Oberlin by inviting the Lane rebels north to enroll at
Oberlin and fortify the student body, by making Asa Mahan the president
of Oberlin and making John Morgan an Oberlin professor. Mahan and
Morgan and the rebels were receptive, but where was Shipherd going to get
the money? He went to New York City to appeal for help from two wealthy
antislavery merchant-philanthropists, Arthur and Lewis Tappan. The
Tappan brothers had meanwhile befriended the nation's foremost revival
minister, Charles G. Finney, who had settled down in New York at the end
of an exhausting run on the revival circuit. The Tappans agreed to finance
the hiring of Mahan and Morgan and six other professorships, if Finney
were also hired to head up the college theological department in which the
Lane rebels were expected to enroll. Shipherd was delighted. Though
Finney had no formal theological training, he was just the sort of star the
college needed. And the Tappans even agreed to throw in $10,000 to guar-
antee Oberlin's financial stability. But there was one catch. No one would
come to Oberlin—not Finney, or Mahan, or Morgan, or the Lane rebels,
and there would be no money from the Tappans—unless Oberlin agreed to
a policy of open admissions irrespective of color. Finney added the condition that he would not come unless the Oberlin trustees agreed to turn over
the admissions program and the entire internal management of the college
to the faculty, with no trustee interference. Finney also wanted a personal
guarantee that he would get three months off each winter for the revival circuit. Shipherd heartily agreed to all this. He admired Finney's preaching,
and, more importantly, he was a strong and eloquent believer in black admissions. But upon completing a series of whirlwind tours to set it all up,

he was dismayed to discover that the people of Oberlin were profoundly unenthusiastic about the whole idea—particularly about the admission of blacks. The townspeople were worried about what it might do to the village. The student body was hotly divided on the issue, with a clear majority (55 percent) against black admissions. The Oberlin trustees at their first meeting on the issue, a meeting filled with "rancour and malevolence," voted to table the question for further study. Some idea of the feeling on the subject may be gained from a letter to Shipherd written by the financial agent of the college:

> Can you bring into one seminary blacks and whites, male and female? . . . I do not believe it. . . . And in trying to do this you will lose the other object, nay, you lose Oberlin. For as soon as your darkies begin to come in any considerable numbers, unless they are completely separate, . . . the whites will begin to leave; and at length your institute will change color! Why not have a black institution, "dyed in the wool," and let Oberlin be? Will it not be better to avoid this collision if possible? The people and the scholars at Oberlin would say nothing about one or two, or even half a dozen blacks as members of Oberlin, but when they should become numerous the subject assumes a different shape and new importance. In my humble opinion, if you do not at least keep the blacks entirely separate, so as to veto the notion of amal- gamation, [the college] will be blown sky-high, and you will have a black establishment. . . . I do beseech you to look at this business well, and in the fear of God.[4]

These sentiments were by no means peculiar to Oberlinians. They were pervasive in white America, and I quote them mainly to indicate the force of the feeling Shipherd was up against in bringing his grand scheme to fruition. All Shipherd had to play against it were his ideals, his eloquence, and the high cards he had been dealt on his trips to Cincinnati and New York. He used them all. In a long letter to the trustees he gave them twenty good reasons to admit blacks. He saved the high cards until the end. Here is reason 18: "The men and money which would make our institution most useful cannot be obtained if we reject our colored brother. Eight professorships and $10,000 are subscribed, upon condition the Rev. C. G. Finney become Professor of Theology in our Institute; and he will not [come] unless the youth of color are received. Nor will President Mahan nor Professor Morgan serve unless this condition is complied with; and they all are the men we need, irrespective of their antislavery sentiments." And here is number 20: "I have pondered the subject well [and have decided] that if the injured brother of color, and consequently brother Finney, Mahan and Morgan, with eight professorships and $10,000, must be rejected, I must join them." This was plain enough. Shipherd was threatening to quit. Faced with the prospect of Shipherd's departure along with everything else, the trustees met again, and on a tie vote, broken by chairman John Keep, they agreed to accept the whole package—black admissions, the Lane rebels, Mahan, Morgan, Finney, Finney's insistence on faculty control of the internal affairs of the college, and the Tappan brothers' money.

This story has been told frequently and in many ways, depending on which part of the package is most important to the teller. There are four major written accounts, each of which focuses on a different aspect. For James Fairchild, the college president writing in 1883, the arrival of the Lane rebels was uppermost—they greatly enlarged the size of the college. For D. L. Leonard, a clergyman writing in 1898, the arrival of Finney and the establishment of a theological department were critical, and his chapter on the subject is titled accordingly. In 1933, a businessman named Wilbur Phillips wrote a centennial history of the Oberlin community, and he stressed the financial aspects of the bargain, which ensured the college's material survival. And Fletcher's *History*, published in 1942, is a tale told by a scholar, a college professor. His chapter is titled "The Guarantee of Academic Freedom." It has not been until recent years that the admission of blacks has emerged to dominate the tale. Each generation asks different questions of the past and comes up with different answers. And the great thing about this particular tale is that the answers are all there. I would simply add: for a visionary country preacher, Father Shipherd certainly knew how to play his cards.

One could go on and say something about the consequences of black admissions for Oberlin over the long haul and changes which occurred in local race relations among Oberlin students after the Civil War. College archivist William Bigglestone has told that story well in a recent article in the *Journal of Negro History.*[5] One might also talk about the process by which Oberlin emerged in the twentieth century as not merely a college with a radical past, but as one of the two or three best colleges in the country in terms of academic quality. That is also an important tale, and a valuable achievement—to my mind, since I am a college professor, perhaps the most valuable achievement of them all. It is, moreover, a tale surrounded with myths that badly need exploring. But I have gone on long enough. Like almost everyone else, I've been captured by the first thirty years.

CHAPTER 2

Asa Mahan at Oberlin: The Pitfalls of Perfection (1984)

On December 3, 1983, Oberlin brought its 150th anniversary to a close with a rousing celebration.[1] We gathered in the First Church Meeting House, the oldest building on the campus (built to house the sermons of Asa Mahan and Charles Finney), to hear short speeches by President S. Frederick Starr, Dean Robert Longsworth, and six other faculty members about our past and our future. Then we each ate a graham biscuit, made from the original recipe of Dr. Sylvester Graham, whose Spartan vegetarian dietary code was one of Oberlin's less successful early reforms. The biscuits were awful, but the ritual grand. The high point of the ceremony had come a little earlier, when a long-lost portrait of Asa Mahan was unveiled.[2] It was altogether appropriate that Mahan's distinguished biographer, Edward Madden '46, was there to help in the unveiling. The portrait earned a long, warm round of applause. I'm sure that Ed Madden couldn't help reflecting, as some others did, on the irony of the moment. That Oberlin should conclude its sesquicentennial with an ovation for its first president would surely have astonished those early Oberlinians who sent him on his way in 1850. Mahan left few defenders when he departed Oberlin.

Mahan and Oberlin had a falling out. I want to explain why that falling out occurred—why Oberlin indicted Asa Mahan in 1850 after receiving him

This portrait of Mahan, dated 1843, was painted while he was president.
Courtesy of the President's Photo File, Oberlin College.

so warmly fifteen years before. It is an intriguing story, and I'll try to tell it with the bark on.

Before beginning, I want to acknowledge a debt that every student of Oberlin history owes to Robert Samuel Fletcher '20. His pages are where we all start, whether we agree or disagree with his conclusions. Fletcher was

also a great classroom teacher. He turned me toward this profession thirty
years ago, and I had the luck to succeed him when he died twenty-five years
ago. He cast a long shadow, and I'm proud to stand in it today.

John Jay Shipherd's decision to found Oberlin in 1833 resonated with a
widespread urge of that day to discover the path to human perfectibility in
the American backwoods. The urge produced a wave of utopian experiments the likes of which would not be witnessed in the country again until
the 1960s.

The reasons for this outburst are complex enough to defy easy summary, but two of the most important ones can be identified. One was the
breakup of Calvinist theology and its tight interlocking assumptions about
human nature and human destiny—original sin, predestination, the salvation of the Elect, irresistible grace for the few, and eternal damnation for the
many. That iron-gray theology no longer had an appeal or made sense in an
age that rewarded people for their personal effort rather than their status
and in a society that celebrated the achievements of the self-made man. The
other cause was the spread of a commercial market economy that was re-
defining the nature of work and depersonalizing relations among people
caught up in the web of the market. To some people the market economy
was a bonanza. To others it was a living cramp.

Both of these social changes plunged many sensitive men and women
into efforts to reorganize their lives in order to fulfill themselves more perfectly and show others how to do it. The breakup of Calvinism made this
seem possible, and the constrictions of a market-oriented society made it
seem necessary. This dream of human perfectibility could motivate people
to blaze many trails. At Oberlin under Shipherd and his friends, it produced
a faith in the capacity of missionary education to promote a full emancipation from original sin—by which they meant selfishness, egotism, and
pride—and thus elevate the tone of human behavior. Oberlin's founders
judged a person by the way he or she behaved. They hoped they could teach
people to behave more perfectly, as individuals and in groups. The covenant
they signed at Shipherd's request concluded with this promise: "We will
strive to maintain deep-toned and elevated personal piety, to provoke each
other to love and good works, to live together in all things as brethren and
to glorify God in our bodies and spirits, which are His."[3] Let's see how it
worked out.

The problems they were trying to solve have not gone away. They faced a challenge that is repeatedly confronted by earnest moral reformers—how to drive toward a goal at odds with the mainstream without wounding and discrediting each other along the way. The egocentric passion of the reformer was often a greater obstacle to reform than the society in need of reforming. The salvation of the world kept getting lost in the struggle to save oneself. Oberlinians never solved that problem—before, during, or after Asa Mahan—nor have American reformers at large.

Mahan came to Oberlin two years after Shipherd. His arrival from Lane Seminary in Cincinnati was a result of that extraordinary fabric of agreements patched together by Shipherd in 1835 to ensure Oberlin's survival. He came designated as Oberlin's first president. Charles Finney came to head the theological department of the faculty and made his arrival contingent on faculty control over the internal affairs of the College.

The acceptance of Finney's tough condition—faculty control over internal affairs—is known to this day as the Finney Compact, and every Oberlin faculty member knows it by heart, or should. It would prove to be Asa Mahan's downfall at Oberlin, but for the moment, like Shipherd, Mahan was delighted with the whole bargain.

In the summer of 1835, they all arrived in Oberlin—President Mahan, Father Finney, Professor Morgan, the Lane rebels, the first black students, and the Tappans' money. Mahan moved into a brick house newly built by the college at the corner of Professor and College, and Finney moved into an identical brick house at the corner of Professor and Lorain, both looking out on Tappan Square. The faculty was expected to line up between them, a nice architectural expression of status arrangements. Mahan got an early taste of the peculiar Oberlin temper when a leading villager complained that $50 of needless luxuries had been built into the president's house. No one complained about Finney's house. Five years later Mary Mahan, the president's wife, was curtly informed by the college prudential committee that she would have to foot the bill on any home improvements she wanted for her kitchen.

But the Mahans were tough people. Their home in Cincinnati had been the target of street gangs during the Lane Seminary controversy, and, as a prominent abolitionist, Mahan knew the meaning of community persecution. In fact, I would argue that his abolitionist experience shaped his public style and behavior as president of Oberlin. Some years ago psycho-historian Silvan Tomkins, in an essay for Martin Duberman's anthology *The Antislavery Vanguard,* applied his expertise in behavioral psychology to a number of well-known abolitionists, including Mahan's acquaintances William Lloyd Garrison, James Birney, and Theodore Weld.[4] Tomkin's analysis of their behavior can be applied to Mahan as well. Like the others, Mahan came from a respected, service-oriented family of New England background. Like them, he had passed through the experience of religious conversion as a young man and thereafter remained preoccupied with personal salvation and sin, in himself and others. These concerns resonated with his attraction to the ideology of Christian perfectionism and the cause of antislavery—saving the slave and punishing the sin of the master in the name of a more perfect world.

The resonance intensified when he began to take risks for the cause in Cincinnati and met with some suffering in consequence. His commitment deepened thereafter to include increased identification with the victims of oppression, hostility toward the oppressor, and contempt for those who, not having passed through the fiery cycle of self-reinforcing commitment, remained uncommitted. Those who are not for us are against us, or, in the catchphrase of the 1960s, if you are not part of the solution, you're part of the problem.

The novelist Nathaniel Hawthorne, who watched the perfectionist reformers of his day very closely, commented shrewdly in *The Blithedale Romance* about their habit of "surrender[ing] themselves to an overruling purpose. It . . . grows incorporate with all that they think and feel, and finally converts them into little else save that one principle. . . . And the higher and purer the original object and the more unselfishly it may have been taken up, the slighter is the probability that they can be led to recognize the process by which godlike benevolence has been debased into all-devouring egotism."[5]

For all the harshness of his phraseology, Hawthorne's perception about the antebellum reform mentality provides a clue to Mahan's troubles at Oberlin. Of course, Mahan was not alone in his driving sense of purpose. The college and the village were filled with men and women, screened through the filter of Shipherd's covenant, with similar commitment to reform and alert to every faltering or wayward step of their neighbors. They created an atmosphere, in their clearing in the woods, where any disagreement over goals or tactics, end and means, was likely to escalate swiftly into fierce, abrasive moral combat. The slightest deviation could ignite it—aberration on a theological fine point, selection of a suspect textbook, a sermon that fell short in rigor or length, a fondness for salt, too many buttons on a winter coat, or a side-long glance at a pretty girl.

In this stern, aggressive atmosphere, Mahan seemed at first to thrive. His mind was razor sharp, his tongue quick and tart, his ego large and muscular, his moral integrity unquestioned, least of all by himself. Only Charles Finney rivaled him as first among equals. But as president of the college, that was all he was—first among equals. The Finney Compact, vesting the faculty with collective authority over the life of the college and reducing the president to the barest level of executive discretion, gave him no more power than his native will and intellect provided. Yet as president his strong opinion was demanded on every issue, every problem, every quarrel, every day. And he was not inclined to duck. Given the nature of the man, the job and the college, the wonder is not that Mahan finally left, but that he lasted fifteen years.

The term "Finney Compact" was not actually invented, as far as I can tell, until 1944, when college historian Robert Fletcher and a couple of colleagues used the word "compact" to describe the 1835 agreement by the board of trustees, at Finney's insistence, to commit the internal management of the college to faculty control. Oberlin faculty members have been happily using the term "Finney Compact" ever since, much to the irritation of our latter-day trustees, and occasionally our presidents and deans. Under the compact Oberlin's trustees ceded to the faculty control over the internal management of college affairs, including issues of admission. Finney's repeated insistence on this, in light of trustee recalcitrance over the admission of black students, may seem a bit strange, since Finney was decidedly unenthusiastic about "racial amalgamation" (as integration was called in those days). He may have taken his cue on the point from his patron Arthur Tappan. Tappan had told Finney, "I do not want you to spread an abolition flag, but carry out your design of receiving colored students upon the same conditions that you do white students; and see that the work be not taken out of the hands of the faculty, and spoiled by the trustees, as was the case at Lane Seminary." There was a sense in which the Finney Compact with the Oberlin trustees was also Arthur Tappan's compact with Oberlin College.

Historians, including Fletcher and Madden, are in disagreement over the merits of succeeding quarrels between Mahan and the Oberlin faculty. Both Fletcher and Madden note in passing how the Finney Compact, which made Oberlin distinctive among nineteenth-century American colleges, shifted the scales in the balance of power between president and faculty. Both then move on to other causes of the combat between them. Fletcher stresses Mahan's imperious and overbearing personality, whereas Madden emphasized Mahan's superior commitment to reform.[6] I think they are both right—that Mahan's behavior was blunt and tactless precisely because his commitments were so unguarded and intense. And I think the Finney Compact, arming the faculty with superior power, was a crucial reality determining the outcome of the combat.

It is easy to show that, from a twentieth-century perspective, Mahan's positions in succeeding quarrels were often more advanced and forward-looking than those of his Oberlin critics. Time and again he was out in front. For example, despite his reservations about William Lloyd Garrison's brand of abolitionism, Mahan defended the Garrisonians' right to a fair hearing at Oberlin, whereas the faculty cautiously resolved that their presence on the campus was "undesirable and unadvisable." The issue of free speech and an open campus was at stake here, and Mahan had the better of it. The same can be said for his stance on equal status for women. Once he had made his commitment to coeducation, he embraced the cause of female equality much more firmly than did the faculty majority. He insisted on equal diplomas for male and female graduates and defended the right of women to read their own essays at commencement—a right not granted by the faculty until long after Mahan had departed. His attitudes toward student discipline and liberal curricular reform were well in advance of his time. As Madden argues, his curricular views anticipated the famous (in some circles infamous) elective system launched by Harvard's Charles Eliot after the Civil War.

On other issues Mahan seems much more a man of his time and place when viewed through the lens of twentieth-century hindsight. He denounced the Greek and Latin classics as heathen texts and implicated himself at one point in a student book burning. Here his position differed little from that of Shipherd, or that of the trustees who voted in 1845 to "expunge from the list of books studied such portions of the heathen classics as pollute and debase the mind." Mahan was also a hearty supporter of Graham dieting at Oberlin in the late 1830s and served as president of the Oberlin Physiological Society to promote that cause. But here again he stood with the local majority—at least until 1841 when a rebellion against the Graham diet broke out among meat eaters, who denounced it as "inadequate to the demands of the human system as at present developed." Thereafter hot meat became legal again in Oberlin.

Three years later Mahan's faculty critics decided they had had enough of him. Stung by his constant criticism of their behavior and by his attacks on what he called their "lukewarm" commitment to Oberlin perfectionism, they made their first open call for his departure. But influential colleagues, including Mahan's fellow perfectionist Charles Finney—who was in a sense waiting in the wings as a presidential alternative—refused to join the attack on Mahan, and it fell apart. In 1848 his critics tried again, seizing on the always potent issue of inadequate faculty salaries. Again they failed. But on the next try, in 1850, they won Finney to their side, and that shift of support was ominous. The faculty now drew up a searing ten-count indictment of Mahan's overbearing behavior and challenged him to confess his guilt and purge his self-esteem. Mahan was trapped. After long weeks of intense negotiations, he suddenly resigned in August 1850. Gathering a small group of friends and students, he left for Cleveland to renew the cycle of commitment all over again. There he founded Cleveland University in hopes of fulfilling his educational and moral goals in a more promising environment. Eight of the first eleven graduates of his short-lived new institution were former Oberlin students who had followed their leader. In some ways it was the Lane Seminary rebellion re-enacted: commitment, risk, persecution, departure, renewed commitment. Meanwhile, back in Oberlin, no one doubted what would happen next. The faculty signed an open letter to Finney that stated, "You are our natural head and leader," and at commencement 1851 he became Oberlin's second president.

Mahan's departure from Oberlin ended the first angry episode in the college's presidential history, but it was hardly the last. At the turn of the century, the Finney Compact was formally written into the college bylaws, where it remains to this day. In 1946 and again in 1973 sharp quarrels about the internal governance of the college produced crises over the modern meaning of the compact that brought Oberlin national attention and new leaders. The crisis of 1973—the worst since 1850—moved the faculty to the brink of unionization in defense of the Finney Compact, ended the shortest and most turbulent presidency in the history of the college, and left us in a state of internal shock from which we took a decade to recover.

Critics of the Finney Compact have long argued that it has made Oberlin a graveyard for its own presidents. Friends of the compact reply that it has been central to Oberlin's twentieth-century academic distinction. One thing is sure. The spirit of the compact has always placed a premium on presidential tact, diplomacy, and self-restraint. These traits were not in great supply among nineteenth-century antebellum moral reformers. For all his eminent virtues and achievements, Asa Mahan did not often employ these traits at Oberlin. In this he was truly first among equals.

In 1844 Mahan tried to define the ideal moral reformer:

> He should never speak as one having authority. He should [always] appear as an honest, earnest inquirer in the boundless field of knowledge—an inquirer who believes he has some important trust and is anxious to present it to the world, and yet fully sensible that he may have connected with that trust some important error. . . . I fully believe that he is among the number who have gained the most complete victory "over the beast and over his image" . . . who together with the most sacred regard for truth and right, is in his own bosom, the most perfectly free from the spirit of intolerance.[7]

If Asa Mahan and his Oberlin friends and critics could have governed their behavior by that high standard, they would have been unique among the righteous moral reformers of that day, or any other. The example of their experience is a warning about what to avoid when people try to create new ideas and new institutions to improve the human situation. Their stubborn faith in its improvement can also inspire us to keep on trying ourselves.

A final footnote: early Oberlinians were not entirely unaware that human nature might be an obstacle to human perfection. They called the quirks of human nature "affections of the head" and regarded them as a puzzling mystery. In the fifth year of Asa Mahan's presidency the college appointed a special committee led by John Shipherd and Charles Finney to investigate the question, "Whether there is any local or assignable cause for the frequent occurrence of causes of . . . affection of the head among persons engaged in intensive intellectual labor."[8] Today, 144 years later, the committee has not yet filed its report, and the mystery remains unsolved.

CHAPTER 3

Father Finney's Church (1997)

$\mathcal{A}$t the northeast corner of Tappan Square in Oberlin, the orange-brick First Church Meeting House, the grandest old building in town, has now been greeting the morning sun for more than 150 years.[1] Construction of the "house," as its builders called it, got under way in the spring of 1842 and was completed in 1844 with the erection of its squat, square cupola. Seating well over one thousand worshippers, the meetinghouse would remain for years the largest religious structure in the Western Reserve. It was a community project that owed its existence to the sweat and generosity of scores of villagers and cash contributions by Oberlin friends scattered from Maine to Michigan. Its creation was also a triumph of the personal will of Oberlin's single most powerful individual, Protestant evangelist Charles Grandison Finney. Oberlin built the meetinghouse to shelter those who hearkened to Finney's word.

Finney is remembered in American religious history as the towering protagonist of a decade of intense revivalism known as the Second Great Awakening that lasted to 1835, the year he left the circuit and arrived in Oberlin. Born in Warren, Connecticut, in 1792, he was brought by his parents to Oneida County in New York's Mohawk Valley at age two. There Finney came of age, a child of the Burner-over District, so named for the blazing waves of religious passion that scorched upstate New York during the early nineteenth century. These recurring conflagrations sprang from the social and emotional turmoil that shook the district as it filled with migrating New Englanders whose Puritan religious roots pulled loose and came apart under the stress of modernizing economic change.

The completion of the Erie Canal westward from Albany to Buffalo in 1825 accelerated the pace of change. The Big Ditch pumped post-frontier commercial growth through the region. This expansion soon spilled over into the Great Lakes region and transformed northern Ohio. The peculiar rhythm of the canal economy—the sunny hustle of the summer months when it throbbed with movements and profits, followed by the long, dark stretch of wintry, indoor introspection while the canal lay frozen over—gave an edge of cyclical uncertainty to people's lives. Finney's revival sermons ministered mainly to the anxious hopes of young men and women struggling to comprehend and master the newness and save their virtue in the teeth of pulsing secular momentum.

Finney himself had been a thoroughly secular young man, beginning a career in law. One night in October 1821, he experienced a soul-transforming conversion while staring into the fire at his office in Adams, New York, and decided to abandon his law books for the Bible. When a client came by the next morning, Finney told him, "I have a retainer from the Lord Jesus Christ to plead his cause, and I cannot plead yours." After three years of informal training in the scriptures, he was ordained a Presbyterian evangelist and began staging revivals, just as the Erie Canal opened for traffic. Over the next nine years, mainly in the wintertime, he seared the canal towns of the Burned-over District from Troy to Rochester with his meetings, working huge crowds as he would a jury, with strong extemporaneous appeals.

The thrust of Finney's message was that his listeners had the God-given natural ability not only to achieve personal salvation in the afterlife but also to transcend their sinning ways and strive for perfection here and now in the lives they led from day to day. For people shaken loose from the grim Calvinistic doctrines of their elders about salvation for the few and predestined damnation for most, this Perfectionist message was welcome but demanding. You could be good, and you had better try. The orbit of Finney's preaching soon widened to include the larger seaboard cities, first Philadelphia, then Boston, and, finally, New York. There, exhausted from the circuit, he settled down momentarily under the sponsorship of Lewis and Arthur Tappan, prosperous clothing merchants and abolitionists who admired Finney's charismatic power.

It was the Tappan brothers who, in 1835, persuaded Finney to move from Manhattan to Oberlin to take charge of the theological department of the newly founded college there and train missionaries to save the raw, young West from the hell-bent sins of Andrew Jackson's America. Finney's arrival in the muddy Ohio village guaranteed Oberlin's institutional survival. Across the next three decades, the village and its college gave the evangelist a welcoming home base for his revival forays, which soon were transatlantic in their reach.

Finney left New York just as his big new church there, the Broadway Tabernacle, neared completion. The tabernacle's interior, somewhat to architect Joseph Ditto's dismay, conformed in close detail to Finney's wishes.[2] Finney was a tall, lean man with hypnotic, ice-blue eyes, aquiline features, and a penetrating tenor voice. He was keenly aware of the psychology and acoustics of large religious gatherings. He favored sermons in the round and insisted on circular seating that surrounded the pulpit and brought every listener within range of his presence and voice.

When Finney left the city, his Manhattan friends gave him a big circular tent to carry to his revival meetings in the West. That tent, pitched on Oberlin's village square, its mast streaming a long, blue banner proclaiming "Holiness to the Lord," served as the community church over the next seven summers, and it housed early college commencement services as well. But winter meetings, crammed into Oberlin Hall and later Colonial Hall, soon nurtured hopes for a larger and more permanent structure.

Finney catalyzed those hopes. In defiance of the hard times that gripped the community after the Panic of 1837 (which broke his main benefactor, Arthur Tappan), Finney gathered his Oberlin congregation on a cold February morning in 1841 and told them: "We must build a church. Now come together tomorrow at one o'clock, all of you, and we will talk this over and lay our plans, for it can be done."[3]

An inspired congregation went to work. Within two weeks the needs were defined—a brick building, plain and substantial, seventy feet wide, one hundred feet long, seating twenty-five hundred people. It would be the largest meetinghouse west of the Alleghenies.

Professional architectural talent was clearly needed for the project. Finney turned to a rich Boston builder, Willard Sears, who had succeeded the Tappan brothers as college benefactor and who was paying Finney's salary. Sears, in turn, asked Richard Bond, a prominent Boston architect with a thriving practice in northern New England, for detailed plans. In December 1841 Finney went to Boston to inspect Bond's plans, which called for an unembellished Greek Revival hall with seating in the round similar to that in Finney's Broadway Tabernacle. Finney approved the plans and mailed them off to Oberlin.[4]

Now the village went to work. The executive committee of the Oberlin Society followed Bond's plans with deference tempered by majority rule. Each major detail was voted up or down—steps, doors, windows, and cornice. The most striking deviations from the plans are the absence of an entablature defining the span of the front gable, a shortening of the length of the church by ten feet, and most surprisingly a radical departure from Bond's circular seating plans. The curving second-story gallery alone survives as evidence of Finney's preference for sermons in the round. Financial necessity no doubt explains these differences, as has so often been the case in Oberlin's physical development.[5]

Another change was the decision to build the roof frame entirely of wood, joined in pegged mortise-and-tenon construction, rather than use a more modern system of iron bolts prescribed by Bond. One possible consequence of this choice was reported twenty-nine years later in the newspaper account of the storm of December 1871 that blew one-third of the roof—rafters, roof boards, and shingles—clear off the church onto the horse barns in the yard below. Apparently the timbers had shrunk so much over the years that rafters slipped off their pegs in the rising wind.[6]

Ground was broken for the church in March 1842. Deacon Thomas P. Turner, a master carpenter who had migrated to Oberlin from Thetford, Vermont, had charge of the construction. Great blocks of sandstone were hauled from nearby Amherst quarries for the foundation. Walls made of locally fired bricks, 400,000 of them, laid in common bond, rose over the next fourteen months. Seventy-foot crossbeams, hewn from tall whitewood trees on a farm just west of town, spanned the walls below the roof frame. It took 60,000 shaved pine shingles to cover the roof. Bond's plans had not included a tower. The congregation voted to add a cupola, modeled after a drawing in one of Asher Benjamin's pattern books, complete with bell and clock. In the end, even these modest flourishes proved too costly. The cupola went up, but the clock and bell were never installed. Years later, after the Civil War, when high Gothic taste arrived in Oberlin, it occurred to some that the tower of First Church was unfinished and that a proper modern spire should now be added to what the village paper called "the squatty old cupola."[7] Pete Seeger embellished the story a few years ago by telling us that whenever enough money was gathered for a tower, it was always spent instead on the Underground Railroad. This is a nice legend, more accurate than some in its symbolism, and ought not to be completely scotched.

As the interior took shape, according to a tale passed down from Finney's grandson, a makeshift platform on carpenter's benches was moved about on the floor of the church while Finney tested his voice against the hall, until just the right spot was found for his pulpit.[8] On the architect's plans, which survive in the Oberlin College archives, a rough pencil sketch is added, with sight lines carefully drawn from the preacher's eyes to the eyes of seated figures in each tier of the rear gallery. Finney knew the power of his eyes as well as his voice, and he wanted no parishioner beyond the reach of either weapon.

When the meetinghouse neared completion late in the summer of 1844, it was clear that the community had been drained by the project. The last $500 needed to finish the job could not be raised. The ensuing debate provides yet another index of community evolution. At issue was the wisdom and morality of selling pews at auction to raise the needed money. Selling pews, or assigning the best pews to those who paid the highest church tax, was an old established New England custom. But Oberlin had intended to be different. And Finney's Broadway Tabernacle had been a "free church," with pell-mell seating. Nevertheless, after consultation with Finney, the seating committee, chaired by Prof. Cowles, recommended to the Society a plan whose most controversial section, Article 3, called for renting pews for four-year terms to the highest bidder. James Dascomb's terse minutes seem to record a heated discussion on this plan—several motions to strike, motions to table, and finally, "The question was taken on the third article, and the Society rejected it."[9]

A week later one David McBride (who may have had a nose for political winds—he became village postmaster a few years later) brought in a radically opposing plan. It called for choosing seats by the simple device of drawing slips out of a hat—democratic, chancy, and free. It was an appealing proposal, and it passed. But at the next meeting, after a no-progress report on efforts to secure the $500 loan, McBride's plan was reconsidered and tabled, and the original plan for auctioning pews to raise the $500 was formally adopted. Provisions were included to seat the aged, infirm, and deaf immediately in front of the pulpit and to reserve prominent pews for the theological faculty. All remaining pews went up for auction five days later. At rates ranging from $1 to $17 per pew, $745 was pledged.[10]

The resulting seating arrangements, preserved in the records of the Oberlin Society for 1844, is a rough blueprint of the emerging social hierarchy of the village. The wealthiest families clustered front and center, and rent-free seats were scattered in the farthest corners. In Oberlin's beginning, financial duress had helped enforce the Covenant. Now financial duress forced the church to acknowledge and exploit those very divisions of wealth that Shipherd had aimed to circumvent a decade before. Within a few more years, families were carpeting their pews to suit their income and taste, and a vivid mix of fabrics and colors mottled the ground floor. One village historian reported that the view from the gallery was fearful to behold.[11] One wonders how it looked to Father Finney in his pulpit.

As the largest meetinghouse in the Western Reserve, First Church had many potential uses beyond religious worship. The Society was hesitant at first to open it for purely secular meetings. The Sons of Temperance were denied its use in 1848, and in 1850, when the Whig candidate for governor asked to speak there, the Society voted not to open the house to political meetings. But when the New Hampshire antislavery leader John P. Hale visited two years later, the political prohibition was formally rescinded, on the condition that his listeners not defile the house with tobacco. Hale thus started a precedent that endured, ensuring a lively future for the house over the century to come.[12]

Despite long and frequent absences on the revival trail in America and England, Finney remained minister to First Church from 1837 to 1872, when membership in the church made it the second largest congregation in the United States, surpassed only by Henry Ward Beecher's Plymouth Church in Brooklyn, New York. Finney also served as president of Oberlin College from 1851 to 1865, binding the religious passions of the college to those of the church with his powerful personal presence.

His temper mellowed as he aged. The Perfectionist heresies he preached in the 1830s, marking his break from the orthodox Calvinism of his youth, slipped into history along with Calvinist orthodoxy itself. Compared with many of his Oberlin contemporaries, his commitment to all moral causes other than the salvation of human souls was graced with a moderation that sometimes provoked criticism from more hotheaded true believers. His fondness for aesthetic pleasures was an improvement on the village norm. Alfred Vance Churchill, an Oberlin boy who became an art historian and curator at Smith College in later years, recalled that Finney's communion table, with its silver tankards and white linen, was the most beautiful he ever saw. Finney loved music, sang well, played the cello, and, in old age, bought a pump organ and played hymns on it with one finger. He admired beauty in women, their hair, their dresses. He was a devoted planter of trees.

The old man mellowed, but he did not go soft. His personal relations with colleagues and parishioners were easy enough, sometimes verging on the cordial. But in the pulpit, he remained a terror. Listeners searched for adequate metaphors to capture the anxiety he could inspire. His sermons crashed through complacency, one recalled, "like a cannonball through a basket of eggs." Another testified that "Finney was a storm, like the lightning and thunder of a dark, cloudy tempest. His eye and glance, of indescribable power, pierced you through and through." He possessed "accusing sternness."

Finney's great days on the national and international revival circuit ended in the 1860s. He staged his last Oberlin revival, aimed at local businessmen, in the winter of 1866–67. The "accusing sternness" of his First Church sermons spared no one. On Easter Sunday 1865, two days after the assassination of Abraham Lincoln, he called Lincoln an amiable, kindhearted man who nevertheless stood in God's way of punishing the South for its sins. Finney's fierce attacks on Freemasonry in 1868 so angered Deacon Thomas P. Turner, the master carpenter of the meetinghouse a quarter-century earlier, that Turner walked out of church, packed his belongings, and moved to Chicago.[13]

In the summer of 1870, the congregation sustained one of Finney's last jeremiads as he flayed his fellow villagers for their indulgence in rich living and decorative display. "They mind their houses and grounds more than God," his sermon notes read. "As bad as the cities." He then proceeded to name the names of local sinners on this score. One of them was Jabez Lyman Burrell, deacon of the church, a charter member of the college board of trustees, a prominent prewar abolitionist, and, back in 1842, a major contributor to the building fund for First Church. But the grounds around Deacon Burrell's Greek Revival farmhouse were too fancy. In the court of Finney's judgment, few went wholly free.

A mood of quiet, respectful relief passed through the congregation when, at age seventy-nine, Father Finney finally resigned his pulpit and retired to his austere, red-brick home a hundred yards west of the meetinghouse. Oberlin was proud of its famous old man. Villagers watched for his regular morning journeys around town in his black buggy pulled by an old yellow mare. He was their connection to a remembered time of virtuous privation and bedrock piety. But a new, more variegated post–Civil War world of academic growth and commercial prosperity awaited the college and town, and Oberlin was eager to get on with the changes.

In August 1875 Finney's last village stroll took him back over to the meetinghouse, to stand with his wife on the lawn outside at sundown and listen to the opening hymns of the Sunday evening service. He died later that night. The taut, vibrant forty-year bond between American's greatest nineteenth-century evangelist and his Oberlin church was now eternal.

CHAPTER 4

Finney's Oberlin (1975)

$\mathcal{T}$his essay dwells on the mundane physical and visible arrangements of the village where Charles Finney came to live in 1835; it establishes an environmental setting against which his Oberlin career may be freshly measured.[1]

Last summer, while on a long family camping trip across the continent, I read Robert Pirsig's *Zen and the Art of Motorcycle Maintenance*. I recommend it to wilderness insomniacs everywhere. By Coleman lantern, one chapter per night was just about right. It draws a distinction between the university of the free, reasoning mind and the university as an institution, a campus, a physical place. The real university is of course the first one—universal, beyond time and place, paying no dues but to the god of truth. It is a free-floating state of mind. The second university—the bricks and mortar, the notebooks, the habits of the community—is the ruck of local circumstance, crass and frustrating at worst, pedestrian at best.[2] This is a distinction dear to the academic mind. It sets up a polarity between cosmopolitan and local that recalls the classic historical images of, say, Jonathan Edwards at Northampton or John Scopes at Dayton, Tennessee, or Thorstein Veblen moving like a one-man university rebellion from campus to hostile campus. It is the split between the "church" and the "location," the universal idea versus the parochial place.

Here I will focus on the place. The interaction between the big pulsing ideas for which Oberlin made a home and the year-to-year behavior patterns of the village is an intriguing subject. The local tensions and local resolutions precipitated by the big ideas endowed those ideas with a tier of meaning that is subtler than is sometimes reckoned. What did the growing pains of the village do to the ideas that Oberlin was established to advance? Woodrow Wilson once remarked that "the history of a nation is only the history of its villages written large."[3]

Remember that Oberlin was just one of the many utopian communities founded across the 1820s and 1830s in America. In every one of these new communities, whatever its distinctive bent, hard, elemental problems about living arrangements, possessions, and ownership arose. Should land and goods be held in common or should the ethic of private property be tolerated? What constraints must the community impose on its members in their use of land, their pursuit of profit, their instinct for self-assertion and display? Oberlin confronted these troubling issues as surely as did the good people of Brook Farm, Oneida, or New Harmony. Their resolution at Oberlin was ambiguous and shifted swiftly over time. The consequences can be read from the physical development of the community more clearly than from its theological and educational debates.

Oberlin's geographical location has often been defended but seldom praised. Charles Finney, always a man of blunt opinion, called the site "a mud hole"—"unfortunate," "ill-considered," and "ill-judged." He generally spent the winter elsewhere.[4] Although the village was chopped out of the woods, it was a frontier community only in a local way. Six thousand people already lived in the county surrounding the site, having made a wide arc around the forbidding landscape of southern Russia Township. Elyria was seven hundred strong in 1833. Cleveland was a city of two thousand and growing fast; its population would triple by 1835. Three hundred miles to the west, Chicago was founded the same year as Oberlin. Beyond that, the line of settlement had moved as far as western Missouri. Oberlin was born in a post-frontier environment on the brink of modernization. The entire region south of the Great Lakes was about to be swept by a wave of technological development that would enclose its people in the culture of the commercial machine age—a culture Oberlin would challenge but not escape. The moral baggage of its founders gave them scant protection from the emerging norms of the region they came to save.

Three technological breakthroughs had recently occurred that would profoundly affect the region and the village in the decades just ahead—the railroad, the steam-powered circular saw, and the mass production of machine-made nails.[5] These would combine with the astonishing American habits of social mobility to produce relentless pressures shaping the town's growth over the next generation. When Finney arrived in 1835 Oberlin was a relatively homogeneous cell of Christian moralism. Forty years later, though the mark of its founders still fixed its separateness from regional neighbors, Finney's village was by comparison with its own beginnings a hive of social pluralism. Let's see how this happened.

John Shipherd, whose dream started it all, was a Christian radical. He knew the meaning of opposition to his views. His revival meetings in and around Elyria in 1832 had provoked gunfire, accusations of adultery against him, and a vote of dismissal from his own church.[6] The following year, when he launched his Oberlin colony, he was determined to keep the project unsullied by dissenters. The Covenant he carried with him on recruiting journeys made clear his vision for Oberlin. Among its crucial provisions were the following: "We will hold in possession no more property than we believe we can profitably manage for God, as his faithful stewards"; "We will hold and manage our estates personally, but pledge as perfect a community of interest as though we were a community of property." Any surplus over expenses would be used to spread the gospel. The Covenant went on to pledge plainness and durability in the construction of homes. It renounced fancy furniture, fancy carriages, tight dresses, and other ornaments of personal pride. Plain food, no tobacco, no strong drink—liquor, coffee, or tea.[7] Despite these stern prescriptions, the Covenant fell short of Christian communism. Property—land and housing other than that owned by the college—would remain in private hands. Access to property in Oberlin, however, was open only to those who pledged themselves to the Covenant. The five thousand-acre grant that Shipherd secured from dealers in New Haven, Connecticut, would be sold only to the godly and pious at $2.50 an acre. The Covenant meshed with the land title restriction to impose a highly selective filter on the sort of people who settled the town. That at least was Shipherd's aim.

His cofounder Philo Stewart doubted that Oberlin could survive as an oasis of purity. He told Shipherd he thought that they ought to "dispose of some of the colonial lands to persons of certain character who are not pious." This might be better, he speculated, "than to have the colony very small, and surrounded by a corrupt and irreligious population."[8] It was not at all clear in the beginning that Stewart's intuition would prevail over Shipherd's dream.

Throughout Oberlin's first decade, the selective filter kept the communal impulse toward purity alive. The Oberlin Society, the governing body of the community in its earliest years, periodically debated moves toward common ownership of property in emulation of the primitive Christians. Failing this, the Society resolved in 1837 that "it is inconsistent with our Covenant obligations to encourage any settlers among us who are immoral or unfriendly to our institutions, or to dispose of our lands to those we have no reason to believe seek the furtherance of our object."[9] Meanwhile at least one colonist accused of selling some of his land for personal profit was formally condemned for his behavior.

The college tried hard to enforce Shipherd's strategy. As the early owner of the steam-powered sawmill near Plum Creek on South Main, the college could govern the sale of lumber to townsmen, and its first account books show the college selling nails as well. Private merchants soon took over these functions, but the college remained the largest landowner in town and strove to use this leverage to good purpose. The college prudential committee minutes note in June 1840, "Whereas it has come to the knowledge of the committee that two building lots belonging to the Institution have been leased without binding the lessees and occupants to an adherence to the principles of the Oberlin Covenant, therefore *Voted* that the agent . . . is hereby expressly instructed to embody these principles in all leases of land hereafter. . . ." And three years later the committee instructed two of its members to commune with one Samuel Abraham, a newcomer who wanted to buy a college lot on North Main. The committee was "strongly impressed with the conviction that S. Abraham's family are not a desirable family to locate upon the Institution's land." No more was heard from Mr. Abraham.[10] (The prudential committee (1835–1962) managed the college's day-to-day affairs.)

Of course the college was mainly concerned with the character of students and faculty. Apparently signing the Covenant was not required for them. Finney, for instance, never signed it. But the college promised quick departure for violators of its solemn rules for student conduct, and faculty recruitment included careful screening of personal habits. As one example, Finney himself was instrumental in bringing Amasa Walker to Oberlin to start course work in political economy in 1842. Walker was a prize catch. His prowess in his field was as well known as his contributions to abolition, temperance, and the peace crusade. But his religious credentials and urban lifestyle were troubling. He had been converted twenty years earlier but had not attended church much since. Finney pressed him on this point during a Boston interview and came away satisfied. "He knows fully what we expect of him," Finney wrote home. "He calculates and wishes to conform fully to Oberlin habits of living. To sell his furniture and get it made there, etc., etc., . . . His piety will I trust improve."[11] Walker arrived and received his college lot the following summer. Finney had worked him through the filter.

(I will only add here an opinion that this sort of moral screening did not operate to diminish the intellectual quality of the early Oberlin faculty. Shipherd, Mahan, and Finney were remarkably successful in persuading men of the caliber of Morgan, Dascomb, Cowles, Walker, and others to come to Oberlin. Finney's own decision to come was only the most spectacular example of Oberlin's pull on a highly cosmopolitan and competent band of teachers.)

Like most nineteenth-century academic communities, Oberlin began with only the most rudimentary spatial plans. These followed the precedents of the nineteenth-century New England township as modified by the purpose of the college. A rectilinear grid of streets and lots extended outward from a thirteen-acre central open space. It was assumed that the permanent buildings of the college would stand on this space. That is why Tappan Square is so much larger than the average village green. Private houses of the colonists would cluster on the east side of the square. The college manual labor farm extended westward from the square. The faculty was to be housed in homes built and owned by the college along the western edge of the square—thus the peculiar name Professor Street. Even this simple scheme was destined for quick modification. As Philo Stewart remarked to Shipherd early on, "You will recollect that to lay a plan is not the same thing as to carry it into execution."[12]

Wood has always been the great democratizer of American architecture, and Oberlin was a wooden colony. The first building was the log house put up by carpenter Peter Pindar Pease at the southeast corner of the square in the spring of 1833. Most of that first summer was spent converting the dense forest of the site into stump-strewn open space. Almost every tree on the square and along the main streets was removed and turned into lumber. The woods were both the main enemy of community development and its chief raw material—not only for shelter but also for walkways through the mud between buildings. For lack of cut stone, Oberlin's early sidewalks were wooden planks, some of which were still in use sixty years later. By the end of the first summer about a dozen log houses clustered near Pease's cabin along Main Street. Oberlin Hall, built of lumber imported from South Amherst, was soon completed on the southwest corner of the main intersection and housed the entire facilities of the college for the next three years. When the sawmill was installed in the fall of 1833, wooden frame buildings made from locally milled materials were possible. A hotel, the first version of the Oberlin Inn, went up on the corner opposite Oberlin Hall. Ladies Hall, the first woman's dormitory in North America, rose in 1835 on the site of the present Oberlin bookstore, and Colonial Hall and Cincinnati

Tappan Square with campus buildings (left to right): College Chapel, Tappan Hall, Council Hall, and First Church. The double "coed walk" to the left kept a respectable interval between male and female. Courtesy of Oberlin College Archives.

Hall soon followed. These were all built of heavy timbers for sills and posts, with mortise-and-tenon construction at major joints. For lack of stone, even the foundations were made of stout oak pillars.

Each of these buildings was a laborious community project, made more difficult by the absence of hard liquor, the traditional fuel of the region used to energize civic instincts at raising time. When Ladies Hall was lifted into place in 1835, college classes were suspended for three days to complete the job.[13] Meanwhile, in line with the communal impulse, the colonists pondered the language of the Covenant as it affected the appearance of their homes and decided that a uniform color on exterior walls would confirm the common purpose of those within. The color chosen was red. But consensus on this point soon broke down. Only four buildings were painted red, and these not for long. Within the decade white had replaced red as the semi-official paint tone of the Oberlin community. Here the colonists conformed to the tastes of the surrounding population. The application of white paint to wooden clapboards was an important means by which early nineteenth-century Americans tried to assimilate the ancient forms of classical stone architecture to a wood-frame building technology.

Most of the early homes were one or one-and-a-half-story frame boxes of two or three rooms. Few colonists arrived with much cash, mortgage money was as yet unknown, and obedience to the Covenant on housing was a necessity as well as a virtue. Many houses began as gabled sheds, set back on the lot, to which in due time the owner added a larger front section, which then became the main part of the house. In later years would come further additions—a wing to the side, a loft to the rear, even a porch in front. From the outset, then, a severe but cumulative and highly eclectic sort of wood-frame gable-roofed architecture emerged to set the tone of the village.

In 1835 the first brick buildings began to go up. With bricks came a sputter of controversy. The main patron of the college at this point was New York City merchant Arthur Tappan. Now came the world's first intrusion on the colony in the woods. Tappan's attitudes toward slavery and education are well known; his architectural views, less so. In June 1835 he wrote to the trustees, advising them to pay some attention to style and good taste in the design of the campus and its permanent buildings. At little extra expense a standard of architecture could be achieved that, in Tappan's words, would have "a refining influence on the character, and add immensely to the enjoyment of life."[14] The new brick college buildings of 1835—Tappan Hall near the center of the Square and the houses for Mahan and Finney at either end of its western edge—suggest that Tappan had in mind chaste, neoclassical lines of buildings like those that Charles Bulfinch had planned for Harvard a generation before and the designs popularized in the contemporary architectural guidebooks of Asher Benjamin.

The new designs were chaste, but not chaste enough in the eyes of some. The tall, imposing tower of Tappan Hall was judged to be unsound both structurally and spiritually—Shipherd thought it defied the principles of Christian simplicity—and so the upper half of the tower was removed in 1840, leaving a boxlike cupola similar to that of First Church. When President Mahan's home neared completion, the colonist T. S. Ingersoll, who later became a leading promoter of the stern dietary rules of Sylvester Graham, fired off a protest to the trustees. Mahan's house was altogether too lavish in detail, Ingersoll believed, calculated only to "please the taste of a vitiated world." Precious dollars were being wasted on presidential frills. "There is," he wrote, "a plain, neat, simple style of building which commends itself to every man's enlightened good sense, and still will not be highly esteemed by the world, neither is it an abomination in the sight of the Lord." Where were the trustees getting their advice, he asked—"from the word of God, or from the word of [Asher] Benjamin, or some other human architect?"[15] Ingersoll's complaint was only the first among many, sounding a theme that would be heard from his day to ours, as each new addition to the campus seemed to violate the Oberlin spirit. In its architectural dimension, this spirit has grown steadily more elusive. Frictions of the sort raised by Ingersoll were doubtless part of the reason the college dropped its plan to house the faculty all in a row along Professor Street. Finney bought his house (which was identical to Mahan's) from the college in 1851, and thereafter professors were expected to fend for themselves.

None of the buildings discussed so far has survived. With one exception, the entire physical campus built during Oberlin's first fifty years has disappeared. The exception, of course, is First Church. No public building in the village was so carefully designed to meet the needs and tastes of one man, and no building is today more widely admired. As Robert Fletcher noted long ago, the church went up like a medieval cathedral, in the sense that it rose from the talents and offerings of the whole community.[16]

The early 1850s brought important changes for Oberlin, accelerating growth toward pluralism. In 1852, after a long wait, the railroads arrived. Oberlin was now connected to the world by rail east and west. This made the town vastly more accessible to travelers, who until now had trekked westward by canal, lake, and overland stage. It also linked Oberlin to a regional consumer market for goods and services, which added a brisk new tone to the town's commercial life.

That other railroad, underground, had helped build up the black population of the town to over 10 percent by 1850. By 1860 the figure was 20 percent. Not all were escaped slaves, of course. Probably a majority were free persons of color on arrival. Many were mulattoes. Most came from North Carolina and Virginia. Then, as now, their homes clustered in the southeast quarter of town, though patterns of residential segregation were not as clear as they would become by the end of the century. Their village leader, John Mercer Langston—Virginia-born, Oberlin-educated, Ohio's first African-American lawyer—broke a color line of sorts when he moved into his new house on East College, the town's most prestigious residential street, in the spring of 1856.[17]

A successful college effort to raise a permanent endowment through the broadcast sale of scholarships doubled the student population in 1851. The college manual labor farm, which had long since become a precarious economic venture, now joined the limbo of other early efforts to achieve self-sufficiency. The college farmland on the west side of town was opened for building lots and leased to holders who promised to house students and give them domestic labor. From the outset, the college had depended on townspeople to provide rooms for male students. Now the student population suddenly doubled, and the housing need became urgent. Professors joined townspeople in taking in student boarders to improve a narrow family budget.

This may account for the many new houses and house additions dating from the 1850s that combined large size with light construction and few frills. The new balloon frame was ideally suited to this sort of housing. Balloon framing, which originated in Chicago in 1833, was revolutionizing building technology throughout the Midwest. Based on the availability of machine-milled two-by-fours and mass-produced nails, balloon framing replaced the arduous old mortise-and-tenon techniques for joining heavy hewn timbers and radically lowered the costs of house construction.[18] The

East College Street, Oberlin, Ohio, 1878. The building marked "Photograph Gallery"
is Oberlin Hall, the college's first building. It burned with the rest of the buildings
on this street corner on May 2, 1886, and was replaced by the Carpenter Block.
Courtesy of Oberlin College Archives.

experience of living in one's own home was now opened to a vastly larger
proportion of the whole American population than ever before, anywhere.
In this connection it is significant that the 1860 Oberlin census returns indicate that the number of houses in the township fell just fourteen short of
the total number of families: 586 houses, 600 families. In an overwhelming
majority of cases, families owned the homes they lived in. The village paper
noted in 1866 that "a house advertised for rent in this town would draw a
larger crowd than a panorama."[19] The earliest mention I have found of balloon frames in Oberlin dates from 1866: "The frame of a house which Mr.
Copeland was putting up for Mr. Vaughn, on Groveland Street, was blown
down in the heavy wind last Saturday. It was a balloon frame and was well
splintered."[20] The language of the report suggests that the term was already
a part of the local vernacular. There is no doubt that balloon framing had
become a standard method of construction well before Gervase Wheeler
publicized it nationally in a book of 1855 titled, significantly, *Homes for the*

People. Professional architects scorned the proliferation of wooden housing made possible by the new method. Calvert Vaux, for example, bewailed the "bare, bald, white cubes" it produced as appealing to people "with little or no cultivation of higher natural perceptions"; others questioned the long-term durability of such houses. In reply to this criticism, a proponent of the new method replied, "Sir, we are Christians, you know, and therefore we take no thought for the morrow."[21] If Oberlin's Christian minds had not been justifiably locked on other issues in the 1850s, that reply might well have served to rationalize the patterns of local growth.

Although Oberlin was growing, it could not match the pace of neighboring towns like Elyria or Norwalk. Despite the lag, or perhaps because of it, turnover in the population was high. Oberlin shared in the remarkable surge of demographic mobility that historians have identified as a salient feature of nineteenth-century America, urban and rural. Of course, the rhythms of the college and its big new student body added an unusual element of flux. But the local adult population was also turning over. Of the 147 identifiable names on the membership list of the Oberlin Society from 1841 to 1856, only fifty-two (or 35 percent) appear in the city directory of 1859–60.[22] The old guard was being thinned out, by death and departure. The Civil War income tax returns, published in the local newspaper, reveal even more striking evidence of turnover and social mobility. Of the seventy-one men listed as the wealthiest in town in 1865, only thirty-six (or 51 percent) had been living in Oberlin five years before. Almost half the town's most prosperous families had moved to town from somewhere else since 1860. Most of the new money was commercial. Of the ten wealthiest people on the list, only three were connected with the college: James Dascomb (sixth on the list), George Kinney (eighth), and Charles Finney (tenth).[23] The richest man in town was Marx Straus, a German-born Jew who arrived to open a clothing store in 1852, at age twenty-two. Straus, possibly the first Oberlinian to smoke cigars in public, gradually acquired much valuable downtown real estate, including the Oberlin Inn, which he would deed as a gift to the college in 1895.[24]

The monopoly of First Church over the religious life of the town ended in 1855 when the Episcopalians organized. Christ Church on South Main was completed in 1859. With Episcopalians came the celebration of Christmas, and with Christmas came Christmas buying, to the delight of local merchants. The village newspaper gloated in 1866, "O Ye Puritans, we love you for many good things, but in that you would not keep Christmas, we pity you."[25] A few prominent Episcopalians, including postmaster E. F. Munson and lawyer Anson Dayton, were also leading Democrats. But authentic competition between political parties lay far in Oberlin's future. Republicans outnumbered Democrats by almost ten to one in the 1860s, and as late as 1884 the newspaper commented, "If a member of the college faculty should ever vote the Democratic ticket, we imagine that the Oberlin soil would open beneath his feet to receive him."[26]

The town's most notorious Democrat, Chauncy Wack, ran a tavern by the railroad tracks on South Main until one of the Munsons succeeded him. By 1870 Oberlin had two saloons, one for blacks, one for Democrats, and both on South Main near the tracks. Oberlin's first prostitute, a visitor from Cleveland, was arrested in 1871. The first raid on a local bordello, on East Lorain, occurred in 1876.

Other, less ominous recreations also flourished after the Civil War—baseball beginning in the late 1860s, football in the early 1870s, balloon ascensions, and velocipede racing on West College Street. The town awoke one morning in July 1870 to see a stuffed gorilla swinging by the neck over the newly erected Civil War monument, dressed in skirts stolen from the clothesline of the new Ladies Hall. In 1873 the young women of Ladies Hall were further shocked when an aged Oberlin colonist came to eat with them. He crumbled his bread in a bowl of milk and ate it with a fork.

The town's appearance kept pace with the new era. Coal-gas lamps now illuminated the streets, replacing the hickory torches of the pioneers. A handsome board-and-batten railroad station went up in 1866, and the picturesque landscape of Westwood Cemetery replaced the grim old burial ground near the town's center. The local architectural deposit remained relatively modest. The lack of any commercial base other than local retail business precluded the sort of architectural show that Milan's grain export business underwrote before the war and Wellington's cheese industry supported after the war. This was a constant frustration to village boosters. "In this go-ahead age, Oberlin must either bestir itself or be left far in the background by its most enterprising neighbors," the town paper grumbled in 1871. "Let us manufacture something besides brains, if it is only toothpicks."[27] Still, a number of substantial homes went up before and after the war, most of them in the modish Italianate style that swept the country in the 1850s. The mansion of Marx Straus on South Main led the parade with its elaborate cornice, round-arched windows, and brightly painted cast-iron stag and mastiff guarding the front lawn. That house has long since disappeared. The brick villa of Oberlin's Civil War hero, General Giles Shurtleff, built on College Place in 1866, is the best surviving example of the new elegance.

For the less wealthy, the advent of the power lathe and jigsaw placed wooden gingerbread details for porch and eaves within easy consumer reach. The fresh wave of home improvement delighted the village editor. "Our town is looking like a bride," he wrote. "New buildings, street improvements, and door-yard embellishments are making the Puritan village as beautiful as any sister place of whatever age or descent." Again: "The house painters are rioting in colors this summer. All the shades of yellow, orange, straw, slate and purple shine through the trees of front yards. The old standard white is being superseded—and more than temporarily, let us hope."[28] As village homes yielded more and more of their economic functions to the store and factory and local farmers, the appearance of the domestic landscape reflected a new attention to the aesthetics of family pride. Machine-mowed lawns, flower plots, and croquet grounds appeared in side and back yards, often replacing former vegetable gardens and chicken runs. Here and there a new fountain graced a front lawn. The wooden fence, once used mainly to confine pigs and poultry, now combined with evergreen hedges to define property lines. The first flagstone sidewalks made their appearance, and the massive stone carriage block, complete with iron horsehead hitching posts, became a village status symbol. "Possibly we are getting a little proud in our old age," the editor acknowledged, "and like to put on a touch of style, now and then—simply to contrast with former poverty, of course."[29]

What did Charles Finney think of all this? He spent more time in the village now. The great days of the winter revival circuit were mostly behind him. His tall, lean figure was familiar to the village—in the First Church pulpit or standing on the southwest corner of the square in earnest talk with John Morgan, his favorite colleague (who now lived in the Mahan house), or riding about town in his leather-top wooden buggy, pulled by an old yellow mare. Back in 1835 John Shipherd had told the colony he did not think there was a man alive who could serve both church and college in a dual role. But if they sought such a person, he advised, "be sure to settle [on] a man who will encircle the Colony in one arm and [College] in another, holding them as a church in inseparable Christian union."[30]

Finney had tried. Now toward the end, unity was coming apart. This did not fill him with despair. Finney cannot be numbered among Oberlin's diehard fanatics or purists for any cause. When he is measured against his local contemporaries, a trace of prudent moderation can be detected in the man. It showed in his attitudes toward the Covenant, Graham dieting, abolition, and even the Oberlin Perfectionism with which he is chiefly identified. His early biographer, George Frederick Wright, caught this quality when he said of Finney, describing his personal characteristics, "according to his theory, everything was sinful when out of place, and when permitted to usurp the position of the supreme end of being."[31] When neighbors complained that his young widowed daughter dressed too richly in her mourning, he called her in, looked her over, and said, "Your dress is black and plain, and I think you are all right."[32] He was a man of iron opinion, and, from long pastoral experience, he knew how to draw the line.

One Sunday morning in July 1870 he drew the line for his congregation on issues of "village improvement" and all the new secular enjoyments of the postwar era. His text was Philippians 3:19, "They Mind Early Things." Like most of Finney's sermons it cannot be recovered, since he spoke from skeletal notes, and much of what he said was extemporaneous. But from the surviving sermon outline and the contemporary newspaper report it is clear that his anger was aroused, and Oberlin was his target. The old meetinghouse echoed with a jeremiad that Sunday morning that matched the strongest tradition of New England Puritanism.

Finney spoke about a class of self-deceived people who were too blind to suspect their own hypocrisy and mistook their self-indulgence for piety. He named names, local names, prominent names. Some excerpts from the sermon outline will convey his message to his townsmen:

> They exult in their good living.
> Proud of their luxuries . . .
> They mind their houses and grounds more than God . . .
> As bad as the cities . . .
> Was this class ever more numerous than at present? . . .

Why is it not right to cultivate taste? It is Christian civilization.
It is refinement . . .

It is the most delusive form of sin. Because it does not involve
what is generally regarded as immorality. Very much of it is
admired and applauded. Many are ambitious to excel in this
direction. In dress, in grounds, in luxuries . . .

In [the] direction of the World.[33]

The sermon caused a commotion. It had been Finney's purpose from
the outset of his ministerial career to revive the tension, again and again, between possessing the world and reaching beyond it. The people of Oberlin
valued that tension. They had lived with it and grown accustomed to it,
along with the strong voice and flashing eye of their great revivalist. They
were proud to have him in their midst. Perhaps they did not want to be reminded so bluntly and harshly of the distance Oberlin had traveled from a
simple separate colony of virtue back toward the larger world. But the evidence was all around them. Some called it progress. Others would call it
history. Finney called it the most delusive form of sin.

Finney knew he could not win them all. Years before, according to a
cherished village tale, he had tried without success to convert the saucy
daughter of a local merchant. Nothing seemed to work. One day he met her
walking across the square and decided on direct words. "Good morning,
child of Satan," he said. "Why hello, Father," she replied. A moment passed
and Finney broke into laughter.[34] An economy of scarcity governed Finney's
laughter, and its memory must have been valued by those who ever heard it.
It seems a gentle note to close on.

CHAPTER 5

Oberlin and Harpers Ferry (1972)

*A*s someone said at the time, John Brown's raid on Harpers Ferry was a stone tossed into a dark pool; it sank to the bottom, but it caused a wave.[1] The raid began on Sunday night, October 16, 1859, when John Brown led his small band of followers through the rain down a Maryland hillside into the Virginia town of Harpers Ferry, where the Potomac River meets the Shenandoah, sixty miles west of Washington, D.C. John Brown intended to seize the federal armory and rifle works at Harpers Ferry, distribute the weapons, and lead a liberation army of rebel slaves and free blacks through the South from Virginia to Alabama. This was his plan for ending slavery in America. Among his personal effects found after the raid was a constitution he had written for a new state, to be located somewhere in the mountains of Appalachia, as a base of operations for his cause.

He started down the hill with seventeen other men—twelve white, five black—each armed with two pistols, a Sharps rifle, and a bowie knife. Among the five blacks were Lewis Sheridan Leary, an Oberlin harness maker who lived here on East Vine; John Anthony Copeland, a former Oberlin College student who lived with his family on the corner of Morgan and Professor (his father was a master carpenter who built many houses in nineteenth-century Oberlin); and Shields Green, a friend of the abolitionist Frederick Douglass, who visited Oberlin several times across the 1850s. Leary and Copeland had probably met John Brown in Cleveland the previous spring, during the trial of the Oberlin-Wellington Rescuers. Copeland had taken part in that rescue, which made a strong impression on John Brown. Some people thought Brown was a madman. Douglass, while sympathetic with Brown's goals, regarded the Harpers Ferry project as suicidal and refused to join it. But Leary and Copeland and Green committed themselves to Brown. They joined him in the hills above Harpers Ferry on October 15, 1859, the night before the raid began. Their arrival was what triggered his decision to move. He told them: "We have here only one life to live, and once to die; and if we lose our lives it will perhaps do more for the cause than our lives would be worth in any other way."[2]

The raid was over in thirty-six hours, completely crushed. Instead of igniting a black insurrection, the raiders found themselves surrounded by several thousand armed militia and a troop of federal marines dispatched from Washington under command of Jeb Stuart and Robert E. Lee. Leary and Copeland, who had helped seize the rifle works, tried to escape through the mist across the shallow Shenandoah. Leary was shot on the rocks in the river and died the next day. Copeland was taken prisoner and narrowly escaped lynching on the spot. Shields Green was captured with John Brown in the railroad engine house after the door had been battered in by marines. The surviving raiders were imprisoned and tried in a Virginia court for murder, treason, and conspiracy to provoke a slave rebellion. By all accounts they bore themselves with dignity, were treated well by their jailers, and received a fair trial. Copeland and Green were defended by a young lawyer from Boston named George Sennott. Along with John Brown they were found guilty and sentenced to death.

A few days before his execution, John Copeland wrote a letter to his father and mother in Oberlin, in which he said:

> Dear Parents, my fate so far as man can seal it, is sealed, but let not this fact occasion you any misery; for remember the *cause* in which I was engaged, *remember it was a holy cause*, one in which men in every way better than I am have suffered and died. Remember that if I must die, I die trying to liberate a few of my poor and oppressed people from a condition of servitude against

which God in his word has hurled his most bitter denunciations, a cause in which men, who though removed from its direct injurious effects by the color of their faces, have already lost their lives, and more yet must meet the fate which man has decided I must meet. If die I must, I shall try to meet my fate as a man who can suffer in the glorious cause in which I have engaged, without a groan . . . [3]

That was Harpers Ferry.

Eleven months later Abraham Lincoln was elected president. A month after that, South Carolina seceded from the Union. The war that followed cost the nation 530,000 lives. Oberlin, college and town, gave a fair share to that number. The names of some of them are carved on the memorial plaques over in Wright Park. It seems reasonable today to add to the head of the list, as the first Oberlin casualties of the Civil War, the names of Lewis Sheridan Leary, John Anthony Copeland, and Shields Green.

CHAPTER 6

Oberlin Starts the Civil War (1990)

$\mathcal{T}$he main thing I learned from reading Nat Brandt's book on the Wellington Rescue was how much I didn't know about the Rescue.[1,2] On the hunch that others may be also in the dark, I'll start by telling briefly what happened, beginning on Monday morning, September 13, 1858. The account that follows is drawn almost entirely from Brandt's splendid narrative.

A black fugitive slave named John Price, living in Oberlin since his escape from Kentucky the previous winter, was riding north out of town on Oberlin Road that morning, on his way to dig potatoes, when he was overtaken and seized by three slave catchers. They drove him in a carriage out through East Oberlin to the Point, then west on what is now Route 20, then south along Diagonal Road toward Wellington, where they planned to put him on a train back to Kentucky. On the way to Wellington the carriage was spotted by an Oberlin abolitionist named Ansel Lyman, who heard Price call out for help. Lyman hustled back to Oberlin and spread the news. Soon dozens of armed Oberlinians thundered down the road to Wellington to rescue Price. Also in Wellington, watching carefully, taking names, was Chauncey Wack, Oberlin's saloonkeeper and the most stubborn Democrat in an overwhelmingly Republican town. Wack had put up the slave catchers at his place the night before, and he would later testify against the Rescuers

The Oberlin Rescuers.
At Cuyahoga Co. jail April 1859

| 1 | 2 | 3 | 4 5 6 | 7 8 9 10 11 12 13 | 14 15 16 | 17 | 18 | 19 | 20 |

1 J. R. Shepard. 5 W. Evans. 9 S. Bushnell. 13 A. W. Lyman. 17 J. Watson.
2 O. S. B. Wall. 6 C. Boyce. 10 J. Scott. 14 J. Bartlett. 18 J. M. Fitch.
3 L. Wadsworth. 7 R. Plumb. 11 M. Gillett. 15 W. E. Lincoln. 19 R. C. Peck.
4 D. Watson. 8 H. Evans. 12 C. Langston. 16 H. Winsor. 20 J. Williams.

This photograph by Cleveland daguerrean J. M. Green was widely circulated.
It was taken in the courtyard of the Cuyahoga County Jail in April 1859.
Courtesy of Oberlin College Archives.

in court. After several hours of tense negotiation, the Rescuers succeeded in hauling Price out of a Wellington hotel, into a wagon, and back to Oberlin, with Rescuer Simeon Bushnell at the reins. After hiding for several days in the home of Professor James H. Fairchild on South Professor, Price left for Canada, never to be heard from again.

Three months later thirty-seven Rescuers were indicted by a federal grand jury in Cleveland for violating the Fugitive Slave Act of 1850. In retaliation, two months later a Lorain County grand jury, more sympathetic with the abolition cause, indicted the slave catchers for kidnapping John Price. Of the thirty-seven Rescuers, twenty-five were from Oberlin—twelve black, thirteen white, including four college students and one professor. Most of the other Rescuers were from Wellington.

In early April 1859 the trial of the first Rescuer, Simeon Bushnell, got under way in Cleveland before an all-white, all-Democratic jury. When he was found guilty, the rest of the Rescuers insisted on being jailed without bond as an act of protest. The Rescuers remained in jail for eighty-three days and became the object of rising passion all over the United States.

My colleague Grover Zinn, professor of religion, recently showed me a book about the Congregationalists of northern Iowa, who in 1859 sent the following resolution to the Oberlin Rescuers: "Be courageous in enduring wrong for the sake of right. We believe that the result of your case will have an important bearing on the cause of liberty throughout the whole country." God, they decided, was using the Fugitive Slave Act to advance the cause of antislavery. To help out, they sent $46 to the men in jail.

Meanwhile the Democratic Buchanan administration in Washington, eager to rid itself of abolitionist critics, was trying to shake loose from Oberlin and its antislavery martyrs. Finally in July 1859 a deal was cut to free the Rescuers and simultaneously drop kidnapping charges against the slave catchers, and the Oberlin twenty-five—now reduced by attrition to thirteen—returned to their village in triumph. The *Cleveland Plain Dealer,* no friend to the abolition cause, showed its awareness of a shift in public opinion when it reported: "The Government has been beaten at last . . . and Oberlin with its rebellious Higher Law creed is triumphant. . . . As goes Oberlin, so goes the United States. . . ."

That whole story passed into local folklore, but for the next 130 years its full details were never told. A decade ago Oberlin's Bill Long, former manager of the Co-op Book Store, wrote a short play about the rescue, called *Feast of Felons.* Bill later sent a copy of his play to a New York City television producer, Yanna Kroyt Brandt. Her husband, writer Nat Brandt, had just finished his latest book and hit on the idea of the rescue for his next one. Four years later, after several trips to the Oberlin College Archives, as well as work at the Library of Congress, the National Archives, and the New York Historical Society, his new book was complete.

Nat Brandt is a professional freelance historian with a long career behind him in journalism, editing, and publishing. He writes narrative history—storytelling meticulously researched and carefully crafted. It's the kind of history that not too many historians with Ph.D.s have tried to write in recent times. Academic history has its virtues, but storytelling no longer ranks very high among them. Much academic history today reads like retrospective sociology, heavy with research design, comparative models, theoretical constructs, control groups and fine-spun motivational analysis. Next to these priorities, storytelling is often lost. Nat Brandt reminds us what we can learn from a well-told story. There is very little flash or melodrama in his pages; his style is quiet and unobtrusive, and his fidelity to fact seems to let the story tell itself.

But his book delivers strong messages. The most important message I find in it is a vivid reminder that the Civil War that Oberlin helped ignite—for all the tortured debate about states' rights and popular sovereignty and regional pride that led up to it—was a war that ultimately turned on issues that still glow hot among us today, issues having to do with the relationship between skin color, racial identity, citizenship status, and personal rights.

Although Brandt doesn't stress the connection as much as he might have, the rescue and the trial it triggered are a clear sequel to the famous Dred Scott decision handed down by the U.S. Supreme Court the year before, in 1857. Historians who have never heard of the rescue still memorize the Dred Scott case, the case of a Negro slave who sued for his freedom but lost. Dred Scott remained a slave by order of the court, despite having lived for a time in a free state and then a free territory where slavery was outlawed by act of Congress. Dred Scott remained a slave because he was black and his ancestors were black, and black slaves lacked the constitutional rights protecting free white men from slavery. So said the Supreme Court in 1857. The message was that slavery could still reach out and pull down every black American, fugitive and nonfugitive alike.

Brandt's narrative makes clear that the threat of the Dred Scott decision was on everybody's mind when John Price was seized a year later. You can feel the threat when a Rescuer yells out from the crowd in Wellington that "The moment a slave touches Ohio soil he is *free,* and all the South combined cannot carry him back, if we say No!" You can hear it from the federal judge in Cleveland, ruling about John Price that his "dark complexion, woolly head, and flat nose . . . afford *prima facie* evidence of slavery and ownership." You can feel the sting of it in

Rescuer Charles Langston's bitter eloquence when he says to the same judge that he, Langston, had gone to Wellington "knowing that colored men have no rights in the United States which white men are bound to respect [that's a direct quote from the Dred Scott decision]; that the courts had so decided; that Congress had so enacted; that the people had so decreed."

Some people at the time wondered why the Rescuers had risked their necks and their freedom for John Price, an illiterate, club-footed Kentucky fugitive whom few people in Oberlin really knew and who dropped out of sight within days of his rescue.

For the blacks among the Rescuers—particularly Langston, Wilson Evans and his brother Henry, O. S. B. Wall, John Scott, John Copeland, and the Watsons—the motivation was plain. By saving John Price in a world of danger, they were also hoping to save themselves. Not only abolitionist passion and Christian idealism and political martyrdom were on their minds, but plain angry self-interest. Probably even Chauncey Wack understood that.

So the Rescuers, with the help of people like Wack and his slave-catcher friends, by inflaming abolitionist passions, had a hand in bringing on the Civil War. The contemporary humorist Petroleum V. Nasby summed it up a few years later when he said, "Oberlin commenst this war. Oberlin wuz the prime cause of all the trubble." Nat Brandt, in basing the title of his book on Nasby's quip, admits to some exaggeration. But no one in Oberlin will fault him for it.

Brandt's most recent predecessor among historians of the Wellington Rescue was Professor Robert Fletcher, who devoted a long chapter to it in his history of Oberlin College. A year before he died Fletcher gave an assembly talk in Finney Chapel about the Rescue. He ended it this way:

> They say that on dark windy nights in September you can hear Simeon Bushnell's carriage rattling up the road from Wellington, stopping at the light at Route 20, and then sweeping on over the railroad tracks into Oberlin. And don't be surprised if, at midnight, when passing by some lonely field between Oberlin and Elyria, you should catch a glimpse of a shadowy figure digging potatoes where none have been planted for one hundred years—since

> 1858. . . . And, perhaps, if you listen closely, you may hear the pale,
> cold notes of bugles and the sound of many marching men.

Professors don't write history like that anymore. But Nat Brandt comes close. This town is full of stories for him to tell. Maybe one day soon he'll come back to Oberlin and take an evening walk down Main Street to Vine to check out the new Rescue Monument and listen for a moment in the night.[3] Facing the monument across the street is the red brick house, once the home of Wilson Evans, where the Langstons, Learys, Copelands, and Walls gathered in the 1850s to talk about what to do next. Wilson Evans lived there with his wife into old age, until his death in 1898. Next door to them, also facing the monument, is the home of Chauncey Wack, who opposed almost everything Wilson Evans and his friends believed in. Wack lived there until his death in 1900. It may not be too fanciful to wonder if, over those forty years after the rescue of John Price, the two men ever spoke to one another across the fence in the dark about old times. One hopes so. The one man might have learned something from the other.

CHAPTER 7

Spiced Wine: An Oberlin
Scandal of 1862 (1968)

*I*n the winter of 1862 scandal swept the village of Oberlin.[1] Mary Edmonia Lewis, a college student, was accused of poisoning two of her friends with drugged wine. After being beaten by vigilantes, arrested by local authorities, and brought to court, she was finally released to go her way. Before her case was closed, it seared the embarrassed town with a blaze of melodrama. For Oberlin was, of course, no ordinary college town. Nor was Mary Edmonia Lewis an ordinary Oberlin student. She was an unusually talented and somewhat exotic "young lady of color," half Native American, half African. Her Indian name was Wildfire.

Though college records listed her as coming from New York City, she had no real home. Born somewhere near Albany, New York, in 1845, the daughter of a black manservant, she was raised in the tribal life of her Chippewa mother. Her childhood was a wandering wilderness experience of swimming, fishing, and moccasin-making, interrupted by occasional forays into the white world for schooling. She was orphaned while still a girl, and apparently a thrifty brother enabled her to come to Oberlin.[2]

She entered the preparatory department of the college in 1859. Although she had earlier been thought too wild for much book learning, she pursued her studies over the next three years with reasonable diligence. She had a marked artistic bent, but there is no evidence the Oberlin classroom gave her much chance to show it. Small and delicately featured, she was open and cheerful in manner, evidently made friends easily, and enjoyed a good reputation on the campus.

Edmonia lived with a dozen other girls, all white, at the home of the Reverend John Keep, where Keep Co-op now stands. Father Keep, the eighty-year-old dean of the college trustees, had cast the deciding vote in the 1835 decision to admit black students to the college. No man had done brighter service in Oberlin's fight to educate women, achieve total abstinence, and emancipate the black slave. He pursued a vigorous retirement raising money for the college, preaching, chairing public meetings, and playing father to the girls who boarded at his home.[3]

Among her fellow students, Edmonia Lewis was chiefly unusual for her Indian background. Some 250 black students attended Oberlin before the Civil War, and about thirty were enrolled in 1859. Among them were Anthony Burns, the celebrated fugitive, and Mary Jane Patterson, who would graduate in 1862 as the first black woman to receive the college's bachelor degree.[4]

Oberlin's attraction for free blacks as well as fugitive slaves made the town a byword throughout northern Ohio. Six miles north of town a crossroad signboard pointed the way to Oberlin with the picture of a black man running with all his might to get there. The fabled Wellington Rescue was a fresh memory in 1852, and many of its proud participants still walked the streets.

Blacks made up about 20 percent of the population. Then, as now, they lived mostly in the southeastern quarter of the town. They were one of the largest black minorities in any community in the region, and their numbers were growing.

The town was not free from race tension, as an incident in the fall of 1860 suggested. Several black residents had asked the village jeweler to remove an objectionable "image clock," evidently a mechanical blackface parody that winked at passersby from the window of his shop. Despite their protest the clock remained in place, and at dawn one day the jeweler's window was found smashed with a bullet hole through the clock. "An element of rowdyism and lawlessness is springing up in our village," the local paper warned, "that, unless checked, will lead to serious results."[5]

Over succeeding months efforts got under way to promote the migration of black residents of Oberlin to the island of Haiti. Some sixty black villagers had left for Haiti by February 1862. Colonization, always a popular antidote for race tension among anxious Americans, was not without its Oberlin proponents.[6]

Most Oberlinians were confident they could handle problems that came along, whatever their source. The meaning of the place remained bright, exposed for all to see, and worth cherishing. What mattered was to keep the faith and prove it, day by day.

Life was not all grim and single-minded. Commitment to the cause of Oberlin was no longer total. Among the one thousand students scattered among the various tiers of the college, one could detect a growing diversity of aims. To improve one's talents, to brighten one's chances, to meet new people, to taste the excitements of college life—these were reasons enough for coming to Oberlin in the 1860s.

Edmonia Lewis had surely come for some such reasons as these. So, no doubt, had two of her friends at Father Keep's, Maria Miles and Christina Ennes, both respectable young ladies from nearby Ohio towns. Three girls in their late teens, full of the warm impulses of youth, they were none of them above an occasional lark.

It would appear that the strange events of January 27, 1862, began as a lark. The college was in recess between terms, and the three girls whiled away many hours in idle talk. One report had it that the two white girls fell into the pastime of "running on" Edmonia. What their teasing was about, or what it had to do with the events that followed, remains a mystery. At length Maria and Christina decided to improve their leisure with a long sleigh ride, accompanied by two "gentlemen friends," to Christina's home in Birmingham, nine miles away. Launched in girlish gaiety, the outing ended in disaster.

On the morning of January 27 they bustled about, preparing for the trip. The air was frosty, but the pleasures of the ride were promising. Just before they set out, Edmonia invited them to her room to share a drink of hot spiced wine she had prepared to fortify them against the cold. The treat was gladly and hastily consumed. Soon the two men arrived with sleigh and horses. The party bundled into place and pulled away. With what emotions Edmonia saw them off, one can only surmise. Speculation turns swiftly to her recipe for spiced wine. Later medical testimony plainly suggested that one item in the mix was cantharides, the aphrodisiac popularly known as Spanish fly.[7]

Christina Ennes's father was among the leading men of Birmingham. About three miles from home, his daughter was suddenly stricken with deep stomach pain. Her friend Maria was overcome by a similar attack almost simultaneously. Their startled boyfriends hurried the team toward town. Upon arrival the girls were put to bed at the Ennes home, and doctors were summoned. Their examination led promptly to a suspicion of poisoning. There can be no doubt that the girls named Edmonia Lewis as the culprit. The ugly report flew back to Oberlin, where Edmonia was instantly accused of foul play. There was no suppressing the news. Oberlin must have shuddered with it.[8]

Exactly what happened to Edmonia next, or why, is not clear. The secrets of the village cannot be unearthed and reconstructed with any certainty. Shock, indignation, embarrassment, and shame, mixed in a configuration that can only be guessed at, produced a community response that seems—a century later—almost mute. The village newspaper maintained absolute silence on the matter for three weeks. One can only piece together the fragments of evidence that survive.

Despite the suspicion pointed at her, Edmonia was not taken into custody. Village officials may have been reluctant to move against her without clinching evidence, since she was a college student and, in a sense, the ward of Father Keep. At best the police facilities of the village were primitive. The village mayor, Samuel Hendry, looked into the case, but apparently he, the township constables, and the college took no decisive action. Perhaps uncertainty about the exact condition of the bedridden victims dictated delay. More likely, the whiff of scandal surrounding the affair inspired caution and uncertainty about a proper course of action.

The scandal provoked in many people an impatience to see Edmonia punished for it. To friends of the stricken girls, delay in the execution of justice seemed intolerable. The situation demanded an arrest. But still the town took no action. Finally for some the wait was too long. If Oberlin authorities could not handle their colored folks, others would.

One evening as Edmonia stepped from Father Keep's door out into the dark, she was seized, dragged to a nearby empty field, and brutally beaten. When she was discovered missing, the village alarm bell sounded, and a search party, hunting the fields with lanterns in the night, found her lying in the cold, her clothing torn and her body terribly bruised. The identity of the self-appointed vigilantes was never revealed, and there is no record of any action taken against them.[9]

The case was getting out of hand. Hesitation brought to Oberlin not only roughneck vigilantism, but what was in some minds worse—the hot glare of sensation. As the story spread, it threatened (as had so many tales in the past) to smear those values the college most proudly to stand for— the virtue of coeducation, of racial harmony, of straight-laced temperance among its people, of moral probity in the conduct of life. Critics of the place—and every town in the region harbored them—must have slapped their thighs in vindication. Worst of all, perhaps, the story made the *Cleveland Plain Dealer.*

The warfare between Oberlin and the *Plain Dealer* was already, a century ago, a conflict of long standing. As Prof. James H. Fairchild remarked to returning alumni in August 1860, the pastime of attacking Oberlin and all it stood for had become an inveterate habit with the *Plain Dealer.* A Democratic paper in those days, the *Plain Dealer* regularly assailed abolitionists and "nigger-lovers" in all their follies, and Oberlin made a handy target. The paper missed few opportunities to titillate its readers with items illustrating the consequences, salacious and otherwise, of unleashing the Negro on a white man's country. All things considered, the *Plain Dealer*'s treatment of the Edmonia Lewis case was remarkable for its tact.[10]

"Mysterious Affair at Oberlin—Suspicion of Foul Play—Two Young Ladies Poisoned—The Suspected One under Arrest." So ran the column heading in the *Plain Dealer* of February 11. Details followed, though no mention was made of the color of "the suspected one" or of the vigilante action. The paper confessed it had not gotten as full a report of this "very singular case" as it desired and looked forward eagerly to the trial.[11]

Oberlin's own weekly broke silence on the case in its next issue. The *Lorain County News,* founded in 1860 in the cause of abolition, was more or less an official voice in the community. It faithfully carried local items, and its columns are generally an excellent source for the mundane preoccupations of its readers. Its reticence about the Edmonia Lewis case is striking.

The turnover in the paper's management may have been part of the reason. Just as the case broke, editorial control of the *News* came into the hands of an Oberlin College faculty member, Henry Everard Peck. A professor of sacred rhetoric, Peck wielded unusual local influence. An energetic antislavery man, he had achieved wide fame as an oratorical firebrand. As the most prominent of the defendants in the Wellington Rescue case, he was castigated by the prosecuting attorney as "St. Peck," ringleader of the "Saints of Oberlin."[12]

Peck took over the *News* in mid-February 1862. The Edmonia Lewis case was, in a sense, his first big local story. He handled it with extreme delicacy. Even after the paper finally acknowledged the story, it kept Edmonia's identity carefully concealed. "We have hitherto refrained from speaking of the matter," the editor wrote, "because we have supposed that the ends of justice would best be promoted by our silence. We speak of it now to make occasion for correcting the impression, which we hear is entertained by many friends of the young ladies who are said to have been poisoned, that the people of Oberlin are not willing to have the case brought to a trial." Nothing could be further from the truth, the paper asserted. The authorities promised a prompt hearing of the case—and a fair one. The people of Oberlin must see to it that the accused girl, "whose character has been exemplary, who is an orphan . . . and whose color subjects her to prejudice," was guaranteed "the common rights of law."[13]

In her room at Father Keep's, meanwhile, Edmonia lay in her bed while her body mended. She was not without friends and defenders who professed a willingness to see the full facts in the case exposed. In fact, her interests had fallen into unusually competent hands. J. M. Langston, attorney-at-law, had decided to defend her.

John Mercer Langston was one of the most remarkable men ever to live in Oberlin. His life was an authentic nineteenth-century American success story, and his defense of Edmonia Lewis was to be a minor incident in a career that ultimately brought him national prominence. His involvement in Oberlin's history was no random circumstance. In a real sense Oberlin had made him. A graduate of the college, he was apparently the first and only practicing black lawyer in Ohio in 1862. By all accounts (including his own) he was a good one.

Langston was the son of a Virginia planter and one of his emancipated slaves. Like Edmonia Lewis, his mother was half African, half Indian. Like Edmonia, he had been orphaned at an early age. Sent north with his broth-

John Mercer Langston, a former slave, graduated from Oberlin in 1849 and later became dean of the law department at Howard and a member of Congress from Virginia. Courtesy of Oberlin College Archives.

ers to be raised in freedom, Langston entered Oberlin in 1844—his first impression of the place was a rousing Finney sermon—and graduated four years later. He wanted badly to become a lawyer, but no law school he could find would take a black student.

So he returned to Oberlin to pursue his studies in the theological department under, among others, Professor Henry Peck. Armed with his master's degree, he proceeded to read law in the offices of an antislavery judge in Elyria. In 1854, in open defiance of the mores of Ohio, he was admitted to the bar on the polite fiction that he passed for a white man.[14]

Langston came back to Oberlin two years later to practice law, moving into a handsome house in a previously all-white neighborhood on East College Street, just across the street from the home of Professor Peck. He quickly acquired a strong clientele. Ironically, the only people who were reluctant to use his services were black citizens of Oberlin. The black laws and anti-Negro customs of Ohio being what they were, the last thing a black man in trouble wanted was a black man to defend him.[15]

A slim, handsome, elegant young man, Langston was embraced by Oberlin's white majority. Election to the town clerkship, the town council, the board of education, and a leading place in the town's Republican caucus were tokens of his acceptance. He may have been a white man's Negro, but he was no Uncle Tom. Intensely proud of his abilities and his color, he was not above knocking down any man who tried to slur him to his face. He knew the meaning of militance.[16]

Langston took on the defense of Edmonia Lewis against the advice, he later recalled, of many black Oberlin residents, who were apparently willing to concede her guilt in the name of community harmony. Langston was convinced that the case against Edmonia was far from airtight. Preliminary investigation, including a hasty trip to Birmingham to ask a few quiet questions, satisfied him that her accusers lacked the evidence necessary to prove her guilt.[17]

The brutality of Edmonia's nighttime assailants slowed the already halting pace of official action against her. By the time a hearing was arranged, her physical condition made her appearance impossible, and a continuation was granted to allow her to recover from her beating. Finally the case was set for February 26. The local justice of the peace, Daniel Bushnell, had little experience in such matters; so the justice of the peace from Wellington agreed to sit with him on the bench. The two justices presided over what was in effect a preliminary hearing to determine whether an indictment should be handed down against Edmonia.

The case aroused widespread curiosity, and the hearing, held in a large business hall in downtown Oberlin, drew a crowd of several hundred— friends of the girls, college students, villagers, out-of-town visitors, and sensation-seekers of every stripe. The prosecution was handled by two private lawyers, a Mr. Chapman from Birmingham and Charles W. Johnson of Elyria. In Johnson, Langston faced a formidable rival. A prominent Elyria Republican, well read, trained in medicine as well as law, he would a few years later be elected prosecuting attorney for Lorain County. Langston had briefed himself thoroughly in the medical aspects of the case, however, and was sure he could match his adversary.[18]

The hearing lasted two days. (Langston later remembered it as lasting six.) Helped into the room by friends, Edmonia endured the proceedings in silence. An impressive parade of witnesses appeared for the state. They included the celebrated victims, Maria Miles and Christina Ennes; Christina's father, Homer Ennes; an Oberlin doctor named William Bunce; and three college students—Thomas Rayl, the son of the assistant principal of the ladies department of the college, and the two young men who had taken the girls on their sleigh ride, E. R. Pelton and Prentice Loomis.

The critical testimony was given by the doctors who treated the girls at the end of the ride, Dr. Parker and Dr. McConolly. They testified that the symptoms had indicated that the girls were suffering from internal poisoning and that the probable agent was cantharides. If a record of the proceedings was kept, it has not been found, and the substance of the testimony remains mostly in the realm of conjecture. Of course, the intriguing questions center on the identification of cantharides as the poison drug.[19]

Cantharis, or Spanish fly, is the most celebrated of stimulants in the long and legendary history of aphrodisiacs. Its popularity, of ancient origin, had survived centuries of experimentation with rival potions. The most astonishing feats are said to have been performed by both men and women under its influence. In the nineteenth century, with the swift modernization of medical science, the efficacy of various traditional aphrodisiacs came under question. The debate encompassed cantharides, which nevertheless has enjoyed a sturdy reputation well into recent times. A powder made from dried beetles native to Southern Europe, the drug was a strong irritant, whatever its other powers. Applied externally, it blistered the skin; taken internally, it could prove highly toxic. Users risked dangerous inflammation of stomach tissues and violent illness as well. A large dose could be fatal.[20]

The known facts in the Oberlin poisoning case would seem to suggest that miscalculation in the intended effect of the drug may have caused the misery in the sleigh. One wonders, of course, how such a drug as Spanish fly was to be obtained in Oberlin, Ohio, in 1862. It was imported into the country for pharmaceutical sale, however, and presumably the underground distribution and use of recreational drugs is not peculiar to the college students of the twentieth century. Edmonia Lewis somehow kept wine in her room at Father Keep's despite a stern ban. One cannot dismiss the possibility of her having had access to cantharides as well. Obviously the question is relevant only insofar as it touches on the issue of her actual guilt or innocence of the charge against her. Did she drug the wine drunk by Christina Ennes and Maria Miles?

There is no good answer. John Mercer Langston later recalled, in piecing the tale together, that the three girls chatted intimately about their personal health the night before the sleigh ride, but the words he uses to describe their conversation are so veiled in delicacy as to be opaque in meaning. More to the point was his comment that the accusation against Edmonia was *"perhaps without reason"* [italics added]. The edge of doubt in this phrase, coming from Langston, is striking. It lends credence to the theory that Edmonia may well have doctored her wine with Spanish fly, but with an antic motive quite innocent of any desire to inflict pain and illness on her friends. The gap between intention and result has played stranger tricks.[21]

It should be stressed that not a word of speculation along this line has survived from the record of the case itself beyond the naming of the drug and the accusation that Edmonia used it. Langston was chiefly concerned to free his client, not to establish proof of her innocence or reveal the truth as he knew it. He succeeded brilliantly in his purpose. By strenuous cross-examination of the state's witnesses he established that (as he had learned on his trip to Birmingham) no sample of the contents of the stricken girls' stomach or bladder had been preserved or analyzed. When the state rested, Langston—without calling a single witness—moved for the immediate dismissal of the case on the ground that the *corpus delecti* had not been proved.

The maneuver touched off an intensive and climactic legal debate. Newspaper accounts speak admiringly of the forensic quality of the arguments on both sides. The *Cleveland Leader* reported: "At the conclusion of the argument, the prisoner was ordered to be discharged, both justices concurring, as the evidence was deemed insufficient to hold her for trial." Edmonia Lewis was free.[22]

The *Plain Dealer* concluded its account with a parting editorial flourish at Oberlin's expense: "The above trial was a very peculiar one in some respects. The prisoner was black, many of the lawyers were black, at least one of the Justices was black, the color of a large number of the spectators was black—in fact it was a *dark* affair viewed in any *light*."[23]

Professor Peck's *Lorain County News* did not let this slur pass unnoticed. The need for constraint was past. Manifestly relieved that the case was closed, the *News* reprinted the *Plain Dealer*'s comment with a jovial rejoinder:

> That is very mild for the aged P. D. We should have expected something like this—"The above trial was only an everyday affair in Oberlin. The prisoner was black, all the lawyers were black, and both justices were black. None but black witnesses were allowed to testify, and no white person could enter the courtroom but by special permission. Several respectable citizens who ventured some unfavorable comments upon the case were knocked down and brutally beaten on Main St., in broad daylight, by Negro ruffians. Oberlin is fast rivaling Paris in the most frightful days of the old reign of terror."[24]

With this mocking reply to its persistent critic, in terms well calculated to soften the ugly edge of memory for local readers, official Oberlin buried the Edmonia Lewis poisoning case. With relief the village turned to its normal preoccupations: the spring term at the college was under way; President Finney returned to the pulpit after a long illness; John Gough, a noted temperance orator, brought his crusade to town; the maple syrup season was in full swing; a faculty committee was appointed to consider barring vagrant cattle from Tappan Hall; and young men left their friends and families to join the Union army.

Edmonia Lewis left Oberlin a year later. A new career awaited her. The temptation was strong to give up on white society altogether and return to the life of her Indian childhood. Instead she headed for Boston. She decided she wanted to become an artist. Soon she was practicing her skill in a Boston sculptor's studio. Her talent began to show.

Success in executing a bust of Robert Gould Shaw, the young Boston patrician who died leading a black regiment in the war, encouraged her to go to Rome to pursue her craft. There she won quick attention and sympathy from the American colony in the city and embarked on a notable career in neoclassical sculpture. When reports of her progress filtered back to Oberlin in 1866, they were greeted with broad if somewhat startled humor by the *Lorain County News:*

> The papers are noting the advent in Rome of a young colored artist and sculptor—Miss Edmonia Lewis—who is creating something of a sensation in the Eternal City. Report hath it that she is none other than a Miss Mary E. Lewis, who had her brief notoriety here—and for other than artistical efforts—a few years since. If Miss Mary E. is none other than Miss Edmonia, she is indeed enjoying a checkered career.[25]

Meanwhile Edmonia pursued her way. Passionate themes from Native American and African American history dominated her work. Her color, her engaging manner, and her shadowy personal history, perhaps as much as her authentic talent, made her a celebrated figure in artistic circles on two continents in the 1870s. At the Philadelphia Centennial Exposition of 1876 a large grouping of her works was prominently displayed. Thereafter her vogue seems to have passed. Hardly anything is known about her last years.[26]

In Oberlin, the other protagonists of the poisoning case of 1862 dropped from sight one by one in the months and years following Edmonia's departure. Their records make a mixed bag. The four youthful participants in the sleigh ride to Birmingham achieved swift obscurity. None of them returned to college the next year, and little is known of them thereafter. (Five generations of Enneses are buried in the Birmingham village graveyard, but Christina is not among them.)

The other student who testified at the trial, Thomas Rayl, joined the army and died near Nashville, Tennessee, in December 1862. (His name is faintly visible in the weathered marble of the Soldiers Monument on the bank of Plum Creek in downtown Oberlin.)

Samuel Hendry, whose responsibility it had been as mayor to take prompt official action in the case, was voted out of the mayoralty in the spring election of 1862. Thereafter he turned his hand to the manufacture of elixirs and achieved wonderful success with a bottled remedy pronounced by Dr. Bunce to be an effective cure for diphtheria. In September 1862, presumably on the strength of other feats, Hendry was elected to the college board of trustees. He died in 1868.

Daniel Bushnell stepped down as justice of the peace in 1865. The same year, Professor Peck resigned from the faculty to accept the American ministry to Haiti, following the route of the black Oberlinians who had departed for the island during the war. Two years later he died of yellow fever. Father Keep went to his reward in 1870, at the age of 89.

John Mercer Langston remained to tell the tale. In 1894 he published his autobiography, *From the Virginia Plantation to the National Capitol.* The title suggests the dimensions of his achievement. Like Edmonia Lewis, he had traveled far from Oberlin. The true stamp of Horatio Alger mythology marked his career, and his memoirs celebrated the American dream of success. The maxim "Self-reliance the secret of success" graced his title page, and the 534 pages that followed offer ample verification. Written in proud and fulsome prose often bordering on the baroque, they tell an important story.

After helping to raise troops for black regiments during the Civil War, Langston left Oberlin to become inspector-general of the postwar Freedman's Bureau. After that he taught law at Howard University and served for a time as Howard's acting president. In 1877 President Hayes named him minister to Haiti, where he served till 1885, after which he accepted the presidency of a Negro college in Petersburg, Virginia. His crowning feat was election to Congress as a Republican from the predominantly black district around Petersburg, in 1888, an event provoking shock and bitterness among white Virginia Democrats. Langston's forty-year defiance of the convention designed to govern the behavior of black Americans was complete. In the early 1890s he retired in Washington to write his memoirs.

Chapter 13 of his autobiography tells of the trials of Edmonia Lewis— "A Rare and Interesting Case Which Tested his Powers." By then the case was thirty-two years old and safely forgotten in Oberlin. Though Langston named no names (not even Edmonia's), misdated the events by three years (placing them in the winter of 1859–60), and exaggerated the story in certain respects, he told it as if it had happened yesterday. Indeed, the odd mixture of graphic melodrama and technical inaccuracy in his version—the only known account by a participant—led some in later years to doubt the authenticity of the incident itself. Thus, ironically, the poisoning case spilled into the realm of legend with the publication of Langston's memoirs. One wonders how they were received in Oberlin among the villagers who had survived since the 1860s. When Langston died in 1897 the *Oberlin News* printed a long obituary, drawing heavily on his memoirs but repeating not a word about the events of Chapter 13.[27]

Forty-six years later, in 1943, two scholarly works appeared that touched briefly on the poisoning. Robert S. Fletcher's *History of Oberlin College* mentions Edmonia and her "sensational trial" only in passing. James A. Porter of Howard University devotes several pages to her career in his fine study, *Modern Negro Art,* describing her as an unconventional character with an original, if forgotten, talent. Like Fletcher, he cites Langston as his source for the poisoning episode but confesses that the facts as related by Langston are "almost unbelievable."[28]

What has been most baffling about the case is the lack of evidence about it in the official records of the college, the town, and the county. The crucial record, the criminal docket of the justice of the peace for Russia Township, has evidently been lost for the year in question. No letter or committee minute referring to the case has ever been found. It is almost as if the community had entered into a covenant of silence to shroud the facts.

Raw, sordid, and touching, the facts should not be forgotten again. They suggest some durable home truths about the place where it happened, the people who came to live and teach and study there, and how they got along. The range of human behavior revealed verifies the potential of men and women for just about everything short of depravity or perfection. In Oberlin as elsewhere, people could approach the brute as well as the angel. A small place with a large purpose, Oberlin reacted to the scandal of Edmonia Lewis with a protective instinct for its good name. The college weathered the scandal, as it had other crises vastly more severe in its early history. The purpose of the place survived. With the help of John Mercer Langston, Edmonia Lewis survived too.

Middle Years (1870–1945)

CHAPTER 8

Warfare between Science and Religion (1999)

Oberlin debated the validity of Charles Darwin's evolutionary theories as recently as 1983.[1] (Some may ask: That's recent? For historians, 1983 was the day before yesterday.) One spring evening that year a long argument between a prominent evolutionist and a prominent creationist filled Finney Chapel—a rare academic happening in the 1980s. Geologist Jim Powell, acting president of the college at the time, spoke to the issue that same spring. Chemist Norm Craig followed with a critique of Creationist evidence for the Oberlin *Observer*. (The *Observer* was a useful campus forum for faculty, staff, students, trustees, and alumni officers. It lasted twenty years until its disappearance last summer.)

The year 1983 marked a long century since the Darwinian controversy first hit this campus with public force. Darwin published his startling hypothesis in 1859, but its reception in America spread rather slowly, owing to the crisis of the Civil War. Outside the scientific community of the East Coast, serious talk about the issue got under way only after Appomattox. The debate finally broke open in Oberlin in May 1871, when the Reverend Theodore Keep delivered a surprisingly dispassionate lecture on the subject to the Oberlin Society of Natural Science. He pointed to problems with

Darwin's theory and big gaps in his evidence, but the measured and tolerant tone of Keep's critique seemed to lend Darwin a certain plausibility.

Some in Keep's audience could not stand for this. John Morgan, professor of biblical theory, a faculty stalwart for thirty-six years, promptly asked Keep what in the world could be implausible if Darwin's theory was plausible. If anything was more glaringly nonsensical, Morgan announced, he had failed to hear of it. A colleague of Morgan, James Dascomb, professor of chemistry, biology, and physiology, a charter member of the faculty since 1834 and its senior scientist, joined the attack. He charged that Darwin's theory would damage morality and warned that a person who read Darwin was apt to be carried right along with the theory unless he was on his guard. Dascomb cited his personal experience with uncultivated peers to question Darwin.

A younger faculty member, Charles Henry Churchill, professor of mathematics and natural philosophy, who had quietly bought a copy of *The Origin of Species* when it first hit the American market, suggested on the other hand that geologists' discoveries about the extremely long, slow development of the earth's surface lent some credibility to Darwin's notions. Churchill's comment was the only semblance of support for Darwin's theories coming out of the evening with the Reverend Keep.

To concede that Darwin might have altered any aspect of one's inherited religious beliefs could be a shuddering confession in the Oberlin environment of 1871. Professor Churchill's son, Alfred Vance Churchill, who grew up to become a noted art historian and museum director at Smith College, looked back on his Oberlin boyhood with considerable nostalgia. His recollections about absorbing the religious impact of Darwin's message are, however, bittersweet. He belonged to that generation of thoughtful young Americans who tried to adapt their family faith to the scientific newness—the price of lost belief in an anthropomorphic God and the certainty of a life after death. He wrote about it this way:

> The pain—the mental anxiety and spiritual torture—of such
> speedy changes in religious conviction are hard to comprehend
> and can never be fully realized by those who have not shared
> them. Especially to those whose faith has been firmly established
> in early childhood . . . and who are suddenly left alone in the uni-

verse—orphaned because they can no longer believe in the "infal-
lible Word" on which their faith is founded. . . . I shared all that.
Those anxieties and tortures darkened my youth. Fortunately for
their own happiness, the majority of men change their minds
slowly. They succeed in clinging to the beliefs that are essential to
their mental pace, leaving it to their children to complete the destruction and put away the debris.[2]

The psychological wrench recalled by Churchill was felt all over
Oberlin as the warfare between science and religion set in for that generation. Neither college president of the era, neither Charles Finney nor James
Fairchild, is known to have addressed the issue in public. No Finney sermon
spoke to it in First Church, and Fairchild shunned the topic even in private
conversation. The man who finally emerged to mediate the conflict was
Oberlin's nationally renowned geologist, George Frederick Wright, who
was also, like so many early Oberlin professors, an ordained minister.
"There must be a divinity shaping the ends of organic life," he wrote, "let
natural selection rough hew them as it will." Wright's strategies of accom-
modation were institutionalized at Oberlin in 1892 when he was named to a
new academic chair as professor of the Harmony of Science and Revelation.
The chair became a department in 1898, an early college probe into multi-
cultural studies.

The Darwinian hypothesis was now firmly installed in the Oberlin curriculum and entered the twentieth century hand in hand with its main rival.

CHAPTER 9

Oberlin College Architecture: A Short History (1992)

Give or take fifteen years, Oberlin can be defined as a twentieth-century college campus surrounded by a nineteenth-century Ohio village.[1] Hardly any physical trace remains of the campus buildings that existed during Oberlin's first half-century. The built environment of the college as it looked as late as 1885 has almost wholly disappeared. The fortunate exception is First Church, the grand old orange-brick meetinghouse that rose from 1842 to 1844, based on plans from Boston architect Richard Bond as modified by the majority rule of the congregation. Donald Love, college secretary from 1926 to 1962, once remarked that the fact that Oberlin College did not own First Church is no doubt the main reason for its survival.

The transformation of the rest of the campus has been a relentless if often planless process. One summer after the Civil War, a traveling artist from Chicago named C. W. Ruger stopped in Oberlin and executed a bird's-eye view of the town as it appeared in 1867. If we had a set of such views, one for every five years since Oberlin's founding, and if we could flash them in time-lapse photographic sequence, what we would see is a vast deal of commotion in the middle and relatively placid, low-visibility change all around. The raising up and ripping down of college buildings in the middle of a comparatively static midwestern village has been the main theme in the environmental history of Oberlin.

Oberlin's settlers were a plain and thrifty lot. The college was the only reason for their presence here, and despite decades of earnest effort by local merchant boomers, Oberlin never acquired a commercial base autonomous from the college. Therefore the town itself produced a rather modest architectural deposit. Oberlin contrasts vividly in this regard to nearby towns like Wellington, Milan, Hudson, and Norwalk, each of which celebrated commercial success through the medium of architecture.

In early Oberlin, architecture was not much on people's minds. The founders' primary cultural virtues—that tough streak of Christian moral frugality, that constant concern for missionary causes whose boundaries lay far beyond the limits of the village—combined with economic necessity to discourage local aesthetic flourishes. While Oberlinians shared in the stylistic changes of passing decades, they did so in a muted, sober way. The nineteenth-century Oberlin vernacular, like that of the New England Puritan villages from which it descended, was very plain.

The college regarded its earliest buildings with little sentiment or historical veneration. Even the most substantial of them, such as Tappan Hall near the center of the square, were looked upon as expedient and expendable solutions to the problems of early privation. When affluence hit the college in the 1880s, and fresh expansion got under way, new buildings replaced the old with few tears shed for the past. Oberlin regarded its physical past, distinct from its moral past, as something to be discarded and transcended.

Oberlin was not alone among American colleges in lacking firm plans for campus growth. Those which did evolve according to a preconceived design include Union College in Schénectady, New York, whose Federal plans were provided by the Frenchman Joseph Jacques Ramée; Thomas Jefferson's neoclassical University of Virginia; and the Gothic Revival campus of Ohio's Kenyon College, launched a few years before Oberlin. These are exceptions, not the rule.

Still, the peculiar circumstances of Oberlin's early growth—the narrow economizing of the first thirty years, followed by sudden affluence in the Gilded Age—meant that when the time and money for expansion came, there was no cumulative local architectural tradition to build on. No perceived line of local continuity existed to distinguish Oberlin from any other place in mid-America, or to guide its physical growth.

There, as the contracts went out in the 1880s, contemporary, cosmopolitan architectural enthusiasms flourished unhindered. Current national taste rather than any local vocabulary defined the appearance of the new build-ings. Each, as it went up, was a separate, celebrated event, often architec-turally irrelevant to what had gone before or what would come next.

One can cite other local habits that help explain the peculiar appearance of the campus: the Oberlin genius for strong-willed individualism; a certain otherworldly impracticality that flashes among us every now and then; a long-standing insistence on grass-roots decision-making that has sometimes resulted in architectural choices being shaped by local committees rather than architectural experts; and finally a certain brooding, anti-elitist mistrust for trained authority or deference to tradition. All these combined to pro-duce a college campus whose architectural cohesion is at best elusive.

The casual, freewheeling eclecticism of Oberlin today is the result. You can stand on the plaque at the center of Tappan Square, turn on your toes through a 360-degree arc, and almost box the compass of the architectural history of the Western world. If something is missing or redundant, it has sometimes seemed that all you had to do was wait.

Still it is possible to detect some order in the variety. One can identify at least four distinct themes in the chronology of our architecture, each overlapping the next across the past century.

One

The Oberlin Stone Age lasted for a quarter century after 1885. It is rep-resented by Peters Hall (1885), Talcott Hall (1887), Baldwin Cottage (1887), Severance Chemical Laboratory (1900), Warner Gymnasium (1900), Carnegie Library (1908), Rice Memorial Hall (1910), and Wilder Hall (1911). These are all thick, chunky, aggressively solid buildings, made of heavy blocks of rough-textured buff Ohio sandstone. Six miles north of Oberlin is the huge Amherst hole from which many of them came.

The Stone Age can be divided into two modulations. The earlier ex-amples enforce patterns of organic irregularity popularized by the work of America's greatest nineteenth-century architect, Henry Hobson Richardson, a style that acquired the label "Richardson Romanesque." They look a little like Richardson himself, who was a massive, bulging man. Those that went up before the depression of the 1890s—Peters, Talcott, Baldwin, and the old Conservatory of Music—were marked by much surface and interior complexity and by a decisive vertical thrust. They burst in a bold profusion of towers and bays and tall punched windows. Those that survive came from the drawing boards of an Akron architectural firm, Weary & Kramer, who described themselves as "specialists in court house, jail and prison architecture." Affable practitioners, they offered several versions of the Peters tower and invited the college to choose among them. Weary & Kramer's interior spaces—Peters court, Talcott's elegant parlors, and the nook-and-cranny arrangements of Baldwin—have proved very adaptable over the years, gathering warm memories from generations of undergraduates.

The college resumed its building program shortly after the depression ended in 1897. Beginning with Warner Gymnasium, a calmer mood set in. Succeeding buildings were more crisp, oblong, and horizontal in their lines. Rectangularity, predictable fenestration and shallow-pitched red tile roofs characterized their appearance. The turn of the century ushered in less swagger and more repose.

Although the buildings of the Stone Age acquired many loyal friends, they are regarded by some as the old gray elephants of the campus, and their careers have been punctuated by periodic demands for their demolition. American architectural technology and popular definitions of beauty and function have come a long way since Richardson and his local interpreters. It is hard to recapture the profound faith in progress that these buildings vindicated for those who watched them go up. For that generation, they were the promise of a modern future. President William Ballantine said at the dedication of one of them:

> Oberlin College has reached now a new era. The pioneer stage has passed. The true university life has begun. We see no longer slab halls, or stumps and potato rows on the campus. Massive and commodious edifices of freestone will look out across green shaven lawns, and graceful towers will rise above the elms. With the buildings already erected, or at once to be erected, Oberlin will take her place unchallenged among university towns famous for scholastic charms.

The elms are mostly gone now, but the buildings they rivaled remain. One hopes that their preservation will help to sustain some sense of connection to that robust nineteenth-century pride in achievement among those who built them.

Two

The second stage of structural evolution can be called the Cass Gilbert era, stretching from the opening of Finney Chapel in 1908 to the completion of the Quadrangle for the Graduate School of Theology in 1931. In the interim, as consulting architect to the college, Gilbert designed Cox Administration Building (1915), Allen Memorial Art Museum (1917), and Allen Memorial Hospital (1925). Cass Gilbert was one of the first-line building artists of the early twentieth century, although his reputation has been shadowed by his more daring contemporaries, Louis Sullivan and Frank Lloyd Wright. Gilbert was a sound, conservative, academic architect, a close student of historical styles and their adaptation to modern purposes. Whatever you wanted, Gilbert could do it for you, and do it well. Examples of this versatility include the neoclassical state capitol of Minnesota in St. Paul, the Woolworth Building in New York City (a soaring neo-Gothic skyscraper), the George Washington Bridge over the Hudson River, and the U.S. Supreme Court Building in Washington.

For Oberlin he chose historical models from twelfth-century southern France to fifteenth-century northern Italy, a stylistic reach from medieval Romanesque to Renaissance classicism. His Oberlin buildings were mostly dressed in warm, rubbed, tan sandstone, trimmed with red sandstone and roofed in red tile. They lent a certain Mediterranean aspect to an otherwise solemn, Protestant Ohio campus. And, in Gilbert's mind at least, they related well to Warner Gymnasium, which he regarded as the best of the Stone Age structures.

Three

The third phase in our building history spanned the years between the two world wars. This was a time of relatively slow growth, for several reasons. One was the long presidency of the aging Henry Churchill King, which seemed to lose some of its drive after the remarkably vigorous prewar years. King was followed by Ernest Hatch Wilkins, who, for all his other virtues, was not much interested in buildings. Finally the disruptive impact of the wars bracketing this era, and the Great Depression in the middle of it did not encourage building expansion.

The era witnessed three significant initiatives, each of which fell short of fulfillment. The first was a decision reached by the Board of Trustees in 1928 to build a residential campus for men on the quadrangle running north from West Lorain Street to the athletic fields. This would be Oberlin's modest analogue to the residential clusters launched in these years at Harvard and Yale. Its purpose was to gather Oberlin's male students from their scattered locations in private rooming houses all over town, and endow the male social life of the college with more cohesion and vitality. This reflected a long-standing concern to which the college had first addressed itself in the construction of Men's Building (later renamed Wilder Hall) in 1911. In 1928 the trustees resolved:

> . . . that Oberlin shall have a Men's Campus on which the men shall live together in buildings owned and operated by the college, a campus on which the life of men can be organized and developed in such a way as to stimulate scholarly ambition and to create an active masculine social atmosphere.

These are quaint words, especially to the students who live on the North Campus today in chummy coeducational contentment. Only one building of the new men's campus, Noah Hall (1932), went up before World War II intervened. The college met vast difficulties in financing the construction of Noah during the bleakest years of the Depression.

The second impulse of the interwar era was a move toward building in a neo-Georgian style. This caught the current popular taste for things colonial which was pervasive nationally in the 1920s and 1930s. The most influential inspiration for this cult was the Rockefeller-financed restoration of colonial Williamsburg, which got under way in the late 1920s. The best Oberlin example of neo-Georgian architecture is the President's House on Forest Street, designed by Clarence Ward for Physics Professor S. R. Williams in 1920 and acquired by the college for President Wilkins in 1927. Executed in red brick, it bears a resemblance to the best loved of all American colonial homes, the wood-frame Craigie-Longfellow house on Brattle Street in Cambridge, Massachusetts.

The new men's campus was to be neo-Georgian in mood. Noah Hall is faithful to its colonial prototypes, Massachusetts Hall at Harvard and Connecticut Hall at Yale. Burton Hall, completed just after World War II, seems more reminiscent of Tidewater Virginia plantation architecture, although the proportions of the central block between its flankers are distended to accommodate more bedrooms. Burton proved to be the last gasp of the neo-Georgian impulse.

The third interwar initiative was a plan to build a science quadrangle along West Lorain just south of the men's campus. Severance Chemistry Laboratory was to be the southeast anchor for this complex. A leading proponent of the idea was W. H. Brown, a young architect in the art department, who introduced the modern international style to Oberlin in his designs for several private homes. Wright Physics Laboratory (1942) was barely completed before the war intervened. Its anomalous red brick wall patches indicate anticipated points of future junction for the thwarted science complex. As it is, Wright stands as Oberlin's last expression of the round-arched style launched in Warner Gymnasium four decades before.

Four

The end of World War II punctuated the beginning of the fourth phase of Oberlin architecture. Almost half the buildings on the campus have gone up since 1946. When William Stevenson assumed the college presidency that year, he found a badly antiquated physical plant. Zoology was taught in a converted church; humanities classes met in an abandoned high school; converted wooden homes housed botany, geology, and geography, as well as hundreds of student roomers; Carnegie Library overflowed with books; theatrical productions wandered about town like orphans in search of a stage. Stevenson promptly launched a modern building program which continued through the years of his successor, Robert Carr, and on into the 1970s. In this construction drive, two rival trends are discernible. The first is an expedient conversion to bland cereal-box functionalism in postwar dormitory construction. The fraternal twins of 1956, Dascomb and Barrows, are characteristic examples. These flat, anonymous slabs of sleeping space, aptly dubbed "motel modern," may be understood as an unimaginative vernacular version of the Bauhaus style that Walter Gropius helped translate into American collegiate architecture in his Harvard Graduate Center of 1949. The merits of this twentieth-century Oberlin plain-style, elaborated in the gigantism of Kettering Hall (1961) and South Hall (1964), are more economic than architectural. The new plain-style met a need for inexpensive interior space at a time of steady inflation in building costs and the necessity after 1955 to conform to the guidelines of federal subsidy programs. Bearing in mind the dozens of aging wood-frame houses demolished to make room for new dormitories, one can define them as Oberlin's campus version of urban renewal.

As antidotes to this homogeneous sprawl, we have been blessed (outraged? entertained?) with a sequence of striking, theatrical architectural statements by building artists of national renown. These include Wallace Harrison's melodramatic but curiously functional Hall Auditorium (1954), the seventh and final version of a project forty years in the making; Minoru Yamasaki's pretty white Conservatory and King Building (1962–1966), controversial exercises in machine-molded neo-Gothic formalism; Hugh Stubbins' vast, handsome Philips Physical Education Center (1971), which remained a subject of contention right up to the day it opened; and the Mudd Learning Center (1974) by Warner, Burns, Toan, and Lundy, which, owing to its central location and long construction process, provoked more sustained debate about its size, appearance and propriety than perhaps any building in Oberlin's history. The monumental scale and doubtful neighborliness of its facade turned out to contrast vividly with its bright, lavish, and accessible interiors, and while the debate sputtered out, Oberlin's students quietly took possession of Mudd and made it theirs.

No sooner was Mudd completed than attention swung to the other side of Tappan Square, where Robert Venturi's addition to the Allen Memorial Art Museum gave the community's talent for aesthetic polemics a climactic test. Venturi is a thoughtful iconoclast of modern design convention and a self-conscious architectural populist. He met the "impossible task" of expanding a contained Renaissance palace with a purposeful collision between Gilbert's palace and his own checkered billboard. While the setbacks of his addition defer to the older building and relate nicely to the nearby appendages of Hall Auditorium, the Venturi entry on the Oberlin scene easily achieves its own identity. With its staccato surprises at every turn it is, like each of its important predecessors, an insistent demand for personal attention. A trip through Venturi's spaces is a challenging and sometimes puzzling adventure. It is pleasant in the end to walk away from the excitement, returning to the quiet pleasures of Tappan Square.

Five

Over the next decade, until the mid-1980s, a long pause went by for campus architecture. Then, with the arrival of President S. Frederick Starr, a fresh wave of initiatives began to roll. In 1985, Starr organized an international design competition for an ornamental bandstand on Tappan Square. The winning design, by the young Canadian architect Julian Smith, an Oberlin graduate, was inspired by the festival wagons of South Asia that Smith had come to know as a college Shansi representative in India in the early 1970s.

Next, a program of restoration and renovation for Oberlin's main nineteenth-century dormitories—Talcott, Baldwin, and Tank—revived the charm and popularity of these aging landmarks. Carnegie Library underwent recycling for modern uses. Charles Martin Hall's boyhood home on East College Street was restored to its original Italianate appearance. Meanwhile a postmodern core addition to North Hall, designed by Peter Saylor, and a crisp, bright addition to the Conservatory Library, by Gunnar Birkerts, went up. In 1990 modernist Charles Gwathmey's big new dining center, Stevenson Hall, opened on North Professor Street, and the Sperry Neuroscience Building, designed by Reed Axelrod, helped integrate Kettering Hall with its red brick neighbors to the north. [Since the publication of this brochure in 1992, the Science Center (Payette Associates, Boston, 2001–2002) has obscured the Sperry Building.] And in 1992 the John W. Heisman Club Field House, by Spillman Farmer Architects, which defers nicely to Philips Gymnasium despite its own vast size, opened for use.

Each of these arrivals enhances Oberlin's remarkable architectural diversity. The bracing nonconformity of the campus constantly refreshes. Strolling around it, one never fails to discover something new to ponder, depending on the season, weather, time of day, or one's own current mood.

The following chronological listing of extant buildings on the Oberlin College campus through 1992 includes the date of construction and the name of the architect:

First Church, 1844, Richard Bond (Boston)
Allencroft, 1861, architect unknown
Westervelt Hall, 1874, Walter Blythe (Cleveland)
Johnson House, 1885, architect unknown
Peters Hall, 1885, Weary & Kramer (Akron)
Baldwin Cottage, 1887, Weary & Kramer (Akron)
Talcott Hall, 1887, Weary & Kramer (Akron)
Shurtleff Cottage, 1892, Weary & Kramer (Akron)
Tank Hall, 1896, F. A. Coburn (Cleveland)
Severance Chemical Laboratory, 1900, Howard Van Doren Shaw (Chicago)
Warner Gymnasium, 1900, Normand Patton (Chicago)
Old Barrows, 1901, Howard Van Doren Shaw (Chicago)
Memorial Arch, 1903, J. L. Silsbee (Chicago)
Finney Chapel, 1908, Cass Gilbert (New York)
Carnegie Library, 1908, Normand Patton (Chicago)
Rice Memorial Hall, 1910, A. B. Jennings (New York)
Wilder Hall, 1911, J. L. Silsbee (Chicago)
Keep Cottage, 1913, Normand Patton (Chicago)
Cox Administration Building, 1915, Cass Gilbert (New York)
Allen Memorial Art Museum, 1917, Cass Gilbert (New York)
President's House, 1920, Clarence Ward (Oberlin)
Stadium, 1925, Osborn Eng Co. (Cleveland)
Quadrangle, 1931, Cass Gilbert (New York)
Crane Pool, 1931, Walker and Weeks (Cleveland)
Noah Hall, 1932, C. W. Frank (Akron)
Hales Gymnasium, 1939, Richard Kimball (New York)
Wright Physics Laboratory, 1942, E. J. Schulte (Cincinnati)
Burton Hall, 1946, Mellenbrook, Foley & Scott (Berea)
Heating Plant/Service Building, 1949, William Kemmerer/Eldredge Snyder
Jones Field House, 1949, Eldredge Snyder (New York)

Harkness, 1950, Eldredge Snyder (New York)

Fairchild, 1950, Eldredge Snyder (New York)

Hall Auditorium, 1953, Wallace Harrison (New York)

Oberlin College Inn, 1954, Eldredge Snyder (New York)

Barrows, 1956, Potter, Tyler, Martin & Roth (Cincinnati)

Dascomb, 1956, Potter, Tyler, Martin & Roth (Cincinnati)

Hales Gymnasium addition, 1958, Visnapuu and Gaede (Cleveland)

Kettering Hall of Science, 1961, Austin Company (Cleveland)

Williams Ice Rink, 1963, Austin Company (Cleveland)

North Hall, 1963, Austin Company (Cleveland)

Conservatory of Music, 1964, Minoru Yamasaki (Detroit)

King Building, 1964, Minoru Yamasaki (Detroit)

South Hall, 1964, Potter, Tyler, Martin & Roth (Cincinnati)

East Hall, 1964, Potter, Tyler, Martin & Roth (Cincinnati)

Zechiel, 1968, Moore & Hutchins (New York)

Bailey, 1968, Moore & Hutchins (New York)

Barnard, 1968, Moore & Hutchins (New York)

Language and Honor Dorms, 1968, Moore & Hutchins (New York)

Oberlin College Inn addition, 1969, Joseph Ceruti (Cleveland)

Philips Physical Education Center, 1971, Hugh Stubbins & Associates
(Boston)

Mudd Learning Center, 1974, Warner, Burns, Toan & Lundy
(New York)

Art Museum addition, 1976, Robert Venturi (Philadelphia)

Clark Bandstand, 1987, Julian Smith (Almonte, Ontario)

North Hall addition, 1988, Dagit & Saylor (Philadelphia)

Conservatory Library addition, 1988, Gunnar Birkerts (Birmingham,
Michigan)

Stevenson Hall, 1990, Gwathmey Siegel (New York)

Sperry Neuroscience Building, 1990, Ewing Cole Cherry Parsky
(Philadelphia)

Heisman Club Field House, 1992, Spillman Farmer (Bethlehem,
Pennsylvania)

Science Center, 2001–2002, Payette Associates (Boston)

President King and Cass Gilbert: The Grand Collaboration (1982)

*A*merican colleges, with rare exceptions, are notorious for their lack of long-term campus planning.[1] But for three decades in the early twentieth century, roughly spanning the presidency of Henry Churchill King, Oberlin attempted a plan. How it emerged and what happened to it make for an engrossing tale—the play of power, talent, money, and tenacious rival visions among a group of strong-willed men and women.

The tale begins soon after King became president, with the January 1903 fire that destroyed the old chapel on the square, which left the college with three obsolete buildings still on the square and no place for the campus community to come together. Other needs of varied urgency faced the new president—a college library, an art museum, a men's social center, and a home for the administration. King went to work. Beyond the chore of raising money, he was determined to achieve coherence and quality in its spending. He wanted the best the college could afford.

In the spring of 1903 he asked the Olmsted brothers of Boston, sons of the landscape architect Frederick Law Olmsted, to visit Oberlin and chart a durable scheme for campus growth. The Olmsteds lacked their father's creative genius but had absorbed his knack for grounding the long view in close detail. Their thirty-one-page report of June 20, 1903, remains an astonishing

forecast of Oberlin's twentieth-century physical future, complete with specific recommendations and warnings that held fast down through the 1950s
and beyond.

The heart of their report proposed turning what was then called "the
campus" into a vast New England village green—the open space that acquired the name Tappan Square in the 1940s. "It would be very greatly to
the advantage of the long run," the Olmsteds wrote, "to clear the main campus of buildings and to keep it as a spacious and beautiful pleasure ground
for the principal working buildings of the college to front upon." The report
went on to propose sites for each main future building, including an expanded science complex to the west and north of the new Severance Chemistry Lab, with men's dormitories to the north of that and women's dormitories clustered southwest of Talcott and Baldwin.

Controversy promptly focused on the proposal for clearing the square.
This idea won support from King and several influential trustees, including
Lucien Warner, Dr. Dudley Peter Allen, and Charles Martin Hall, a strong
advocate of open space who joined the board in 1905. But a rival faction, led
by college treasurer James Severance and supported by many faculty members, favored a fresh new string of buildings across the square to retain its
functional utility and screen out the commercial ugliness of Oberlin's downtown. The chief promoter of this plan was James Lyman Silsbee, the Chicago
architect whose Memorial Arch went up in 1903 across from Peters Hall.
(He is remembered today in architectural history as the man who gave Frank
Lloyd Wright his first job.)

Treasurer Severance and Silsbee were close friends. Silsbee may well
have designed Severance's handsome house on South Professor Street,
where Ben and Gertrude Lewis now live [1983]. Together Silsbee and
Severance fought the Olmsted plan for several years, until their resistance
was overcome by King's friendly persuasion and some deft trustee commit-
tee-packing. Silsbee was then mollified by the commission for Men's
Building (later Wilder Hall) and the promise that he would design an administration building after that.

Meanwhile, beginning in 1903, President King tackled the vexed problem of creating a new college chapel. Scrapping designs proposed by architects from Indianapolis and Boston, he began to stroke the son of Charles

Grandison Finney for money and advice. Frederick Norton Finney, a tough western railroad magnate, was prepared to finance a memorial to his father and had strong views about what he wanted in a new chapel. He gave King two names to pursue, Kim and Gilbert, noting that the latter was "a very artistic fellow." "Kim" turned out to be Charles Follen McKim of McKim, Mead and White, the country's leading architectural firm. Cass Gilbert was a younger man whose Minnesota state capitol had brought him sudden renown. King chose Gilbert, who took up the project with winning personal energy.

King soon found himself caught in a tense contest of will between Gilbert and Finney's son, who disliked Gilbert's preliminary sketches for the chapel, never quite reconciled himself to the final plans, and in the end denied funds for installing a rose window. For his part, Gilbert asserted his professional autonomy and succeeded in building the chapel *he* wanted for Oberlin.

The architect believed that Oberlin's best existing building was Warner Gymnasium, whose plain horizontal lines, low-pitched roof, and round-arched fenestration were to his eye "serious, quiet and not extravagant"— aligned with the college's mood and reputation. He tried to translate these traits into the smooth-surfaced Romanesque styling of Finney Chapel, economically confining decorative flourishes to the entry facing the square.

His letters to King as well as surviving wash drawings of the interior suggest his hope that over time the chapel might acquire inner warmth, color, and texture from stained glass, memorial tablets, banners, and sensitive mural paint tones. As late as 1915 he wrote wistfully to King, "The chapel will never be complete until this work is done."

Sixty-seven years later, in the summer of 1982, the college finally launched a renovation of Finney that goes far to make up for Gilbert's dismay over its unfinished look.

King and Gilbert got on well. As early as 1904 they discussed a ground plan for Oberlin's future buildings. By 1911, King was ready to confirm Gilbert as Oberlin's master architect. Rival practitioners, including Silsbee and Normand Patton—who had designed Warner Gym and Carnegie Library—protested this move, but King prevailed. Patton had to content himself with one last local commission, Keep Cottage on North Main

Finney Chapel (1908), Cass Gilbert, architect. Courtesy of Oberlin
College Archives.

Street. Silsbee agreed to a quiet settlement over his design for a new administrative complex on the square, and Gilbert was now free to proceed on
his second campus building, the Jacob D. Cox Memorial Administration
Building next to Finney.

The trustees' 1912 decision to name Gilbert general architect to the college is unique in Oberlin's history and testifies to the strength of his bond
with King. The two men shared the dream that Oberlin might become an
architectural as well as educational community, transcending what one
prominent critic of the campus called "the chaos of architectural aberrations
which have, in the course of a rather aimless growth, sprung into existence
without apparent thought, rhyme or reason."

Gilbert and King, products of a generation for whom culture was a
seamless web, agreed that a pleasing physical environment was crucial to
good learning. As King said in 1913, "It is no small part of the obligation
which the College owes to its students to make their environment, as well
as their courses, minister to a discriminating aesthetic taste. In its architecture and grounds, as well as in its courses in literature and music and art, the

College hopes thus to meet the aesthetic needs of its students with increasing satisfaction."

Along the trail of their common quest, one finds here and there a tantalizing might-have-been. In 1911 Gilbert suggested to King that the college buy the surviving stone detail of Henry Hobson Richardson's Cincinnati Chamber of Commerce Building, which faced demolition after a fire. Gilbert produced two pages of sketches showing how Richardson's arches and carvings might be worked into Gilbert's future Oberlin buildings, but there the matter died. A half-century later students at the University of Cincinnati College of Design rediscovered Richardson's ornate granite blocks and built them into a modern historic monument to Richardson and his work.

Better luck attended other Oberlin projects. At the urging of Charles Martin Hall and with Gilbert's strong endorsement, in 1912 the Olmsted brothers were asked to turn the square into an authentic park for use by both college and town. The Olmsteds at first declined the offer, pleading overwork elsewhere. But after King and Gilbert made separate trips to Boston for a bit of brotherly arm-twisting, the Olmsteds changed their minds and became Oberlin's consulting landscape architects, to collaborate with Gilbert in campus planning.

Over the next two years they launched a comprehensive renovation of the square. Programs of underground drainage, soil aeration, and fertilization were started. New crosswalks and border walks—of red brick rather than concrete or macadam, at Gilbert's and the Olmsteds' insistence—were laid. Sickly tree specimens, resulting from long decades of overplanting since the 1850s, were cleared out, and long corridors of American elms of varied vintage now lined the walks. Charles Martin Hall saw to it in his will of 1914 that the three remaining buildings on the square would disappear. The last of them came down in 1927. But for the onslaught of the Dutch elm disease in the 1960s, Tappan Square would survive today as the most coherent legacy of the grand plan.

In 1914 attention swung to the eastern, Main Street boundary of the square, where everyone agreed Charles Martin Hall's auditorium in memory of his mother would rise on the center line directly across from Silsbee's Memorial Arch. Of course, no one anticipated that fifty years and a long train of hopeful architects, Gilbert among them, would pass before its actual

construction. To the south of the auditorium, King envisioned a multipur-
pose town-gown civic center, with space to house the village government, a
new hotel and faculty club, and perhaps a public school.

North of the auditorium site lay the land for Gilbert's next building, the
Allen Art Museum, which he planned in close consultation with the donor,
Dr. Dudley Peter Allen, and later his widow, Elizabeth Allen. For the
museum, Gilbert swung decisively from Romanesque to North Italian
Renaissance associations.

The result was serene, formal, yet inviting. Gilbert's office records show
that he maintained closer control over the details of the museum's appearance, construction, and ornamental detail than he enjoyed in any of his other
Oberlin commissions. Architect, client, contractors, and subcontractors
worked in disciplined harmony to produce his proudest Oberlin monument.

Allen Art Museum (1917), Cass Gilbert, architect. Courtesy of Oberlin
College Archives.

After his appointment as general college architect in 1912, Cass Gilbert went to work on a total solution for the campus of the future. It was published in 1914 and appears in the Oberlin *Hi-O-Hi* of that year. Gilbert's version of the Olmsted Brothers' grand plan is a faithful reflection of the rules that governed American urban planning from the Chicago World's Fair of 1893 to the outbreak of World War I. It was a highly rectilinear plan, with long sight lines across the empty square and through Memorial Arch, enclosed on the block west of the square by a dense cluster of buildings connected by curving arcades. Finney, Cox, Warner, and the old Conservatory of Music would be melded into this scheme, together with new classroom buildings to provide symmetrical balance. Dormitories, athletic facilities, hospital, and power plant stretched out beyond that to the north, south, and west.

Peters Hall, which Gilbert regarded as a standing rebuke to his code of beauty, was the big obstacle to his plan, and he called repeatedly for its demolition.

When President King in 1912 asked for sketches for a modest memorial bell tower to honor his predecessor, John Henry Barrows, Gilbert responded with plans for a huge tower to replace Peters—a 300-foot-tall campanile soaring into the Ohio sky and dominating the landscape for miles around. Its erection would create a central focus for the campus, facing down the large Hall Auditorium planned for the other side of the square, and make Oberlin a Midwestern pivot point of architectural distinction.

Gilbert was by now a world-famous architect, mainly on the strength of his fabulous new Woolworth tower in New York, the tallest building in the world so far, and the most widely admired skyscraper of his generation. Clearly he felt the campus bell tower would be his climactic offering to little Oberlin. A faint trace of condescension now entered his correspondence with the college. "It is over twelve years," he wrote to King in 1916, "since I first began to do work for Oberlin College and though its buildings heretofore have been small and relatively unimportant I have found it a very interesting, not to say inspiring, work and I devoutly hope to see this consummation."

In the bell tower, Gilbert had overreached. No donor was ever moved by the idea, and little campus support gathered for it. As in his earlier hope for a Finney Chapel interior rich with historic and sentimental allusions, so with the bell tower, Gilbert seriously misjudged the Oberlin temper, which has rarely lingered over the aesthetics of tradition or the inessential flourish. The collapse of his dream coincided exactly with America's entry into the Great War and the end of an era in architectural persuasion. The restless modern world of the postwar years made Cass Gilbert, along with the aging Henry Churchill King, begin to seem a bit stiff and old-fashioned—relics of an age suddenly disappearing.

Their collaboration was not quite over, though both men were increasingly preoccupied with other matters, and some distance opened between them. As the war drew to a close and King left for a year of peace work abroad, Gilbert's New York office began work on his next Oberlin project, an elaborate Romanesque quadrangle for the graduate school of theology. Plans and perspective drawings for the quadrangle were ready by 1919, and Gilbert published them in a national architectural journal a year later. But the plans gathered dust in Oberlin for lack of funding.

Gilbert's involvement in Oberlin's long-standing need for a modern hospital brought the first obvious chill to his relation with the college. On the strength of a bequest from Dudley Peter Allen, the Oberlin Hospital Association had in 1916 retained a Cleveland architect, Charles W. Hopkinson, to design a facility that would be owned by the college and shared with the town. Hopkinson produced a design in the newly popular Georgian colonial idiom, which would have contrasted sharply with the architectural mood chosen by Gilbert for the campus. Mrs. Allen and her friends among Oberlin's trustees balked at this point and insisted that the job be done by Gilbert. Then the war intervened. Not until 1920 did Gilbert's office send out a design. Cost estimates for it ran far above funding. After much negotiation, revision, and a big fresh donation from Allen's widow, construction finally got under way in 1924.

Gilbert was now sixty-five, the head of a large firm with a huge clientele, and accustomed to long summers abroad. He had tired of the business dimension of his work. "The price of success in America today," he wrote to his wife in 1924, "is too great to be worth the effort. If I have fifteen minutes out of a day to devote to the *art* of architecture, I count that day as a special one. This sort of thing would have thrown the whole bunch of Renaissance architects of Michelangelo's time into the incurable ward of the mad-house. How I stand it I don't know." One way he stood it was to delegate authority. In 1924 he placed his son, Cass Gilbert, Jr., in charge of the Oberlin hospital project.

The project went badly. Technical complaints accumulated as the hospital, a picturesque single-story stuccoed building with a California mission-style look about it, neared completion. Oberlinians were shocked to discover finally that Cass Gilbert the son, not the father, was the architect in charge. To some this seemed almost like a breach of promise. For all its faults, the hospital served the community for forty-five years before it was swallowed up in its big successor. The hospital was the only Gilbert building in Oberlin to be overtaken by modern times. Two wings of its exterior survive as nostalgic reminders of its colorful village ambience.

King's long presidency came to a close in 1927. The record indicates that by then many trustees and faculty members believed the Gilbert connection was also due for termination. When King's successor, Ernest Hatch Wilkins, took office, he launched a systematic survey of Gilbert's buildings, calling for close appraisals by local faculty and administrative experts familiar with their use.

The reports added up to a harsh indictment. Clarence Ward of the art department, a practicing architect who admired the classical tradition in American architecture and whose enthusiasm for Gilbert's Romanesque creations was well under control, provided a detailed critique of Allen Art Museum and its structural and spatial limitations. Dr. Whitelaw Morrison, Dean Thomas Graham, and presidential assistant W. F. Bohn did the same for the hospital, Finney Chapel, and Cox, respectively. A common theme running through these reports was the stiff inadaptability of Gilbert's buildings, their lack of adequate cellar and storage space, and the high cost involved in their construction and maintenance. Gilbert's own growing inaccessibility was also noted.

When Wilkins next took the matter up with the trustees, he met with mixed reaction. A newcomer to the board summed up a major ground of discontent when she wrote, "I am *not* for keeping Cass Gilbert, *Inc.*, for our architect. I am afraid it is mostly the '*Inc.*' whose services we get." But others, including the sons of prewar power brokers Louis Henry Severance and Lucien Warner, mustered a last-ditch defense of Gilbert and his goal for Oberlin, a campus of quiet harmony and ordered beauty. In the end the board left the decision to Wilkins. Wilkins chose to stick with Gilbert.

No doubt the compelling reason behind the decision was the impressive backlog of detailed plans for future buildings that Gilbert had lavished on the college over the years in pursuit of his dream. One of these was his design for Hall Auditorium, a fraternal twin to Finney Chapel, which the trustees tentatively accepted in 1928. Another was his theological quadrangle, now made possible by a large Rockefeller gift of 1929. Construction of the quadrangle began a year later.

Once again, Gilbert assigned the details to younger partners. When Cass Gilbert, Jr., visited Oberlin in March 1930 to review the project with college authorities, he found himself defending the quadrangle's appearance against strong local doubts. When Clarence Ward questioned its style, the son responded warmly in behalf of his father's historicism: "I said that . . . we were not bound in this century to use any style. We were permitted to use all the details that were available, and that he could find probably every century represented in some part of the work. The stonework was American, the character was based on Northern Italy, and the style was 1930 Cass Gilbert." The quadrangle was Gilbert's last Oberlin commission.

From that point on, the turmoil of public history, clashing personalities, and opposing wills combined to shred the Gilbert connection and end his Oberlin dream. Hard times, triggered by the crash of '29, made fresh building commitments hazardous and simultaneously accelerated local rebellion against the costs and constraints of Gilbert's grand design.

Gilbert and Wilkins never came close to the rapport that Gilbert had enjoyed with King. After 1929 Gilbert was immersed in the most prestigious commission of his life—the U.S. Supreme Court Building in Washington—and gave over much of his Oberlin business to his son. The son predictably had no better luck. "President Wilkins is the world's worst for giving information," he told his father in 1930. And again, "President Wilkins was not in Oberlin. Thank heaven!" As troubles and delays set in over the Hall Auditorium project, the elder Gilbert wrote to Wilkins, "I wish we could get together oftener and go over matters relating to the College personally and more fully." But more was wrong than a failure of communication.

What Gilbert did not know was that the auditorium project had snagged on a legal tangle over Hall's will that would not finally be cleared until after World War II. The problem was compounded by deepening aesthetic quarrels, the local tremors of a global revolution in architectural thought. Homer H. Johnson, the trustee of Hall's will, had concluded by 1933 that Gilbert's auditorium design was unacceptable. It looked too much like a church, too much like Finney Chapel, too far out of line with modern architectural trends. Johnson used these words to describe what he preferred: "brightness, colorfulness, sparkle, snap." (Johnson's son, the young architectural gadfly Philip Johnson, had helped introduce the crisp modern "International Style" to an American audience the year before, and would emerge after World War II as its foremost American practitioner. Homer Johnson cheerfully confessed in later years that he had hoped his son would ultimately win the commission for the auditorium.)

For Gilbert, a self-professed aesthetic and political conservative, the architectural newness of his last years was an ominous portent of erratic vulgarity and barbarism. He called it "this silly modernist movement" and railed against it endlessly. Franklin Roosevelt's New Deal inspired similar emotions in him. He hoped that his Supreme Court building would inspire a reaction against all the newness and a return to settled historical roots in politics, art, and literature as well as architecture.

As for his long Oberlin connection, he now looked back in disappointment. In October 1933, seven months before he died, he wrote to an admirer:

> The buildings there which I have designed are of a picturesque type and quite different from the style of the Detroit Public Library, the Supreme Court and other works with which you are familiar. They have never allowed me money enough for any of their buildings and the matter has strung along for nearly thirty years in which time I have struggled, sometimes ineffectively, to create an environment suitable for a college that would give some impulse toward architectural beauty and distinction and which would possibly have a good influence upon the student body. I have had but little encouragement there in this direction since President King retired.[2]

The college formally ended its ties to Gilbert's estate and his successor firm in 1937. Hall Auditorium was completed in 1954; it was designed by Wallace Harrison, with whom Philip Johnson was then in close association. Cass Gilbert's grand design for the campus was invoked in the late 1950s during disputes over the siting of Minoru Yamasaki's King Building and new Conservatory of Music, and again in the late 1960s during the controversy over Mudd Library.

The campus that has developed since Gilbert's death would no doubt appall him in its restless eclecticism. The shift of student traffic and energy from the quiet of Tappan Square to the busy north-south axis running through Wilder Bowl can nevertheless be read in the plans he developed, along with King and Hall and the Olmsted brothers, beginning eighty years ago.

Gilbert's own campus contributions remain as witness to his art. Finney Chapel is generally regarded as the best large acoustical space in Oberlin. Cox, long since inadequate for all administrative purposes, remains a handsome stone box for sheltering the college's most important officers. Allen Art Museum has survived two major additions with its quiet beauty intact. And the theological quadrangle has proved nicely adaptable to its many new secular needs. Strong, unpretentious, and calm, they have together proved vastly more weatherproof, literally, aesthetically, and historically, than most of their strident neighbors. Today they have more human friends than ever before. But the grand design is lost.

Henry Churchill King and Cass Gilbert had hoped to create a campus that would somehow sustain the sort of cultural community they believed Oberlin ought to be. The fabric of that community began to come apart after World War I. Newer, more pluralistic meanings of community, emerging here and elsewhere between the two great wars, have flourished with growing insistence ever since. After the second war, urgent new building needs, the egocentric impulses of the modern American architectural profession, and the absence of a durable local campus planning system combined to dim hopes for architectural comity among us. But as Oberlin enters its sesquicentennial year, ideas for enhancing the visual cohesion of the campus in the teeth of its variety are on the rise.

CHAPTER II

Saving Peters Hall (1997)

*P*eters Hall was a crossroad for thousands of students in the past and will be again now for thousands to come.[1] We've waited three decades to be able to say that. For almost eighty years, from 1887 into the 1960s, Peters court gathered Oberlinians on their way somewhere—to nearby classrooms, or to upstairs physics or psychology labs, or basement bathrooms, or a visit to a dean or registrar, or the faculty room—which was originally Adelia Field Johnston's teaching room—in the southeast corner off the court. With the opening of the King Building in 1964, Peters began attracting fewer visitors, but memories of its original centrality lingered on.

You could always count on seeing friends there. A young alumnus testified eighty years ago that "hardly a feature of College life can be called to mind which did not depend to some degree on Peters court. Friends were more easily found there than anywhere else on campus." When you climbed the stone steps from the sidewalk and pulled open the heavy doors, you could always count on meeting folks you knew inside, running their errands or maybe waiting for you, from eight in the morning until sundown. All day long for a century now, the tall glass window wall has opened the court to the changing western sky. In the winter through the 1920s there were crackling fires in the big fireplace. Until the 1960s, there was cool drinking water in the granite fountain. That fountain has been returned and placed in its old location, and we are trying to see if it will work again.

The restoration of this remarkable nineteenth-century space, surrounded by splendid new learning facilities for the twenty-first century, thanks to many generous donors—including especially Paul and Edith Cooper—is what we celebrate today.

The space has history. Antiwar protesters filled its air with the stench of burning human hair in the 1960s. Peters became a royal castle for a film parody of Shakespeare called *Omlet* in the 1950s. Later that decade, freshmen marched on Peters with a moose head from a Wilder lounge, chanting "The moose is loose," and, as a gift to the dean of men, they ran their dorm counselor's illegal 1947 Ford up Peters main steps.

Until 1935, the year the new dance hall opened in Wilder (then called Men's Building), most dances and proms were held in Peters court, with live bands on the stair landing, crepe paper drifting from the balcony, and the brass chandelier dimmed low. If you were there with someone you liked, it could be magical.

Sports rallies in the court were common in the 1920s on Saturday mornings before the game. Early in the presidency of Henry Churchill King, in 1904, King solemnly threatened to expel upperclassmen who prevented freshmen from standing on the hearth of the fireplace. An alumna from wartime 1940s recently recalled that she used to neck at night with a V-12 sailor friend under the north entry to Peters after studying in Carnegie until nine at night. It's fun to wonder if the first Peters kiss occurred in the nineteenth century or the twentieth.

In the early 1960s I had an office on Peters' second floor with Bob Neil and Nate Greenberg in offices nearby. We often stayed up there writing lectures until well past midnight, and one night when I left I found a high-level administrator crouched downstairs in the dark, hoping to catch students who had broken into his office to ransack his files the night before. When I told Nate Greenberg about that recently, he replied, "Ah, there were giants in those days."

The prehistory of Peters, before it opened on January 26, 1887, was faithfully told at the building's dedication on that brisk winter afternoon 110 years ago. Much of its subsequent history is nicely captured in the Mudd

Library exhibit put together by archivist Roland Baumann and his staff. Rather than echoing these records, I want to explore the meaning of Peters Hall—first, as an architectural event; secondly as a clue to the changing character and quality of Oberlin, a college already well on its way in 1887 toward academic distinction; and finally as a twentieth-century study in the perils of historic preservation.

Alumni who came to celebrate Peters Hall, old and new, could see at a glance the gifts of the early classes—the clock, the friezes, the chandelier, and the lampposts, all lovingly donated nearly a century ago.

The dedication brochure of 1887 for the opening of Peters pronounced it "the most perfect college building in the United States." Let's see why they thought so.

The architects of the building are not prominent in the annals of American architecture. Frank Weary from Cleveland and George Kramer of Ashland had joined forces in Akron in 1875 and collaborated on the design of courthouses, churches, jails, and campus buildings all over the Midwest before they parted company in the early 1890s. The structural integrity of their buildings and the resulting survival rate among them are quite impressive. Their stylistic taste had been profoundly touched by the reigning master of their generation, Henry Hobson Richardson, the first American architect to have a style named after him—Richardsonian Romanesque. Richardson was a huge man whose grand manner and living style, as well as his buildings, made him a legend in his profession long before his early death at age forty-eight in 1886. He left his impress everywhere, and Weary and Kramer brought it to Oberlin.

Viewed from a distance, Peters is a less coherent, more restless presence than Richardson's masterpieces; he was not easy to adapt or imitate. Frank Weary told his Oberlin clients in fact that the vertical thrust of Peters's pinnacles were a "type of Gothic architecture . . . somewhat domesticated and Americanized." He offered to moderate the pinnacles if Oberlin desired, and at Oberlin's insistence he eliminated almost all decorative flourishes of the sort that delighted Richardson in his own buildings. Carved stone decoration is virtually absent from Peters's exterior, except for the spandrels over the main arched entry.

What has set Peters apart on this campus is Weary and Kramer's superb interior arrangements. There were no corridors in their design—Peters Hall has no halls. Immediately surrounding the central court were two great rings of teaching space. Nine classrooms opened directly on the court, and eight more looked out on the balcony above. The crisscrossing traffic; the polished red oak woodwork of the staircase, balcony, and ceiling; the absence of tight dark passageways between classrooms; and the big windows in each classroom all made for a warm and airy interior, a welcoming contrast to the soaring gray stone exterior one contemplated on approach.

The transition from outdoors to indoors was abrupt, but not without its psychological rewards, especially in the northern Ohio academic wintertime. Class gifts in the building's early years enforced the contrast—the fireplace in 1890 (a more Richardsonian structure than Peters itself), the casts of the Parthenon frieze in 1900, the chandelier in 1901, the brass lampstands on the stairposts in 1907. Meanwhile, Peters's state-of-the-art forced-air ventilation system installed at the outset—which made it a very modern building when it opened—changed the air in each room every twenty minutes, or so the furnace people claimed.

The most costly renovations of 1996 brought a comprehensive new heating, ventilation, and air conditioning system to Peters, new plumbing and fire-proofing, and a new elevator to bring the building up to code. Solving the aesthetic issues involved in meeting the Americans with Disabilities Act was a major challenge well met. The redistribution of interior space in Peters's upper stories was a response to the new definition of the building as a center for language learning and international studies and to the radically shifting ratio between classroom space and office space that has marked the academic campus everywhere in recent decades. In 1887 there were three classrooms in Peters for every office; today there are four offices for every classroom. Meeting all these needs inspired intense debate through the mid-1990s and produced, one hopes, effective and durable solutions. Those who dissented from some of those solutions were assured by the architects in charge of the renovation, Peter van Dijk and his associates, that when the time comes sometime next century for another Peters renovation, future designers can make spatial rearrangements by moving temporary inside walls around. The building itself was built to outlast us all.

The arrival of Peters in 1887 was a clue to the changing future of Oberlin College. The money that made it possible came from a personal old-boy network carefully cultivated by James H. Fairchild, president of the college from 1866 to 1889. Alva Bradley, a Great Lakes steamship owner, gave the first big sum. He was one of Fairchild's closest boyhood friends; their families had migrated together from western New England to Brownhelm Township, just north of Oberlin, in 1817. Bradley's gift was soon followed by a larger one from Richard Peters, a Michigan timber king. The career of Richard Peters, in contrast to his building, was not all that stable. He moved from rags to riches and back to rags again twice in his lifetime. He would die blind and penniless at the age of ninety-eight in 1927. Oberlin caught him in his riches. An upstate New York Congregationalist farm boy by origin, he enrolled at Oberlin in 1857, got married in his first year here, and was therefore promptly expelled along with his wife Evelyn. They evidently left without rancor. Peters's next move, into Michigan timber, brought him better luck. Soon he was prosperous enough to endow an Oberlin professorship. A few years later, in 1883, Oberlin tightened its bond with Peters by lending him several thousand dollars to prop up his business. Meanwhile, his wife Evelyn moved to leadership in the Christian temperance movement, a cause in which Oberlin led all colleges in America at that time. Oberlin professors became frequent preachers at Peters's Congregational church in Manistee, Michigan. All this was prelude to that jubilant telegram home from one of them announcing Peters's big gift of 1886: "With God all things are possible . . . Captain Bradley's work completed." An Oberlin trustee later nailed down the meaning of the gift: "Here is Peters, and upon this rock will I build my college."

I think the crucial details in that story may be Mrs. Peters's faith in temperance, which her husband shared, and Oberlin's dogged missionary visits to the Peters's Congregational church in Manistee. And those details are symptomatic of a larger pattern, sometimes obscured by automatic thoughts about a gilded age of robber barons.

Peters Hall was one of six new buildings to go up, suddenly transforming the campus, between 1883 and 1887. Each had its philanthropic donor. If one could fashion a collective portrait from the careers of Lucien Warner, Charles Spear, Alva Bradley, Richard Peters, Elbert Baldwin, and James Talcott, and, later on, Louis Severance, Willis James, Frederick Norton Finney, Herbert Wilder, Jacob Cox, and Oberlin's own Charles Martin Hall, the resulting profile would be instructive. It would tell about a group of earnest, pious men, born into active churchgoing homes, who made it big in the onrushing age of business enterprise that followed on the Civil War, but who never forgot their families' antebellum origins and never lost their admiration for Oberlin's perfectionist commitments to antislavery, women's rights, and temperance.

As the biographer of Oberlin's Lucy Stone once put it, "Many men who knew that riches were there for the earning believed also that man and society were infinitely perfectible. The American myth, even when it is materialistic, is [also] idealistic." Oberlin's post–Civil War leaders, led by President Fairchild, understood that, and they proved to be remarkably skillful in trading on their college's moral-reform heritage to coax money from sympathetic moguls. Their goal was to launch a new Oberlin toward the century ahead.

Of course buildings alone did not make a new Oberlin. Their arrival throughout the 1880s was of a piece with the college's first decisive moves toward academic modernization. In the midst of all the fresh construction, as the walls of Peters were rising and the cornerstone of Baldwin was being laid, Professor William Ballantine, who would soon succeed Fairchild as president, gave a talk about what was going on. It merits reading:

> Oberlin College has reached now a new era [Ballantine said].
> The pioneer stage has passed. The true university life has begun.
> . . . Massive and commodious edifices of freestone will look out
> across green-shaven lawns, and graceful towers will rise above
> the elms. With the buildings already erected, or at once to be
> erected, Oberlin will take her place unchallenged among univer-
> sity towns famous for scholastic charms. . . . [To our alumni] the
> Oberlin of today is a new Oberlin. . . . We should like to keep
> the precious past just as they knew and loved it. But that may
> not be. . . . We must move onward into the future. That Oberlin
> should become a great and fully equipped university was the in-
> evitable result of the past. . . . Grand as was the work done by
> the old Oberlin, it could not render that service to learning
> which continuous progress demands. . . . Libraries and laborato-
> ries, and suitable buildings, are essential tools of learning.
> Scholars who are to lead at the frontiers of science cannot be
> frontiersmen of the backwoods.

Ballantine went on to identify those values from the Oberlin past that ought nevertheless to remain part of the Oberlin future. It makes an interesting list:

Religious concern: "We believe in teaching theology to undergraduates. The theology upon which Oberlin is founded is an urgent one—[it is] a missionary theology."

Social concern: "The living questions of the day, in education, in social morals, in politics and in religion, have always found here a free platform. . . . Every law practice, fashion or opinion may be called upon to give account of itself."

Racial diversity: "Every human face, black or white, red or yellow, shall find at this door cordial greeting. . . . Already Oberlin numbers among her sons and daughters those of every complexion and every sky, and with the increasingly easy inter-communication of nations the proportion of foreign students must largely increase."

Income diversity: "The poor must not only be invited to Oberlin; they must be made to feel welcome. Plain clothes and frugal habits must be at home here. . . . Social habits which increase the expense of living must be frowned down upon."

And, finally, community cohesion, fellow feeling, comity: "In the early Oberlin perfect harmony reigned among citizens, teachers and students. All had the same principles and aims. Each [group] confided in the others. This state of sentiment must be maintained."

On balance, all things considered, not a bad prescription for the future.

Ballantine had at the outset of his talk called on Oberlin to join the trend of the day among Eastern colleges and become a university. The faculty rejected that change as overly pretentious. But in fact the decade of the 1880s witnessed breathtaking transformations. The endowment tripled, the student body doubled, library holdings doubled, and the faculty grew by 50 percent, with an ominous number of newcomers lacking a proper Oberlin education.

The elective system, imported from Harvard, came on strong across the 1880s—too strong, some felt. A math professor grumbled that the curriculum was becoming so liberal that "a student could make everything elective and graduate without going through cube root." The new teaching technique of lecturing arrived, replacing rote recitation sessions, which were called "hearing your classes." Old habits died slowly, though, then as now, and in its early years Peters was still referred to as "the New Recitation Hall."

Laboratory work in the sciences flourished under Professor Frank Jewett, though Jewett had to wait fourteen more years for the gift of a modern laboratory building from Standard Oil magnate Louis Severance. Student interest in lab science grew so fast in the early 1880s that President Fairchild feared the traditional humanities might suffer from the competition. He added, however, that "as yet there is probably no occasion for alarm." One reason for this was the arrival of attractive new course work in modern language and literature, often taught by newcomers uninitiated in Oberlin's peculiar ways. When Peters opened in 1887, only one teacher of modern language graced the faculty, and he was fired for plagiarism a year later. H. H. Powers (of travel grant fame) came in from Wisconsin to replace him, but Powers left after four years, his religious and moral views under a cloud. It turned out his social concerns favored the abolition of the family, state-controlled childbirth, and legalized prostitution. Meanwhile Oberlin's first Ph.D., Charles Harris, arrived from Leipzig to teach German in 1888, but left after five years, complaining that the college wouldn't buy the books he needed.

A popular young literature professor, William Thomas, arrived from Tennessee by way of Berlin in 1889 to start a modern English department. In 1893 he decided to become a sociologist instead. He left for the University of Chicago, wrote a startling book, *Sex and Society,* and a few years later was fired by the university for violation of the Mann Act with the young wife of a soldier fighting overseas. The case made headlines. That was the trouble with these new language and lit professors brought in from other places: you couldn't count on them; they were often too secular and cosmopolitan; they didn't fit in. The new Oberlin was not supposed to be that new.

The fast-growing Conservatory of Music posed a similar problem. When a wave of old-fashioned religious revivalism hit Oberlin in October 1891, the college suspended classes for it, but the conservatory did not. A history professor wrote in his diary, "At the faculty meeting [today], the lack of religious activity in the Conservatory was deeply lamented."

The college, as you know, survived all the young Turks who came to teach in Peters, and its new neighbors, then and later on, and benefited from most of them.

One other young Turk merits attention. Alumnus John R. Commons returned to Oberlin from Johns Hopkins in 1891, and in the single year before he left, he introduced the modern social sciences at Oberlin—the first course in institutional economics, first course in sociology, first course in modern American history. He went on to become the leading labor historian of his generation at the University of Wisconsin.

How Peters itself managed to survive is my last concern. I'll deal with the story briefly because it's been told before, and the tension in the tale has now happily disappeared. The castellated Romanesque appearance of Peters became problematic sooner than anyone anticipated. The long Richardsonian moment in American architecture ended abruptly with the Chicago World's Fair of 1893 and the surge of Beaux Arts neoclassicism it inspired. One up-and-coming young architect whose taste was changed by the Chicago fair was Cass Gilbert, who had been a strong admirer of Richardson in earlier years.

When Gilbert visited Oberlin for the first time in 1903 to start designing Finney Chapel, he was dismayed by the rest of the campus, including Peters, which he regarded as altogether too awkward, fussy, and dated. But in deference to what else he found here—he liked Warner Gymnasium, for example, and he liked the red tile roofs of Baldwin, Warner Gym, and Severance—instead of moving the full distance toward formal neoclassicism, he chose a more picturesque, Mediterranean theme for his Oberlin buildings, evolving from twelfth-century southern French Romanesque to fifteenth-century Italian Renaissance.

He also championed the concept of the City Beautiful, another legacy of the Chicago World's Fair, and, along with Frederick Law Olmsted, Jr., and others, he helped develop the design of the Mall in Washington, D.C., a model of City Beautiful planning. He later collaborated with Olmsted to lay out a City Beautiful design for the twentieth-century Oberlin campus, a design marked by broad rectilinear subcampuses taking off from Tappan Square to the east, north, and west, with grand vistas in each direction terminating in picturesque new buildings to be designed by Cass Gilbert.

Peters was in the way of this plan, and as early as 1911 Gilbert made President King promise that Peters would come down as soon as possible—meaning as soon as the college could find the money to level it and distribute its functions to new buildings. That proviso saved Peters, because the college never did find the money, and alumni raised hell whenever campus planners brought the matter up. When word leaked out just after World War I that

Peters was doomed to make way for Gilbert's grand design, and alumni started growling, the college took another look at its budget and announced it wasn't going to happen after all. In the early 1970s, when several influential trustees tried to revive Cass Gilbert's dream in the site planning for Mudd Library, which threatened both Peters and Warner Gym, again a storm broke and the site of Mudd was moved instead. And in 1992, faced with costly maintenance problems, and the news that Peters—by now an administrative annex loaded from the attic down with paper and beaverboard—had become a firetrap, campus planners again considered demolition. President Fred Starr, a committed preservationist with a few tricks up his sleeve, then proceeded to orchestrate a successful campaign to save Peters one last time.

So here we are back at the crossroads. At Peters's first dedication in 1887, the main speaker predicted that "fire and cyclone and earthquake excepted, [Peters] will still be standing and doing good service when the twentieth century shall strike its midnight hour." The oldest survivor on this campus, now new again, Peters has made it, with three years to spare.

CHAPTER 12

A Century of Oberlin Football, 1891–1991 (1991)

*I*ntercollegiate football arrived at Oberlin one hundred years ago this fall.[1] Oberlin played its first home game against Cleveland's Adelbert College (later renamed Western Reserve, then Case Western) on October 31, 1891. A sizable crowd, filled out by a trainload of fans from Cleveland, lent color to the gray, windy afternoon, as Adelbert's cherry and white rivaled the hometown crimson and gold. Oberlin won, 12–6.

The sport that drew the crowd was an evolving American hybrid of English rugby—a rough mix of kicking, running, tackling, and slugging that Oberlin men had been playing among themselves on Tappan Square since the 1870s. Now with the faculty's grudging approval, the best players on campus began to challenge other schools, plugging the college into a drive for intercollegiate competition that spread rapidly from the Eastern seaboard through the Midwest across the 1880s. Dressed in baggy canvas knee pants, tight-laced vests, and thick turtlenecks, the squad played a game that was heavy with signals for the future of American popular culture.

Crucial rules governing the game changed almost yearly. In the early 1890s they dictated a sequence of compact head-on collisions between opposing rush lines, the offensive team trying to advance the ball by pounding a wedge of bodies through the resistance. The most spectacular tactic was the flying wedge, until it was outlawed as too dangerous in 1894.

Excited observers of the sport noted the disciplined, pistonlike precision in its rhythms, and began using industrial and military metaphors to describe what they watched, which contrasted vividly with the more pastoral, meandering preindustrial flow of English football (soccer). Hostile critics disliked the difference and regretted the pounding physical aggression promoted by the American game. Some Oberlinians wondered if it squared with the Christian values of their college. But players and their fans found it an exhilarating release of energy and read into it a test of character and discipline unmatched by any other sport. The game promptly generated campus heroes.

In 1892 two special heroes emerged for Oberlin. John Heisman, recruited and hired by students, arrived at age twenty-two, fresh from his playing career at Brown and Penn, to mold a winning team as its player-coach. His biggest victory that fall came in Ann Arbor, where in the waning moments of a close game he threw the block that sprang halfback Charles Savage for a ninety-five-yard dash to clinch a win over Michigan, just in time for Oberlin to catch the last train home. (The game's outcome is disputed to this day, however. See Chapter 13.)

After two seasons at Oberlin, Heisman went on to become one of the most successful big-time coaches of his day, climaxing his career at Georgia Tech. Meanwhile Charles Savage, after graduate training at Harvard, returned to Oberlin to become director of athletics. Savage spent the rest of his life campaigning against the growing intensity and commercialism of the big-time game and tried to promote the rival concept of the amateur student athlete playing with his friends for the fun of it.

When President Theodore Roosevelt in 1905 demanded reforms to reduce football's alarming injury rate, Savage joined a national committee (along with Chicago's Amos Stagg and Yale's Walter Camp) that devised new rules to moderate combat along the rush lines. The most transforming innovation to come out of these deliberations was the forward pass. Once quarterbacks mastered the knack of the spiral, the passing game decisively opened up the field of play and broadened the sport's crowd appeal. By the 1920s football had arrived as America's most exciting autumn spectacle, played in huge new university stadiums by recruited specialists who brought pride, publicity, and revenue to their academic sponsors.

Meanwhile at Oberlin, with support from college president Henry Churchill King, Savage and his disciples struggled on to maintain a simpler, less frenzied version of the spectacle. Before World War I, nevertheless, the local team ranked among the strongest in the region, although menaced by its upstart rival in Columbus, Ohio State. After winning 65 percent of its games since 1891, the Oberlin program momentarily collapsed in 1915 after a mass expulsion of team members for belonging to a secret society. Oberlin lost to Ohio State that fall, 128–0.

After splitting two more games with the Buckeyes, Oberlin settled into a less ambitious small-college schedule in the 1920s. Two undefeated seasons, 1921 and 1925, stirred the community, whose streets would be clogged on game day with Model Ts headed for the north campus stadium. The excitement even touched a few professors, including one of its most respected sages, Kemper Fullerton, an Old Testament scholar in the theology school. Reporting an Oberlin victory to his son in 1921, Fullerton drew a firm moral lesson from the outcome: "Our men are better trained and the fact that they don't smoke and live a fast life as so many of the men do in other colleges does tell in the long run." The search for meaning in the game again came down to character and discipline.

In a 1926 chapel vote, Oberlin students chose "Yeomen" over "Savages" and "Kingbirds" as a nickname for their varsity teams. The name nicely captured durable Oberlin priorities—hard work on and off the field, "Learning and Labor" brought up to date. Twenty years later the *Oberlin Review* decided that "Yeomen" lacked luster and sponsored a contest that hit on a new name for campus athletes—"Crimson Knights." But traditions, once fixed, can be stubborn. "Yeomen" met the challenge, hung on, and prevailed.

In 1930 Lysle Butler, star of the undefeated 1925 team, became Oberlin's head coach and held the job longer than anyone else, twenty-eight years. He cultivated the values planted earlier by Savage, always insisting that football, like physical education in general, find its proper place as part of a balanced learning experience for student athletes. For Butler, winning was far from the only thing, but he knew how to seize his chances when they came along. In the 1940s, when World War II filled Oberlin with military trainees and veterans returning from the war, he patched together some of the most interesting and rewarding teams he ever coached. Each of his successors could point to similar moments of satisfaction, although, as one of them once cracked, there were some Saturdays when they felt lucky to win the coin toss.

Since midcentury, debate over the role of football at Oberlin has flared repeatedly. The arrival in the 1950s of platooning and free substitution required bigger squads and bigger budgets. Coaches' efforts to recruit talented players ran up against rising academic standards, financial aid constraints, and Oberlin's long-standing male admissions problem. Team practice time competed with scholarly demands on players. (This was an old complaint. Back in 1913 Savage wrote, "I view with considerable alarm the gradual encroachment here at Oberlin of the schedule of classes, seminars, field work and laboratories upon the play time of the students." He added, "I am sure many members of the faculty are so driving themselves that their own efficiency is suffering from the lack of recreation.")

The ongoing football debate is unlikely to fade. The culture of the game today runs counter to so many Oberlin preoccupations that playing it and watching it sometimes seem to be not merely a pleasant diversion but an outright release from prevailing campus norms. Maybe that is its most useful function, as it was one hundred years ago.

Against stiff odds, the Oberlin version of the game—a game for grim-faced, happy amateurs—plays on. For players, coaches, and diehard fans, its rhythms, rituals, and flashes of hope provide memories that are hard to forget. One autumn afternoon some years ago, when Oberlin climaxed its first winning season in thirteen years by beating Denison in the last home game, an aging English professor ran on to the field to help tear the goalposts down. Some of us are still waiting for our chance.

CHAPTER 13

The Day Oberlin Beat Michigan— or Did We? (1999)

To stress the perils of documentary research for students writing seminar papers, historians urge skepticism about everything they read until it can be verified by another source.[1] To underscore the point, I used to teach that possible exceptions to this rule were newspaper reports about yesterday's weather or the scores of yesterday's ball games. Nobody bothers to lie about those. But when looking at the history of football at Oberlin a while ago, I learned that even on the playing field the truth about outcomes can be wonderfully elusive.

On a cold Saturday afternoon in November 1892, Oberlin's team took the field in Ann Arbor against a heavily favored Michigan eleven that had trounced them handily the year before. Notable among the Oberlin visitors was their new player-coach John Heisman, who had been hired away from the University of Pennsylvania by the Oberlin Athletic Association (a student-run enterprise in those days) and who brought an undefeated team with him to Ann Arbor. The team's fastest running back was Charles Savage, who a few years later would become Oberlin's director of athletics and, like Heisman, a nationally prominent figure. Oberlin's best lineman was theology student John Henry Wise, half-German, half-Hawaiian, who after graduation returned to his island home and joined a nationalist drive to overthrow the Hawaiian government. He was charged with treason and sent to prison for three years. Oberlin's team trainer, "nurse to the wounded," was premed student Clarence Hemingway, who would go on to practice medicine in Oak Park, Illinois, and pass on his love of hunting in Michigan to his son, future novelist Ernest Hemingway.

The game in Ann Arbor was close all the way. At halftime Michigan led 22–18. The team captains agreed on a shortened second half, to end at 4:50 P.M. so Oberlin could catch the last train home. With less than two minutes remaining, Michigan drove to the five-yard line before Oberlin stopped them and took over on downs. Then halfback Savage entered the mists of Oberlin athletic legend by dodging through the line and sprinting ninety yards to the Michigan five, where Michigan's star player, George Jewett, caught him from behind. Two plays later Oberlin made its final touchdown. Score: Oberlin 24, Michigan 22, with less than a minute to go. As Michigan launched its last drive, the referee (an Oberlin sub) announced that 4:50 p.m. had arrived, time had expired, and the Oberlin squad trotted off the field to catch the train. Next the umpire (a Michigan man) ruled that four minutes remained on the game clock, owing to timeouts that Oberlin's timekeeper had not recorded. Michigan then walked the ball over the goal line for an uncontested touchdown and was declared the winner, 26 to 24. By that time the Oberlinians were headed home clutching their own victory, 24 to 22.

The Ann Arbor mood that night was muted: Oberlin, much better trained than the year before, had surprised the home team, and Michigan's victory was a squeaker with an odd taste. Oberlin's victory was less complex and more emphatic. When news of the outcome arrived on campus, students raided the box and barrel pile of every downtown store, and soon a monstrous bonfire lit up the square. (By mistake, a box of clothing in front of Johnson's dry goods was tossed in to brighten the blaze.) The team rallied on its return with an oyster supper enlivened with town-and-gown toasts, player's responses, and a medley of college yells and fight songs celebrating what turned out to be Oberlin's only victory over Michigan in nine games played between 1891 and 1905.

In 1906, long after Heisman's departure for the big time, Charles Savage, after graduate training at Harvard and Columbia, became Oberlin's director of athletics and pursued a simon-pure sports program until his retirement, one year before the first Heisman Trophy was awarded in 1936. When Savage died twenty years later, a Cleveland sports writer recalled his greatest personal athletic achievement: "Those of us who knew him and loved him hope that at the moment he was departing this earth he was once again galloping over that Michigan gridiron with the ball tucked under his arm, his straight-arm working to perfection, and the goal posts getting nearer and nearer and nearer."

Who really won that game in 1892? A newspaper scan yields these results: *The University of Michigan Daily*—Michigan; *The Detroit Tribune*—Michigan; *The Oberlin News*—Oberlin; *The Oberlin Review*—Oberlin. To this day, the two schools dispute the outcome. The official records of the University of Michigan claim the game for Michigan, as if the Wolverines needed it, while the official records of Oberlin College, hungry for victory from any source, claim the game for Oberlin. You can look it up.

CHAPTER 14

Tobacco at Oberlin: A Backward Glance at Moral Reform (1999)

*T*he ongoing battle against the cigarette on campus today inspires a backward glance at the tangled history of Oberlin tobacco policy.[1] Right at the outset, the community Covenant of the 1830s banned smoking, chewing, and snuffing for reasons best captured some 230 years earlier by King James I. James warned his subjects in fine Elizabethan prose that if any one of them should use tobacco "as a drowsie lazy-bellied god, he shall vanish in a lethargie." In post–Civil War Oberlin, the campaign against tobacco was second only to that against alcohol among incentives to moral reform. In January 1880 antitobacco agitation surged momentarily out in front. A newspaper in nearby Wakeman put it this way: "The moral village of Oberlin is again on the rampage against one of the evils of its society. This time, tobacco has to suffer."

Nonconformists could be found. Marx Straus was the town's leading clothier, running his shop out of Park House, the old Oberlin Inn. He owned the inn until he gave it to the college in 1895. A prospering Bavarian Jew who had arrived in the 1850s, Straus lived in a handsome Italian villa on South Main. Large, affable, and flamboyant, Straus was the first man in Oberlin to smoke cigars in public. Small children stared at him. Most adults looked the other way. Mass production of cigarettes began in Durham, North Carolina, in the mid-1880s. After that, furtive smoking began to spread across the Oberlin campus. All sorts of people got involved. Raymond Swing, son of the eminent church historian Albert Temple Swing, and later eminent himself as an international radio correspondent, started smoking secretly at age fourteen. "I wanted to be good," he later testified, "but it was too much for me." A young English instructor from Princeton joined Raymond and his friends for late-night smokes around a campfire in the woods on the edge of town. The famous academic reformer Robert Maynard Hutchins of the University of Chicago, who grew up in Oberlin and went to college here just before World War I, testified that he longed to defy the tobacco ban but "was not robust enough" to smoke. The novelist Sherwood Anderson recalled that when he was a young man selling paint in Elyria, young faculty couples from Oberlin would come over to smoke and drink and talk books behind drawn curtains in his living room. The popular young Professor Henry Churchill King, on the rise in official Oberlin, set himself against all this. The covert use of tobacco violated the love of truthfulness, he told his students. As president after 1902, he called for a "New Puritanism" in Oberlin, an activist self-denial that prized "heroic service" over "passive self-indulgence." In January 1914, responding to King's dogged insistence, the men's senate resolved to try to enforce the campus tobacco ban, even though students regarded it as unenforceable and therefore "absolutely foolish."

World War I damaged that sort of grudging deference. The war and its aftermath took King from the campus for a stretch of diplomatic service. In his absence, in a general reaction against the Progressive civic morality that informed king's prewar mood, the year 1919 witnessed a major surge of restlessness among students and younger alumni against Oberlin's demanding behavioral traditions. An angry pamphlet, originating in New York City, circulated among alumni to arouse concern over Oberlin's current problems: inadequate faculty salaries, listless athletic policies, closed-minded college administrators, and the need for change in student social rules, namely the hoary rules against smoking and dancing. On his postwar return to Oberlin from abroad, King acknowledged that the time for change had arrived. In November 1919 the faculty lifted the smoking ban for men. A month later, social dancing also became legal. The 1920s brought few flappers, flasks, or raccoon coats to Oberlin, but the college did meet the decade with a careful arm's-distance embrace.

In May 1931, as the roar of the twenties faded into the anxieties of the thirties, the college faculty, after wrenching debate, voted to let women smoke in the privacy of their own rooms. After that, there was no controlling the tapping finger and the blue haze in dorm lounges, in the Campus and the Varsity, and later in the Snack Bar.

The Surgeon General's report persuaded millions to drop the habit, but the culture of choice that set in across the 1960s at Oberlin and elsewhere protected diehard smokers from organized constraint. Finally, in 1993, the college turned on the cigarette and banned smoking from almost all indoor campus spaces. The ban worked. Oberlin shares in the success of a project in behavioral coercion of national dimensions. This historic campaign, though hardly a clean sweep (outdoor smoking remains highly visible) is so remarkable that schoolkids may soon be reading about it just as we all once studied Prohibition. Prohibition—that cause had many origins. Some of the most important of them, come to think of it, sprang up in Oberlin, Ohio.

CHAPTER 15

Professor Geiser's Heresies (1992)

$\mathcal{F}$or over 150 years now, people who have heard of Oberlin have gotten used to thinking of its college as a hothouse of offbeat notions—most of them pretty radical.[1] Anyone who knows anything about Oberlin history can rattle off its radical heresies quite easily—the idea that you could educate women right alongside the men; that you could educate black Americans right along with white Americans; that when it came to eating food you could and should get along without meat (as long as you ate enough graham biscuits); that the consumption of tobacco and alcohol was a moral evil to be proscribed; that since capitalism on the face of it is problematic, various kinds of socialism (Christian and secular) are worth studying and trying out from time to time; that the same goes for organized pacifism, interracial dating, co-op living, and coed dormitories. Try them out.

Many of these wild presumptions have turned out to be not so heretical after all. Historically, most Oberlinians have been quite proud, even smug and righteous about them. Oberlin has always been pleased with itself about being out in front, ahead of the pack, challenging the pack to catch up. The heresies of the left are part of our normal heritage.

Heresies of the right—conservative heresies—are another matter. They have not broken out as frequently in Oberlin or attracted many converts. In

Karl Geiser was one of the prime movers in inaugurating the city-manager form
of government and served on the first city council under this system.
Courtesy of Oberlin College Archives.

fact they can sometimes be downright embarrassing and tend to be purged and forgotten about as soon as possible. That's what happened to the heresies of Professor Karl Geiser.

In November 1938, Professor Geiser was awarded the Merit Cross of the Order of the German Eagle for his outspoken sympathy for Nazi Germany. The award came from Adolf Hitler. This made headlines in the local papers, and it made the *New York Times*. It was big news, as when Charles Lindbergh received a similar award that same autumn. Yet when Geiser died thirteen years later in 1951, in his obituaries—local and national—not a word was whispered about the medal or the reasons for it. The familiar rule—of the dead, say nothing but good things—was carefully applied to the dead professor. Understandable perhaps. But even back in 1938, after a short uproar, the code of embarrassed silence set in very quickly.

One of the few people in Oberlin today who remembers Karl Geiser is Richard Lothrop, a retired educator who has been very active in Oberlin town politics over the past twenty years. Dick Lothrop was a young teenager, the son of an Oberlin chemistry professor, who lived just a block away from Geiser's home in 1938. When he heard about Geiser's medal from Hitler he was fascinated by it. So without telling anyone he walked over to Geiser's house to see the medal. Geiser was surprised and pleased with his young visitor and happily showed him the medal—"a beautiful thing," Lothrop recalls, "red in the form of the German Cross with its edges etched in gold," with a red and white silk ribbon for wearing around the neck. His curiosity satisfied, Lothrop thanked Geiser and went home. Many years later Mrs. Geiser told Lothrop's mother that Dick was the only person in Oberlin, town or gown, adult or child, who ever asked about the medal. Aside from Lothrop, dead silence. Ostracism.

It wasn't as if the medal surprised too many people in Oberlin. Given Geiser's behavior and statements about Germany, some Oberlinians who had been around over the previous twenty-five years could see it coming a long way off. And a historian poking around Geiser's biography with the benefit of 20-20 hindsight can see it coming almost from Geiser's birth.

He was born in 1869 in Fairbank, Iowa, the son of a German immigrant. Geiser's father broke with the local German-speaking Lutheran community of Fairbank to bring his children up in a secular, English-speaking atmosphere. And the family suffered an ostracism that Geiser had occasion to remember for the rest of his life.

After going to college in northern Iowa, Geiser went east to Yale for graduate work and earned his Ph.D. in 1900. After some postgraduate research at the University of Berlin (his first trip back to the fatherland), he joined the Oberlin faculty in 1908, as its first full-fledged political scientist—one of a big cluster of fresh young Ph.D.s who helped turn Oberlin into an outstanding liberal arts college in the early twentieth century.

This was a time when political science, like the social sciences in general, was a relatively new field, and its practitioners were charged with a sense of mission—a mission not only to bring out the truth about human political behavior but to reform that behavior by sweeping away ignorance and advocating better, new, more modern ways of doing things. Geiser shared that sense of mission, which resonated with the general progressive reform movement of those years. As a rising star on the Oberlin College faculty, he specialized in municipal government and international law. Trim, handsome, and blunt, he was a forceful campus presence.

Then came World War I. Now Geiser committed his first heresy. In May 1915, when a German submarine sank the British liner *Lusitania*, killing 128 American passengers and touching off a fierce anti-German public opinion backlash, Geiser challenged the backlash by announcing that the Germans had every right under current international law to sink the *Lusitania*, since its cargo hold was filled with munitions bound for England to be used against the Germans. As it turned out, he was right, but it was blasphemy to say so. When the U.S. joined the war against Germany two years later, wartime passions and the demand for superpatriotism gripped the campus along with the rest of the country, and the hunt for heretics got under way. One superpatriot dug out Geiser's statement about the *Lusitania* and mailed copies of it anonymously to every member of the Oberlin College board of trustees and sent another copy of it to the Bureau of Investigation in Washington. The Bureau promptly cleared Geiser of subversive pro-German tendencies. But the trustees, clutched by wartime jitters, decided to tell Geiser to find another job.

That was easier said than done. Geiser's good friend Kemper Fullerton, a highly respected Old Testament scholar, rallied the faculty to resist the trustees in the name of academic freedom, and after a six-month faculty investigation the faculty voted 38–2 to oppose Geiser's firing. And after heated debate, the trustees reluctantly backed down. But for Geiser, the experience left an ugly scar. Twenty years later he called it a moral lynching. That memory, reinforced by his belief that he had been absolutely correct in exposing the truth about the *Lusitania*, convinced Geiser from then on that when it came to any debate about Germany and German national behavior, he was right and Oberlin was wrong.

Across the postwar decade of the 1920s, Geiser spent the happiest and most useful years of his life. He led a drive to convert Oberlin to the city-manager system—one of the most successful progressive municipal reforms of the day—and was elected to the city council for six straight years to help implement the new system. He moved into a handsome new red-brick neo-Georgian house on Oberlin's most prestigious residential street—Reamer Place—just across the way from his friend Kemper Fullerton. Their children played together and became best friends.

And Geiser remained an effective teacher. Felix Frankfurter, who was teaching at the Harvard Law School before going on to become a Supreme Court Justice, said this about him: "I really believe that the best teacher of political science in the country is Geiser out in Oberlin. For fifteen years he has been sending us the best men we've been getting at the Harvard Law School. . . . I don't know what Geiser does to them or how, but they have background and are really educated. He must be a great teacher." High praise from the most distinguished law professor in America.

In 1924 Geiser made his first trip back to Germany since the end of World War I. He was dismayed by what he saw. Defeat in the war had prostrated the country, and the harsh peace terms imposed by the Allies in the Treaty of Versailles kept the country pinned down. Meanwhile the German middle class was being ruined by runaway inflation. Geiser came home and reported what he saw in an article for *The Nation* titled "Will Germany Live Again?" His forecast was glum. The German story was, he said, "a story of patient suffering amid discouragement unparalleled by any state in modern times."

Five years later, in 1929, he returned to Germany again for a sabbatical year. Now he found the country on the brink of revolution—but he prophesied a revolution of a different kind. Revolution German-style will not begin in the streets and work upward against the bayonets of the state, he said; it will begin at the top by a vote in the Reichstag, and since the Germans are a law-abiding people, it will be supported by the entire nation. "A vote in the Reichstag may change the course of history," he concluded. A perceptive prediction, as it turned out. The Berlin correspondent for the *Baltimore Sun* said that Geiser was "the first man since the war who has observed Germany and knew what he was talking about."

Geiser's next trip to Germany came in the summer of 1932. The country was now boiling with revolutionary change—street riots, mass demonstrations, communists killing Nazis, Nazis killing communists. Geiser was excited and also fearful about it all; he confessed it shook his nerves. But mingled with the fear was hope. He found the source of hope in Adolf Hitler's Nazi headquarters in Munich. Geiser's visit to the headquarters enormously impressed him. He wrote about it this way:

> I dare to say, judged from the indications I saw, they have the most scientific and complete organization in the world. There is, moreover, an atmosphere . . . of cleanliness and order, and the personnel is made up of fine appearing young men, so that the Hitler movement, from its mechanical and physical aspect, commands respect, if not admiration. . . . It is religious, Puritan, cultural, temperate in habits of life, though not of thought, and it is, above all, idealistic.

Geiser's first glimpse of Nazism at its source reminded him of elemental German virtues—order, discipline, energy, control. A couple of days later he got the full dose. He joined 50,000 Germans in Munich's big new municipal stadium for a six-hour Nazi rally. It was an awesome spectacle. As he described it, storm troopers marched in and out of the stadium in complex mass formations while pretty young women danced around them with colorful banners, and a 150-piece brass band pounded out party anthems. When night fell, a 12,000-man torchlight procession entered the stadium and formed a gigantic flaming swastika. Then over the loudspeakers came the climactic signal: "Achtung, Achtung, der Fuhrer Kommt!" Up in the black sky searchlights picked out an approaching airplane that circled the glowing stadium before landing nearby. Minutes later der Fuhrer strode into the stadium through a thunder of "Heil! Heil! Heil!" Hitler spoke to the crowd in a mounting frenzy: for thirteen years, he shouted, Germany had worked and starved and waited, while the world laughed. Democracy had ruined the fatherland. All established political parties must now be abolished. The misery must end. The misery *will* end. Geiser ended his description of the rally: "Here at last was the savior of the German people." He went on to analyze the meaning of the event for *The Nation*'s readers by drawing a parallel between Hitler and William Jennings Bryan, the great folk protest leader of Geiser's midwestern youth. As with the prairie evangelist, so with the Nazi spellbinder: "Those who had lost all, or feel themselves the victims of injustice and unavenged wrongs, naturally turn to him who promises relief." Six months later Hitler became the chancellor of Germany.

In March 1933 Hitler confirmed his power in Germany's last free election of the decade and won from a shattered Reichstag the historic vote that turned Germany into a dictatorship. Also in March 1933 Franklin Roosevelt launched the New Deal in Washington. For the rest of the decade Geiser struggled to make sense of these two rival responses to a world in crisis. At the outset he admitted reservations about the Nazis now that they were in power. They tended to carry things to excess in their sudden centralization of all power in Germany—the totalitarian aspects. And he regretted the Nazi's anti-Semitism. But he reported conversations with German friends who argued that the hounding of Jews was no worse than the acts of American lynch mobs against Negroes; the number of German Jews suffering discrimination was small compared with the mass of American blacks victimized by race hatred and segregation.

As for Hitler himself, Geiser began to warm to the man. His personal habits were a model of the simple life: no alcohol, no nicotine, no feasting. Hitler was bringing Germany strength through joy. No one who had seen the marching columns of German youth, "clean and strong, singing their songs of home and fatherland," could doubt that this Austrian provincial, "now the leader of a great people, has given new meaning and a new purpose to the great masses who make up the Third Reich."

In the mid-1930s the Oberlin campus blazed with ideological fervor. Visiting speakers pounded home their rival theories to eager listeners: Rex Tugwell for the New Deal, Norman Thomas for socialism, Earl Browder for communism, Lawrence Dennis for fascism. Meanwhile the faculty social science club heard colleagues debate Nazism with Geiser. At Oberlin, as in classrooms, country clubs, corporate offices and political workshops across the country, a polarizing either-or mentality emerged, as the extremes of left and right battled for the future. In this hot atmosphere of rival "isms," Geiser's clinching argument for Hitler was that he had organized Germany into the strongest bulwark in Europe against the spread of the red menace. Geiser described Hitler as "a Siegfried slaying the dragon of communism."

Meanwhile Geiser's attitudes toward Roosevelt's New Deal moved from initial admiration to growing mistrust. He thought Roosevelt's early brain trusters were responsible, forward-looking intellectuals—one reason being that the head of the brain trust, Raymond Moley, had once been a student of Geiser's at Oberlin. But by 1936 Geiser condemned the New Deal as "an ill-planned and wasteful extravagance which hinders rather than helps recovery."

Geiser retired from teaching at age 66 in 1935. By that time he was running out of close friends in Oberlin. His old companion Kemper Fullerton, who had come to his rescue back during World War I, was now a strong New Deal liberal and an outspoken antifascist and was no longer on good terms with Geiser. In fact these two Oberlin neighbors stopped speaking to each other, though their children remained good friends. When Fullerton died at the end of the decade, he left funeral instructions naming Geiser as one of his pallbearers—one way of asking that their feud now cease. Geiser obeyed, and this became a minor Oberlin legend.

Geiser led a very active retirement. In early 1938, while on a research and lecture tour in Germany, he had the honor of a fifteen-minute audience with Hitler. He came home and in a talk to the Elyria Lawyers Club described Hitler as a calm, impressive person "with eyes like searchlights and a face as innocent and guileless as a child's." Hitler would go down in history as a great man—"Greater than Bismarck, he came to Germany like a Lincoln, from the common people." Geiser forecast peace, stability and prosperity for Germany and for Europe, but he added: "I am not so sure about America. Unless things improve here, I am not so sure of my faith in democracy as we know it."

While Geiser spoke to the lawyers of Elyria, Nazi troops were completing their occupation of Austria. Six months later came the Munich Conference, and Neville Chamberlain's capitulation to Hitler on the future of Czechoslovakia. Two months after that came the Nazi attacks on Jewish synagogues—*Kristallnacht*, the night of shattered glass. Then on November 25, 1938, Karl Geiser received his medal from Hitler.

News of the medal, coming on the heels of Munich and *Kristallnacht*, ignited a small firestorm in Oberlin. The college faculty met in special session, and students held a mass meeting, and both groups passed resolutions condemning Nazi persecution of racial and religious minorities and the Nazi track record on free speech and human rights.

Geiser wouldn't let up. In a talk to the Cleveland City Club he defended the Munich settlement before a big, hostile crowd. He said, "When the Munich Pact causes hopes to rise and the stock market to go up, and whenever Roosevelt speaks hope goes down and the market falls, what are we to think?" In an answer to a question from the audience, he said, "Yes, I believe in democracy, but democracy is a spirit, and I deny that America is a democracy at the present time."

A year later, in 1940, with World War II well under way and American defense spending on a sudden rise, Geiser called Germany "the greatest democracy in all the world" and said that with Roosevelt seeking a third term, the U.S. was moving toward "a military dictatorship as rigid as anything in the world today." Roosevelt, not Nazi Germany or the Soviet Union, was now in Geiser's mind the main threat to American democratic capitalism.

After Roosevelt's reelection in 1940 and his call for massive Lend-Lease aid to Britain, Geiser spoke in Elyria in what turned out to be his last public address on the war. He condemned Lend-Lease, described Britain as a country dominated by international banking interests led by Winston Churchill, and said that the U.S. should force Britain into a negotiated peace with Hitler. A United States of Europe dominated by Germany was a possible result. If Hitler was unwilling to settle for peace on these terms, Geiser (now 72 years old) said he would shoulder a gun against him. As for America, he wouldn't be surprised to see someone like Charles Lindbergh become the next president—"if there is another president." After Roosevelt, he wasn't sure there would be. With that judgment, Geiser fell silent at last. Pearl Harbor confirmed his silence for the duration.

But four years later, in March 1946, as a shattered Europe emerged from its first postwar winter after the destruction of Hitler's Third Reich, Geiser broke his wartime silence by calling Oberlin's attention to the widespread postwar starvation in his beloved Germany. One of Geiser's former faculty colleagues, Lloyd W. Taylor, a physicist who had known him for twenty years, chose to reply. He told Geiser that the situation in Germany was indeed unfortunate. But he added in cold and unforgiving language: "We have prior obligations to the nations which Germany overran and plundered—Poland, Belgium, France, Norway, Czechoslovakia, Greece, and every one of the pitiful survivors of the German pogram against her own people." That was the last known political exchange between Geiser and his critics on the Oberlin faculty.

Aside from Dick Lothrop, the only person in Oberlin today who remembers Geiser clearly is Professor Andrew Bongiorno, who recently turned ninety-two. Bongiorno sat in Geiser's classes as an Oberlin student shortly after World War I. He returned to join Geiser as a junior colleague on the faculty in 1925. He watched Geiser's friendship with Kemper Fullerton come apart and stood with Geiser at Fullerton's burial. Like the majority of Oberlin faculty members, he broke with Geiser over Hitler.

A decade later, when Geiser had just turned eighty (Bongiorno says he used to think of eighty as an advanced age), he saw Geiser for the last time, wheeling an old bicycle across the campus. Bongiorno congratulated him on still being able to use a bicycle. He remembers Geiser's exact reply: "If I didn't have a clear conscience I would have died long ago."

Geiser carried his conscience with him to his grave. For his tombstone (which is located fifty yards from Kemper Fullerton's grave in Oberlin's Westwood Cemetery) he chose the opening line of an ode by the Roman poet Horace: "Justum et tenacem propositi virum." An English translation on the full passage reads: "For a just man and one with a full grasp of his intentions, neither the heated passions of his fellow citizens ordaining something awful, nor the face of a tyrant before his very eyes, will shake him in his firm-based mind." Geiser died unembarrassed. His heresy might inspire caution for those who believe, on the strength of their training and personal experience, that they have a lock on the truth of this century's turbulent past, or its puzzling future.

CHAPTER 16

Campus Life at Oberlin,
1930–1945 (1998)

Most historians would agree, I think, that the fifteen years from 1930 to 1945, spanning the Great Depression and World War II, were the harshest stretch of time in twentieth-century American history.[1] Yet an impressionistic survey of the Oberlin campus scene throughout those years leaves one with an odd sense that the morale of student life flourished with a resilience that compares surprisingly well with the mood in later years of less searing anxiety and stress.

This essay pokes around for clues with which to puzzle through that paradox.

What follows needs a warning label.

Many Oberlinians come to think of the years just before their own stay here with a particular nostalgia, imagining them as a kind of golden age that they barely missed. As a Depression kid who monitored the war from a safe distance by punching red pins in a National Geographic map of the world, and whose first visit to Oberlin at age fourteen for my sister's graduation in 1946 made it seem a wonderfully serene and pastoral place, I share some of that second-hand nostalgia. My own subsequent student years here and my accumulating obligations to historical detachment have not washed it entirely away. The teenage visitor's soft thoughts about Oberlin may be forgiven. As for the professor's—well, fair warning.

The great educational reformer of the 1930s, Robert Maynard Hutchins, grew up in Oberlin and went to the college here for a couple of years before finishing at Yale. He came back to speak at the commencement of 1934. He called his talk "The Sentimental Alumnus," but he managed to avoid nostalgia in describing his student days here:

> With a struggle I can remember aspects of the Oberlin of my time. . . . I can remember, for example, that this is the hottest, coldest, wettest, flattest part of the state of Ohio, so uninteresting and disagreeable that Plum Creek, the arboretum, the reservoir, and even the cemetery seemed like scenic gems glowing in a dull setting of yellow clay. I can remember sitting every day in this room on the most uncomfortable of all chapel seats, trying hard not to hear what the speaker was saying. I can remember the dancing rule, the rules confining ladies to their rooms [after dark], and the smoking rule, which I abhorred but was not robust enough to violate. But these items do not disturb me very much. On the contrary, they help me to preserve my illusion of the uniqueness of the Oberlin of my day. . . . My college had the worst climate, the hardest seats, and the silliest rules of any institution in the world. [Hutchins went on to say that Oberlin gave its students the best teaching to be found anywhere. That may or may not have been a lapse into nostalgia.]

In 1934, Rec Hall in the basement of the Men's Building (now known as Wilder's Disco) replaced Peters court as the place for nightly dancing, the faculty having caved in on coed dancing (called "promiscuous dancing" by its critics) back in the 1920s. The student generation of the 1930s was born dancing, intoxicated with swing. In the fall of 1939, it celebrated the sudden arrival of the jitterbug.

After long faculty debate and deep misgivings, required chapel was dropped in 1934, replaced by "expected regular attendance," a term suggesting that even back in those days the faculty had a knack for useful euphemisms. The next year brought another change—President Wilkins called it a "drastic change"—the mixing of men and women in chapel seating. From then on you could sit next to a person of the opposite sex for religious purposes.

Student demographics began to change decisively across the 1930s. More students were coming from the urban East. President Wilkins called this a Depression phenomenon: Oberlin was attracting easterners, he said, because it offered an eastern education at western prices. Geographical diversity brought growing religious and cultural diversity. Until the Depression years, Oberlin remained a Protestant place, in its self-description and its student and faculty composition. The percentages of Jews and Catholics, infinitesimal in 1930, rose steadily across the decade—in the case of Jews, from 1 percent to 5 percent. The Depression was clearly the catalyst for this long-term shift. Asians and African Americans remained few and far between. Not until the 1970s would Oberlin's white homogeneity begin to disappear, and with it a degree of cohesive community sameness. When students in the 1930s talked about racial diversity, they did so with a certain wistful longing.

Despite the Depression (or maybe because of it) graduate school loomed as an ever more alluring post-Oberlin choice. In the early 1920s fewer than 20 percent of Oberlinians went on to graduate school. By 1940 the figure was over 50 percent. In those lean years, graduate school was a valuable avenue of rising expectations, of hope for job security and satisfaction some day. The percentage of women going on to graduate studies tripled between 1920 and 1940. College teaching was the fastest growing profession of choice for both sexes; the ministry and missionary work, the fastest shrinking. Clearly, teaching was replacing preaching in an increasingly secular world.

The Depression energized campus politics. In the presidential election of 1932, a straw poll among the students recorded 69 percent for Republican Herbert Hoover, 22 percent for Socialist Norman Thomas, and 8 percent for Democrat Franklin Roosevelt. These results were squarely in the Oberlin tradition: strong Republican family voting habits going back to Lincoln, Emancipation, and civic morality, spiced with a strong dose of social concern and a serious mistrust of Democrats. Oberlin villagers, also firmly Republican, complained when Roosevelt's New Deal started governing with borrowed money. A lot of that borrowed money went to relief agencies like the

Federal Emergency Relief Administration and later the National Youth Administration, both of which funneled job money to college students. By 1935 some 225 Oberlin students had FERA grants. This work relief may be one reason why the Democrats fared better at the next election. In 1936 the student body still tilted Republican, but by a much smaller margin: Landon, 51 percent; Roosevelt, 43 percent; Thomas, 4 percent.

A Republican resurgence occurred in 1940, the year of Wendell Willkie and the ominous third term issue. A bus caravan of several hundred students went to hear Willkie whistle-stop in Elyria, and in the poll of that year he took 64 percent, as against 26 percent for Roosevelt and 8 percent for Thomas. (The faculty was barely to the left: Willkie, 59 percent; Roosevelt, 39 percent; Thomas, 2 percent.) At the student mock convention the previous spring, several state delegations collaborated in an effort on the fourth ballot to stampede the nomination of W. C. Fields. Convention leaders were alarmed; mock conventions were serious campus business in those days.

In both 1936 and 1940, the mock conventions featured live elephants. But behind those elephants and the sturdy mainstream they stood for, a good deal of ideological ferment and anxiety divided students over where the real world was headed. With other Americans, they coped with an either-or global crisis environment: democracy versus dictatorship, capitalism versus communism, peace versus war—lots to worry about, and therefore lots to debate.

Campus political organizations, long dormant across the 1920s, suddenly flourished, most of them well to the left of center. The Liberal Club of the twenties became the Radical Club of the thirties and promptly got into trouble with President Wilkins and the faculty for attacking the college's complicity in the wealth of ALCOA. "A large proportion of the President's time," Wilkins told the trustees, was spent dealing with "the problems created by the doings and desires of a small but active group of radical students"—a complaint echoed in one way or another by each of Wilkins's successors. Meanwhile, a steady run of visiting speakers kept minds open and lively across the whole political spectrum from left to right, to a degree that really hasn't been matched since. In 1933–34, for example, Rex Tugwell came for the New Deal, Norman Thomas for socialism, Earl Browder for communism, and Lawrence Dennis for fascism. A full platter, its equivalent no longer widely desired today.

The largest campus political organization of the decade was the Oberlin Peace Society, founded in 1930 at the initiative of President Wilkins, for whom it was by all odds the most important cause on campus. "What is the use of giving four years of laborious and expensive education to these fine young men and women," he asked, "if their lives are presently to be shattered, in one way or another, by war and the consequences of war?" He proposed an undergraduate major in peace, hoping to ensure that pacifism did not slump into passive isolationism.

Roughly half the student body belonged to the Peace Society by mid-decade. In 1936 an Oberlin chapter of the Veterans of Future Wars was formed, called the Peter Pindar Peace Post. Its stated aim was to win from Congress an immediate $1,000 bonus for each future veteran so that he could "enjoy his government's generosity before he is blown up."

As the decade neared its end, prospects for peace grew more grim each month as events began their dark slide toward war. In March 1938, Nazi troops goose-stepped past Adolf Hitler through the streets of Vienna as he joined Austria to the Third Reich and called it "the greatest accomplishment of my life." More accomplishments soon followed. As college opened the following September, the young nation of Czechoslovakia was dismembered at Munich. Then came *Kristallnacht*, the night of shattered glass for German synagogues. Oberlin could not isolate itself from these events. A mass campus protest meeting passed a solemn resolution: "We, the students of Oberlin College, fully realizing that we in the United States are not above insidious action toward minority groups, do abhor and condemn the racial and religious persecution now taking place in Germany, and all persecution of minority groups everywhere." Nine months later mechanized German armies rolled over the Polish frontier and the second war was under way.

Campus debate mounted over what America should do. President Wilkins and Dean Wittke led one side of the debate, in favor of prudent neutrality. Wittke told students that "if fascism comes to America, it will not be because of a foreign invasion but because of internal decay." Political scientist Oscar Jaszi and historian Freddie Artz marshaled twenty-three colleagues behind a militant reply: "This war seems certain to be long and bitter, but all its waste cannot be compared with the evil consequences of capitulating to Hitler."

Then in the winter of 1939–40 the war seemed momentarily to go away, and students could concentrate a while on pleasures close at hand. Sergei Rachmaninoff, Rudolph Serkin, and Marian Anderson (fresh from her rebuff by the DAR, and her invitation to the White House by Eleanor Roosevelt) performed in Finney Chapel. *Gone With the Wind* began smashing box office records. *For Whom the Bell Tolls* hit the best-seller list. Harry James came to play for the junior prom, Eddie Duchin for the senior prom.

Suddenly the dark realities exploded. Hitler's *blitzkrieg* turned west, overran the Low Countries, cracked the Maginot Line, and forced the Dunkirk evacuation. The Battle of Britain got under way that summer. When college opened in the fall, 237 men registered for the draft in Warner Gym, 14 percent of them as conscientious objectors.

Over the academic year 1940–41, a faculty majority gathered around American intervention. Freddie Artz wrote an eloquent pamphlet, published by William Allen White's national committee to save the Allies, about the possibly terminal damage that fascism was inflicting on Western civilization. In class, Artz interrupted his own lectures repeatedly to drive home the warning. He circulated a letter supporting Lend-Lease aid to Britain, which President Wilkins opposed. In May 1941, 90 percent of the faculty signed a call for armed convoys to get the aid across the Atlantic. Not many students were quite so convinced. One wrote to the *Review:* "Our Daddies are running around signing petitions for convoys, and it is youth that is going to be blown full of holes when those convoys are sunk and we go to war." A *Review* poll indicated minimal student support for American entry but also massive opposition to strict American neutrality. So what to do?

Some students favored waiting until the war came to America, where it could be fought to better advantage; others, perhaps influenced by President Wilkins, favored a negotiated peace with Hitler. In the end there was no satisfactory solution.

In October 1941, the *Review* startled readers by publishing a long, anguished editorial, written mostly by future college trustee Victor Stone '42, in favor of an immediate declaration of war against Hitler. The heart of it merits quoting:

> We young people of the inter-war period have ever been activated by the hope that we were living in a postwar period. We

hoped that we could look back with historical objectivity upon the mistakes which led our elders into world-wide slaughter and destruction, that we could recognize these errors and, by avoiding them, could shape our lives as we chose. We were wrong. If we go to war, we will temporarily relinquish democracy. It is better to relinquish democracy for the duration of the war than to relinquish it indefinitely in a Nazi-dominated world. We shall brutalize, conscript, and regiment ourselves for the duration of the war in the hope that we can thus avoid being forced to do so for the next fifty years or more. That is the only hope.

The Japanese attacked Pearl Harbor on a Sunday morning seven weeks later. When President Wilkins spoke to a packed crowd in Finney Chapel about it on Tuesday at noon, the chapel was never more still. "I offer you no illusions," he said. "Fate has given you a job to do, a job which is in its essential nature a terrible job. But it is your job." Scattered in the crowd he spoke to were nine students whose names, along with those of sixty-six others forever young, are on the new memorial alongside Finney Chapel. Wilkins honored every one of them and wrote personal letters to other Oberlin servicemen all over the world throughout the war.

After Pearl Harbor, the college immediately went over to a three-semester accelerated wartime calendar. Commencement Illumination Night was canceled for the duration. As volunteers and draftees began disappearing from the campus, Wilkins opened negotiations with Washington about a military unit to replace them. A 700-man navy V-12 unit finally arrived in July 1943. Faculty members discovered untapped skills in engineering, personnel management, and navigation to try to teach them.

Meanwhile, among remaining students on campus, thoughts about a more democratic postwar world, led by a stronger version of the League of Nations, dominated conversation about the war itself. This led in March 1942 to a multi-college conference on the role of youth in postwar planning, keynoted in Finney Chapel by Eleanor Roosevelt. She arrived on a Greyhound bus, having traveled all night alone by train from Washington to Cleveland to get to the conference on time.

The war hardly curtailed domestic concerns in Oberlin. Anti-black racial discrimination in the deans' offices, in downtown barbershops, and

in the local public schools came in for student censure. An anti-Semitic
English professor was publicly condemned for his outbursts. A few students
began to call for student course evaluations, a brash idea whose time would
not come for another twenty-five years. A feisty *Review* columnist named
Midge Myers shocked her readers by coming out for sexual freedom and
no-fault divorce. The *Review*'s next April Fool issue announced that she
was scheduled to be stoned to death on Tappan Square by the Women's
Board for her indiscretions, but predicted that she would probably survive
the ordeal since "she who is without sin shall cast the first stone." An ad hoc
wartime feminism emerged as women took charge of the *Review* and *Hi-
O-Hi* staffs. When seventeen veterans of Japanese-American internment
camps enrolled at wartime Oberlin, one of them, Kenji Okuda, was
promptly elected student body president. Meanwhile, the wartime fighting
blasted on.

Finally came that summer night in August 1945 when the war's end arrived in Oberlin, so much sooner than expected. A loudspeaker near the
Historic Elm blared the news by radio. Police sirens, fire sirens, car horns,
church bells, and train whistles raised a raucous chorus of relief. The Navy
V-12 unit marched briskly once around Tappan Square, and happy teenagers
snake-danced across the square itself. At last the killing was over.

Most student survivors of the Great Depression and World War II had
their lives disrupted or delayed, in some cases by many youthful years, before savoring what they hoped would be "normal" life from now on beginning in 1946. Yet in their years at Oberlin there is little evidence of despair,
resentment, or alienation. Denied the American illusion that most of their
parents and grandparents had once shared, that the future would surely be
better than the past as they came of age, they learned to hang in there any-
how, eager for hard times and then wartime to stop.

Meanwhile, as Oberlinians, they tried very earnestly to understand
what had happened to them and to the world they had grown into. I believe
that there has not been a time since then when this academic community—
president, deans, faculty, and students—worked harder to educate one another through blunt, open, reasoned debate about the scary times they lived
in. They met reality head-on and dealt with it in balance and civility. Five
decades later that still seems quite remarkable.

CHAPTER 17

Oberlin and the G.I. Bill: Forty Years Later (1987)

$\mathcal{A}$t 7 P.M., Tuesday, August 14, 1945, the end of World War II arrived in Oberlin.[1] The village went wild. Crowds gathered by the Historic Elm, where a loudspeaker blared the radioed details over the clamor of police sirens, fire sirens, church bells, and hundreds of car horns. The navy V-12 unit at the college marched briskly once around Tappan Square, and teenagers snake-danced across the square itself. The Plug, Oberlin's last surviving passenger train, passing through en route to Toledo, blew its whistle in a sustained, delirious wail. At long last the fighting was over.

In the months that followed, the nation's huge military force of fifteen million underwent massive demobilization, to "get the boys home by Christmas." Soon a substantial fraction of the veterans, some 2,230,000 of them all told, headed for the country's campuses to exploit the unprecedented largesse of the G.I. Bill, which few of them had heard of much before war's end.

In Oberlin by February 1946 over one hundred veterans had shown up, 65 percent of them returning to resume schooling interrupted by the war, 35 percent of them newcomers. Twenty percent of the veterans were married. These percentages held steady as the numbers mounted. Two hundred more veterans arrived for the spring term. The real deluge came in fall 1946, when the largest enrollment in Oberlin's history thus far—2,050—swelled the campus. Fully half the students were male. For the first time in a long time, Oberlin enjoyed an equal balance between civilian men and women. An overwhelming majority of the men were veterans—832 of them by final count that academic year. Three hundred more men were turned away for lack of housing.

The campus physical plant was not quite up to the stress of big numbers. ("The college's building needs are terrible to contemplate," Trustee Erwin Griswold '25 had told President Ernest Hatch Wilkins on the eve of the war.) The campus possessed as yet only two substantial men's dormitories—Noah Hall and Men's Building (Wilder)—plus a shabby though well-loved collection of recycled nineteenth-century wood-frame houses to cope with the overflow. Warner Gymnasium and the auditorium in Men's Building were converted in September 1946 into emergency sleeping barracks. The big main reading room in Carnegie Library and classrooms in Peters, Severance, and Westervelt thronged with crowds beyond anyone's memory. Professors smiled grimly at the thought of their first tall bluebook stacks. Bobby-soxed coeds and khaki-jacketed veterans checked each other out, savoring the sudden prospects of peace.

Together with their counterparts on other campuses, the veterans of the G.I. Bill ushered in what turned out to be the happiest crisis in the history of American higher education. Although the crisis passed quite quickly, four decades later the transforming impact of the bill on the concept of "college" can still be felt. Today, as the surviving veterans of World War II quietly approach and enter their retirement years, the force of their broad collective presence at Oberlin and elsewhere in the early postwar era is worth remembering.

In the popular imagination of that era, the G.I. Bill was the country's reward to the heroes of the Good War, the soldiers, flyers, and sailors who saved the world from the fascism of Nazi Germany and military Japan. In its inception it was something else—a plan to ward off unemployment among returning veterans and cushion the country from the worst effects of postwar depression. Most experts believed that peace, by ending wartime spending and production, was going to bring back the flat economic circumstances of the 1930s. (Carl Arlt, a young Oberlin economics professor freshly returned from three years of naval combat in the North Atlantic, spoke to the local Rotary Club in November 1946 on "The Coming Depression.") From the White House on down, politicians worried about the prospect of restlessness, alienation, and political turbulence among unemployed veterans. They must not, President Roosevelt declared in a fireside chat in July 1943, "be demobilized into an environment of inflation and unemployment, to a place on a bread line or on a corner selling apples."

To avert this grim prospect, FDR entered into an expedient arm's-distance collaboration with the American Legion, the chief lobby for expanded veterans' benefits, to soften up Congress for the G.I. Bill of Rights. The collaboration worked better than anyone expected. The Servicemen's Readjustment Act, the formal name for a comprehensive program of unemployment checks, easy home mortgages, and educational benefits, passed quietly through a unanimous Congress on June 13, 1944, just a week after the Allied cross-channel invasion of Normandy, an event that riveted public attention overseas. Most servicemen learned about the law only when they were being mustered out.

The bill's educational benefits turned out to be especially generous—college tuition for up to four years, payment for fees, books, and supplies, and monthly subsistence allowances. Over the decade after the war, these federal payments to colleges and veterans added up to $5.5 billion. In economic effect the G.I. Bill was a notable de facto commitment to Keynesian spending policy, pumping big bucks out into many hands across the country to ward off a return to hard times.

As it turned out, however, the bill proved less important for its economic consequences than for its educational impact. Postwar consumer spending on new cars, new TV sets, and other postponed pleasures, together with cold war spending on military hardware and foreign aid, all combined to end fears of mass unemployment. Meanwhile, the bill greatly democratized assumptions about access to a college education by those on modest incomes. The veterans were the vanguard for millions of young Americans who across the 1950s and 1960s would flock to public universities—and pricey high-quality private colleges like Oberlin—for educations (often subsidized) that their parents and grandparents had realistically assumed were out of reach. What the government had defined as a "right" for veterans became a widespread expectation among the postwar young. In 1945–46, just over two million students (12.5 percent of the college-age population) were enrolled in American colleges and universities. Twenty-five years later, by 1970–71, the number had climbed close to eight million (32.1 percent).

One reason, among others, for the success of the G.I. revolution was the ability of colleges and veterans to come to terms with one another in those earliest postwar years when the return of the veterans was at its flood. In the understated language of that day, it was a "period of adjustment" on both sides. The balance of this essay will look at how Oberlin and the veterans got along. The details are local, but the patterns of adaptation touched every campus in the land.

One Oberlin veteran spoke recently for many when he wrote simply about his return from the jungles of the South Pacific: "I remember a feeling of calm when I came back to Tappan Square." For college administrators bracing for the flood it was anything but calm. A change of presidents in the summer of 1946, attended by a harsh struggle between faculty and trustees over the internal governance of the college, complicated matters. But the new president, William E. Stevenson, was a fortunate choice. He was in a sense a veteran himself, having headed Red Cross operations in Britain, North Africa, and Italy from 1942 to 1944. He promptly applied his brisk executive talents to improving the college's antique physical plant.

Housing remained the college's most elemental problem. Oberlin's solutions were no more expedient or bizarre than those elsewhere. Rensselaer Polytechnic Institute in Troy, New York, for example, leased four surplus LSTs (landing ship tanks) and moored them on the Hudson River, where six hundred veterans turned them into floating dormitories. Harvard, always more elegant, rented the top six stories of a downtown Boston hotel to house its married vets.

At Oberlin, one remedy for the crowding arrived in the form of Federal Hall, a well-worn, prefabricated wooden dormitory used by wartime factory workers at Willow Run outside Detroit. Planted just east of Noah Hall on the North Campus, it sprawled out in four directions from its core of toilets and washrooms and quickly acquired the nickname "Spider" among the two hundred men assigned to its flimsy beaverboard compartments. Meanwhile, a homely army-surplus cafeteria for veterans, borrowed from an ordnance depot in Sandusky, occupied the future site of Mudd Library.

Married veterans and their wives inspired the most distinctive emergency housing solution. With help from the Federal Public Housing Authority, fifty-three trailers were installed on makeshift pads on the North Campus on the northeast corner of Lorain and Woodland streets. Named Botany Lane, this mud-spattered trailer camp looked like something out of a Steinbeck depression novel. It represented Oberlin's grudging response to the first large numbers of married undergraduates in the college's history. (Cohabitation, legal or covert, among ordinary students of course still carried the risk of prompt expulsion.) Conditions at Botany Lane were primitive, worse than at its counterparts on other campuses, President Stevenson acknowledged. Each trailer—eight feet by twenty-two feet, expandable for couples with babies—had a two-burner electric cook stove, a kerosene space heater, and no running water. Couples fetched water in buckets from nearby pumps, and bundled up to head for showers and toilets located in community trailers equipped for those purposes. For many it was a very basic introduction to marriage, but it beat military life and wartime separation. By all accounts morale was strong. J. Daniel Lyons '48, who with his wife (then a registered

Botany Lane provided trailer housing for married veterans and their families.
From 1946 to 1952 it stood near the northeast corner of Lorain and Woodland streets.
Courtesy of Oberlin College Archives.

nurse at Allen Memorial Hospital) may have lived at Botany Lane longer than anyone else, recalls:

> In the trailer camp we were, by and large, a close-knit "family." We had much in common—all veterans, close in age, limited finances, newly-wed, new babies in many cases, and in a hurry to complete our education. The most common social activity, as we recall, was an evening of bridge; one couple supplied the coffee, the other brought some cookies. Undoubtedly, the community toilets and showers, and the community laundry, enhanced the close relationships. There were few secrets about our personal lives.
>
> Both the college and the community had some difficulties in adapting to us. Our time in the military service and our relatively greater maturity had sharpened our abilities to identify, shall we say, poultry droppings in the rules and regulations of both the town and the college. And we were more inclined than the average student (of that time) to question the authority of both entities.

Botany Laners developed quite a sense of turf in Oberlin. When one couple found a college housing administrator inside their trailer "inspecting" it shortly after the camp opened, residents used the incident to establish the principle that the trailers were private homes, not dormitories subject to college intrusion. In time the college learned to look the other way when it came to cars and alcohol among married veterans, thus establishing unacknowledged precedents that would resurface over drugs and mating on campus in the 1960s. On another front, the veterans and their wives waged a running fight with village election officials to establish their right as year-round residents to vote in Oberlin. Life in Botany Lane was pretty feisty while it lasted. The camp was phased out, along with Federal Hall and the veterans' cafeteria, in the early 1950s.

Morale among single veterans, the great majority of the total, was more uneven. In the nature of things, many of them lacked the close camaraderie of Botany Lane. Except for the tiny scattering of female veterans (fewer than a dozen), they concentrated in the three big male dorms—Men's Building, Noah, and Federal—though many moved off campus after their first year. That first year could be rough. For R. Andrew Lee '47, a veteran of Patton's drive into Germany in the spring of 1945 and the Occupation that followed, the speed of the transition back to college seemed unreal

"At times during that first semester of 1946, it became almost too much and I wanted to escape, could not settle back into the academic routine," he wrote recently. But he was not alone, and "we were always able to talk it out and ease the pressure." He remembered that certain professors, including Andrew Bongiorno and Warren Taylor, "seemed to have an insight into what had happened to us and would occasionally bring it up in their classes. Understanding on all sides really helped in that readjustment we all went through." Dean Holdeman, the college veterans counselor, a Navy veteran himself, is also remembered for his help and empathy.

Some veterans who were newcomers to Oberlin found its special atmosphere hard to take. "Without the G.I. Bill there was no way I could have gone to any college," one recently recalled. "However, I was academically, economically, socially, and emotionally unprepared for nearly everything I encountered. As a result I am and always have been alienated from Oberlin. . . . Yet," he concluded, "perversely, Oberlin remains the best thing that ever happened to me."

Another veteran remembers: "My two years at Oberlin were valuable ones. I met some great individuals and absorbed some relevant teaching. I wasn't happy enough to stay there, however." He experienced a growing disenchantment with Oberlin's "value system" as too parochial and idealistic. "At times the place seemed utopian, and having come from the Army experience, I didn't quite mesh—or mix. The campus and its constituents sat there in isolation, and I suppose I wanted out." Then this postscript: "Forgot to add that 3.2 beer at Oberlin was a real downer from Army beer and the other poison served in Japan." He transferred to Harvard for his final years on the bill.

Dissatisfaction was not confined to students. A freshly hired sociology professor named John Rowland, a Navy veteran, startled his seminar halfway through fall semester 1946 by announcing his resignation. Oberlin's rigorous academic standards, he decided, created an "unhealthy atmosphere," which was compounded by all the silly social rules. "There is not enough machinery for bringing couples together," he told a *Review* reporter. He added that most Oberlin housemothers, the custodians of decorum in the dormitories, were "repressed and emotionally unstable." Rowland left for the University of Pittsburgh at semester's end.

Most veterans rolled with Oberlin's peculiar punch and managed to make do. One remembers that he wobbled a bit academically before discovering a pleasant arrangement to circumvent dormitory rules. "I found a woman graduate student who lived off campus to shack up with now and then. My grades improved noticeably." William Parmenter '47, whose army career included four rocky months in a prisoner-of-war camp in eastern Germany, recalls that his return to Oberlin was like "coming back to a great buffet of . . . general good living," centering at Embassy, where the housemother regularly cleaned out the veterans at poker. "The social rules," he wrote, "did not trouble us particularly; we simply ignored them for the most part, and the administration had sense enough to leave us alone."

Another hallowed Oberlin tradition that the veterans scorned was freshman hazing. When the day came for new students to dress in bed sheets and submit to upperclass jeering, many first-year veterans made a point of wearing their G.I. fatigue jackets. Upperclassmen quickly got the point, and—for veterans at least—"the dumb ritual" stopped. Varieties of hazing—beanies and pajama runs—lingered on into the 1950s, then disappeared unlamented.

Tension between veterans and non-veterans seems to have been minimal. One reason for this was the enormous respect the veterans enjoyed for what they had come through. Another was the veterans' desire to merge and melt back into the civilian scene as smoothly as possible. "We were really Oberlin students first and veterans second," James W. Moore '47 remembers. The veterans at Men's Building were insistent on this point. The caption for their 1946 *Hi-O-Hi* picture carried a jovial complaint:

> Why do you persist in thinking we are different because we are vets? We have wrestling bouts and we flunk bluebooks, we enjoy political harangues and Tommy Dorsey, we make a feeble attempt at a spot on the varsity squad in baseball, we too run up a monumental telephone bill, we bike to the quarry to cool off Sunday afternoon, we live at the Apollo during final week. We are normal, healthy young men who love booze, babes, and boogie as much as you do.

One clue to veterans' attitudes toward their special status was their clothing. By preference or necessity chino pants and olive drab jackets (or fur-collared bomber jackets or Navy pea jackets) became their postwar uniforms, though all insignia of rank and units disappeared. Some even took the trouble to dye their G.I. clothing to enforce the difference between war and peace. Daytime neckties were much less common than before the war. Women figured importantly in the new casualness, having adopted the so-called "sloppy style"—blue jeans and loose shirttails—during the war years. The college, clinging to the more formal dressing habits of the prewar years, primly enforced neckties and skirts at dinnertime long into the postwar era.

The veterans were probably as diverse in their political attitudes as other postwar students. Apprehensions about their being radicalized as a group by their war experience proved entirely misplaced. But that is a judgment in retrospect; many observers at the time remained unsure. As cold war tensions mounted between the United States and the Soviet Union in the late 1940s, feeding fears of communist subversion in Washington and on campuses across the land, Oberlin's liberal reputation made it vulnerable to charges of being unduly left-wing. When a red flag complete with hammer and sickle flew from the Tappan Square flagpole for three days in January 1947 before college workmen managed to bring it down, not everyone who read about it in the local papers believed President Stevenson's dismissal of the incident as a skylarking prank with no political significance. But he was probably right.

A year later the editor of the *Cleveland Press,* an Oberlin alumnus, reported after a visit to his alma mater that the veterans had brought a mood of intellectual and social maturity to the campus, as well as a new look of sartorial informality, but nothing very dangerous in the way of ideology. "No one was sure that he knew of a single communist among the student body," he wrote. "I should advise anyone who is worried about radicalism at Oberlin to relax."

In the late 1940s a new forum of left-wing libertarian debate and entertainment stirred the campus with the arrival of Arch Seven, a lively series of after-dinner speech rallies at Memorial Arch. The most visible speaker at Arch Seven was Paul Willen '50, who was a high schooler during the war. But Willen credited an older man, Emil Abramovic '49, with being the mastermind behind the rallies. Willen's description of Abramovic captures the respect and even awe with which younger students regarded their friends among the veterans.

Emil was my teacher at Oberlin, patient, firm, good natured; he had "vintage" which we lacked: working class, United Auto Workers, authentic-ethnic, service in WW II Navy in the South Pacific; he was mentor to our groups. He was older (probably thirty) wise, careful, seasoned. He knew how to drink beer; he had seen the great strikes of the 1930s, the bloodshed, to say nothing of the war . . .

Maturity was by all odds the salient trait among the veterans. Maturity was not simply a matter of age. Most campus veterans were still in their early twenties, only three or four years beyond the norm. But of course the content of those years distanced them from their teens by a huge psychological margin. Once the transition back to civilian life was more or less over (for some it would never be entirely over), the veterans began a purposeful drive to complete their educations and get on with their lives. "Making up for lost time" was a common phrase among them. Their seasoned, unflagging commitment to academic achievement made them collectively a teacher's dream. Their professors remembered them as the best batch of students they had ever taught. That estimate was borne out in contemporary statistical studies, which showed that veterans across the country performed consistently better in the classroom than non-veterans. Benjamin Fine, education editor of the *New York Times,* reported in November 1947: "The G.I.s are hogging the honor rolls and the Dean's lists; they are walking away with the top marks in all their courses." Fine labeled their performance "the most astonishing fact in the history of American higher education."

The best book on the general subject, Keith Olson's *The G.I. Bill, the Veterans, and the Colleges* (1974), devotes a chapter to the veterans' classroom record. The chapter ends with these observations: "Looking back a quarter of a century later few persons are surprised that young men who, for the most part, were teenagers during the country's greatest economic depression and who took part in a world war, both rather sobering experiences, proved to be serious, highly motivated college students." But as Olson notes, the G.I. Bill was an unprecedented initiative in federally subsidized mass higher education, an effort to defuse the crisis of postwar dislocation, and few of those who launched it anticipated such a happy outcome. He concludes: "In a postwar era filled with disappointment, the record enrollment and academic achievement of the veterans who went to college under the G.I. Bill must be considered one of the country's pleasant surprises."

College generations are short. At Oberlin and elsewhere the veterans arrived and departed all too swiftly. In keeping with one of Oberlin's sturdiest traditions, many of them headed on to graduate study, landed their master's and doctoral degrees, and moved into careers in teaching and research. A decade or so later they were in place on campuses from Maine to Oregon, bracing to cope with the next major crisis in higher education, a much less pleasant surprise, the student rebellions of the 1960s. So the cycle turns.

I will risk ending this essay on a personal note. I arrived as a freshman at Oberlin in 1949. By then most of the veterans had graduated. But over three hundred of them were still around, and they were a felt presence in the classroom, in the snack bar, on the playing fields. Despite their preference for a low profile and their reticence about their military careers, we knew who they were, and we spent a lot of time imagining what they had gone through, and what seemed to make them different. Now, four decades later, trying to capture that difference, I will fall back on words from a veteran of an earlier mass conflict, the Civil War, the first modern war in American history. In a Memorial Day address in 1884, Oliver Wendell Holmes, the future Supreme Court justice, talked about the men who fought the Civil War. He used words that the veterans of World War II might find acceptable:

> We attribute no special merit to a man for having served when all were serving. We know that, if the armies of our war did anything worth remembering, the credit belongs not mainly to the individuals who did it, but to average human nature. We also know very well that we cannot live in associations with the past alone, and we admit that, if we would be worthy of the past, we must find new fields for action or thought and make for ourselves new careers. But, nevertheless, the generation that carried on the war has been set apart by its experience.

The war veterans once on this campus are now scattered everywhere. Today, in memory, they remain an uncommon crowd, set apart not only by their experience in uniform but also by their performance later on.

Later Years (1950–2000)

CHAPTER 18

Observations on Governance at Oberlin: Another Look at Its History (1992)

Owing to Erwin Griswold, Oberlin's faculty governance is a hotter topic than it was in August when I agreed to give this talk.[1] Like others, I was puzzled by Dean Griswold's letter published in the *Oberlin Review* on September 25. The substance of the letter is not surprising. It is vintage Griswold, consistent with views he has held for over half a century. What is puzzling is its timing, the occasion for it. What lies behind it? The long-simmering dispute over the merit component of faculty salaries? The recent faculty investigation of performance management at the college? The new trustee-sponsored strategic issues inquiry now under way? I am not sure.

The *Review* editorialized about the published letter: "Erwin Griswold has fired the first shot" in a potential blood bath over faculty governance. I hope not. Ever since the last blood bath eighteen years ago, I have hoped (as has everyone I know who survived it) that it would never happen again. The faculty won that battle, but you have to put "victory" in quotation marks, because it came at enormous cost in faculty morale, collegiality, and the reputation of the college. Its reoccurrence would be awful. I trust that everyone locally agrees, from Cox Administration Building on down.

But what about the trustees? Let's hope they have a strong institutional memory. Only one currently active trustee was on the board in 1973. Fortunately, he is its current chair.

No one should underestimate Erwin Griswold. Not only was his the longest twentieth-century tenure on the board—from 1936 to 1980—but he was also more actively and intimately involved in the internal affairs of the college over that span than any other trustee, through the presidencies of Ernest H. Wilkins, William E. Stevensen, and Robert K. Carr. In many ways *he* has been the institutional memory of the board. And he waged a steady campaign for over thirty years to contract the boundaries of faculty governance at Oberlin. He has always been foursquare on issues of academic and curricular freedom. As an academic himself, he lectured President Stevenson, a man with no prior professional experience in higher education, on academic freedom during the postwar McCarthy era. But he has regarded the Oberlin faculty mainly as paid employees of the college, and he has serious reservations about how good we are at what we are paid to do and how responsible we are in evaluating each others' merits. Moreover, he believes we have overly inflated pretensions about our ability to help run this college.

He is also an outstanding constitutional lawyer, which makes me wonder about his interpretation of the Finney Compact of 1835 (see Chapter 2). I wonder why he is reluctant to acknowledge the role of habit, precedent, and usage (the "common law") in shaping the long-term functional meaning of the compact, which he dismisses as an interesting event in the early history of the college that "has no bearing on problems of today." In his private advice to presidents he urged a resort to habit, precedent, and usage in seeking procedural change—just as the common law grew step by step, slowly changing customs and expectations. That is precisely how the Finney Compact grew from 1835 to 1903, when it finally entered the college bylaws in the first year of the presidency of Henry Churchill King. It remains there today—Article 15, Section 2—entrusting the faculty with management of the internal affairs of the college. Absent the prior ongoing history of the Finney Compact, the trustees' acceptance of the bylaw of 1903 is inexplicable.

By 1941 the habits and precedents accumulating around that bylaw had grown to the point where Committee T of the AAUP (American Association of University Professors) rated Oberlin as having the most democratic governance of any college in the country. It was also possibly the most complex. Diagram A—simplified to leave out the Graduate School of Theology, which removed to Vanderbilt University in 1966—shows this structure.

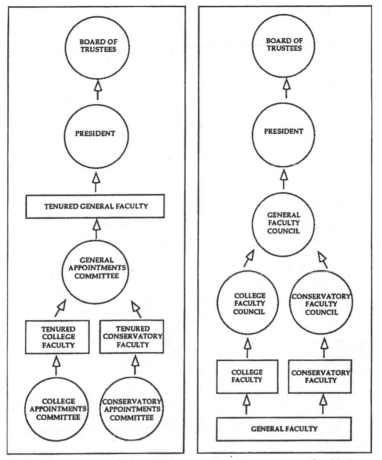

A: Faculty governance before 1946   *B: Faculty governance after 1946*

The arrows indicate the route taken by faculty personnel decisions as they progressed upward from elected appointments committees through the tenured college and conservatory faculties, then to the general appointments committee, then to the large body of tenured general faculty, then to the president, and then to the board of trustees. Though many people shared responsibility for the changes in this structure that were introduced in 1946, President Wilkins and Dean Griswold were the main agents of change. In 1944 Wilkins's dissatisfaction with the need to nurse committee decisions through the divisional faculties and then through the large "town meeting" of the general faculty convinced him of the need for change. Dean Griswold's solution, as it emerged from bylaw changes introduced in 1946 and thereafter, produced a governance system with a different structure (diagram B).

The changes of 1946 provoked the third major crisis over the Finney Compact, the first being the faculty's struggle to remove President Asa Mahan from office in 1851, and the second being the faculty's defense in 1918 of the academic freedom of Professor Karl Geiser against trustee efforts to remove him from the faculty for his heretical views on World War I (see Chapter 15). The faculty lost the fight of 1946, and some of them believed at the time that they had lost the Finney Compact.

In retrospect, in my opinion, Dean Griswold's solution of 1946 introduced a decisive improvement in the structure of faculty governance. It brought more efficiency to the upward flow of decision-making. It replaced the direct "town meeting" democracy of the old system with the representative democracy of the modern council system. And it expanded the political definition of the faculty to include younger, untenured members who had been excluded from the older system. But clearly the main purpose of the changes of 1946 was to relieve the president and deans of the need to debate and justify faculty personnel decisions before the whole tenured faculty.

Over the quarter-century after 1946 the trustees under Dean Griswold's leadership pressed steadily against the boundaries of faculty governance, while the faculty dug in its heels in resolute resistance. In this long academic cold war, both sides believed absolutely that they represented the college's best interests. The trustees thought they were trying to make the place still more governable, more efficient, more responsive to presidential initiative. The faculty thought they were struggling to preserve Oberlin's historic uniqueness, their own collective strength as academics, and Oberlin's educational distinction. The trustees charged that faculty intransigence was making Oberlin the graveyard of presidents who were pecked to death by ducks. The faculty in turn charged that the trustees were bent on imposing hierarchical governance models from the alien world of corporate management or—in Dean Griswold's case—the Harvard Law School.

Here are the important checkpoints in the long struggle:

1. In 1949 a new bylaw gave the president clear authority over the college budget.

2. Also in 1949 the president was given power to appoint deans with the advice and concurrence of a special faculty committee elected for that purpose.

3. In 1959 the trustees passed a controversial bylaw authorizing the president to make separate personnel recommendations to the trustees when he disagreed with the recommendations of the elected faculty councils. That bylaw authority has been used only once, in the early 1960s.

4. Across the 1960s the faculty largely (though by no means entirely) yielded its bylaw authority to govern student life *in loco parentis,* thus expanding de facto administrative responsibility in this sector.

5. Meanwhile, the faculty through its several departments steadily tightened its control over faculty search and hiring procedures and over curricular change.

Then came 1970, and the onset of Robert Fuller's presidency, the shortest and most turbulent of the twentieth century. Fuller arrived with a mandate from those who chose him to launch a radical restructuring of Oberlin's educational and governance arrangements—to bring the college into line with the needs of students as it emerged from the 1960s. His major educational achievement was to persuade the faculty (by a narrow margin) to drop distribution requirements for graduation, so that students could pursue their academic interests unimpeded by traditional definitions of a liberal arts education.

Fuller's downfall began with an administrative proposal to curtail tuition remission benefits for faculty children. It accelerated with the trustee authorization of a governance commission charged with remodeling the internal political structure of the college and faculty insistence that the commission submit its recommendations for the faculty's approval before sending them to the trustees. The power struggle climaxed when the trustees passed, over concerted faculty protest, a new bylaw in June 1973 that gave Fuller authority to change the curriculum by reallocating faculty slots when they fell vacant. This action triggered a faculty unionization drive. That led in turn to Fuller's resignation at the end of 1973, followed by the largest mass exodus of administrative appointees in modern memory.

The college spent the next decade quietly knitting itself back together, under acting president Ellsworth Carlson, the abbreviated presidency of

Emil Danenberg, acting president James Powell, and then under President Starr, who arrived in 1983. Crucial to the knitting process was the decade-long deanship of professor of English Robert Longsworth, from 1974 to 1984. Nothing comparable to the governance fights of 1946 and 1973 has plagued us since.

Two questions remain. First, is Oberlin still different, after all, from other good colleges in its faculty governance? My answer is tentative because I haven't done the comparative research. But my impression is that at other colleges the authority and influence of presidents and deans reach further down into their faculties through closer control over the choice of department chairs, who then do a lot of dickering with deans over the merit of department members. Furthermore, the authority of presidents and deans is less impeded elsewhere by what we have here—a one-person/one-vote democratic decision-making system, beginning in each department and moving up through the elected faculty councils. So Oberlin presidents and deans find their political authority somewhat shallow in its downward reach, and the faculty's political authority reaches higher. The success of presidents and deans (in the eyes of the faculty at least) depends in large part on their ability to accept these limits and work creatively within them, without feeling they are being pecked to death by ducks.

Second, if Oberlin remains somewhat different in its faculty governance, is this a good thing? Prior to the publication of Dean Griswold's letter, the most sustained recent analysis of the Finney Compact I know of was a valedictory talk given by acting president Jim Powell to the board just before his departure from Oberlin to become the president, first, of Franklin & Marshall, and then of Reed. Powell spent twenty-one years at Oberlin, as a geology teacher fresh out of MIT, as department chair, as provost, then as acting president from 1981 to 1983. He got to know the pros and cons of the Finney Compact pretty well. Here is what he told the trustees:

1. On the one hand, the compact is somewhat anachronistic if it is read literally. There are plenty of internal affairs of a large modern college that the faculty cannot manage and does not want to manage.
2. Faculty involvement in governance at Oberlin is not all that different from other schools. It's just that at Oberlin we have this landmark bylaw about it, which has created a tradition and a heightened

      sensitivity about it, which in turn often makes life difficult for administration.

3. Nevertheless, "The principle of faculty governance simply is a *sine qua non* of excellence in liberal education."

4. If the trustees should choose to repeal the compact, "a heavy blow would have been struck at Oberlin College, and things would be worse, not better. Collegiality would be a thing of the past, and the life of administrators and faculty made miserable."

Powell concluded: "I believe it is time for the board to face and admit the inevitability of the Finney Compact, and to try to make it work. The college's best hope is a sincere attempt to have the faculty truly live up to the responsibility and trust which is supposed to be theirs, and which they say they want."

I don't think any faculty member could have put it more simply and bluntly than that.

So what's going to happen? Here I will revert to my historian's role and quote Casey Stengel: I never make predictions, especially about the future.

CHAPTER 19

Memorial Minute for Ellsworth Carlson (2000)

Ells Carlson '39 died last summer in Oberlin at age eighty-two.[1] Over the second half of the twentieth century he ranked among the most important faculty members at this college. For those who knew him well, the words that come to mind are remarkably consistent through his best years and the years of his adversity. The newspaper editors who named him Oberlin's Man of the Year in 1975 got it right when they called him a "direct, warm, modest, good human being." As faculty colleague, department chair, provost, and acting president, he was the sort of person you could agree with or quarrel with as if you were his closest friend. But another constant in his nature was a quiet terrier tenacity, a commitment to purpose against the odds, which some might justifiably call courage and others will call plain guts. From his earliest days at Oberlin to the years of his campus leadership, he was a gentle warrior for what he thought was right.

The son of a Protestant minister, he was born in Bridgeport, Connecticut, and arrived in Oberlin in 1935 as a freshman from Pocatello, Idaho. He took a while to decide what he wanted to become. A determination to somehow improve the world through service was there from the beginning and would never go away. His father wanted him to follow in the ministry, but that ambition fell away early on. His presidency of the Oberlin Peace Society, the largest and most influential organization on campus in the 1930s, led him to believe that social activism was a more certain path to usefulness than academic scholarship. After graduating Phi Beta Kappa in 1939 he headed to China as a Shansi representative and, with his wife, Bobbie Dunn Carlson, spent World War II confined there by Japanese aggression. Only after a postwar stint with the State Department and the O.S.S. did Ells head for a Harvard Ph.D. and a career of teaching and service on the familiar ground of his alma mater, beginning in 1950.

Over the next two decades he contributed far more than his share to the global demands of the Oberlin curriculum. No Oberlin historian has ever taught more different kinds of history than Ells did, and if any were ever asked to do so in the future, they would doubtless file a grievance. Today five historians do what he did then. Chinese history was what he was hired to teach, with Japan and the rest of East Asia thrown in to round things out. Also piled on his plate were Europe from the fall of Rome to the fall of Hitler, the history of czarist Russia and the Soviet Union, and the history of British and postimperial India. In 1966, to enhance his specialty, he created East Asian Studies, Oberlin's first interdisciplinary program. Meanwhile, across most of the 1960s, he served as chair of the history department, presiding over several senior angels of academic discord. Young untenured historians valued his guidance and protection. His departmental leadership prepared him well for those feats of crisis management that he brought off after moving over to Cox in 1969.

Ells served as provost and then as acting president from autumn 1969 to the spring of 1975. The worst crisis broke early on. No one involved at the time will forget those awful days in May 1970 when this campus, like others all across the country, was suddenly locked in the grip of antiwar emotion by the bombing of Cambodia and the Kent State killings. President Carr was out of town. As a large crowd of students marched across Tappan Square to seize Cox in protest, Ells came back to the campus after dark to confront them in the floodlights. "Confront" was too strong a word for him. "I just talked to them," he said later on. After he promised to take their protest to the faculty, the students left the building, and the faculty agreed to meet. The upshot was a special Saturday afternoon meeting of the faculty packed into King 306, surrounded by students and chaired by Ells. After three and a half hours of taut debate, with Bobbie Carlson arriving with sandwiches midway through, an antiwar resolution was finally passed for faculty members to sign as they chose. The regular semester closed four days later to give way to the Liberation College, and Ells served as acting president through the summer as Bob Carr resigned and prepared to leave.

The next three years witnessed an altogether different sort of academic crisis, the Fuller presidency. Ells served Bob Fuller as provost, the president's man, lightning rod and good soldier all the way, from Fuller's arrival to his abrupt departure. At first Ells savored the new atmosphere, in which the white-knuckle survival of Carr's last years was replaced now by breezy, open-ended reform. "I am enjoying my work very much," he wrote to an old friend. He followed with this splendid understatement: "President Fuller is anxious to achieve a great deal in a rather short amount of time." But then on orders from above he began to take on tough issues that bloodied him—cutbacks in faculty tuition remission, a purge of the admissions staff, changes in faculty governance to enhance the power of the presidency, and the resulting faculty drive for unionization.

When it was finally over, and Fuller was gone, the trustees turned to Carlson once more for help. Despite the medical problems that now began to bother him, Ells served for the next fourteen months as acting president, patching a ripped campus community back together again with the help of trusted friends. This was perhaps the most valuable service to the college he ever performed. He now thought he might be named president himself. Many people shared this hope, but the trustees tapped Emil Danenberg instead in the search for a clean slate and fresh start. Ells quietly returned to the faculty in 1975 to teach and write and mend himself until his retirement in 1981.

His colleagues saw a lot of him on campus after that. He and Bobbie kept showing up, for concerts in Finney, dramatic performances in Hall, gatherings of historians and East Asian scholars, and—what he seemed to like most of all—visiting speakers from the outside world. He loved to hear them out and then hit them gently afterward with tough questions to find out what their answers were. He never lost his intellectual curiosity, his appetite for new ideas, and the chance to chew over one more way he and the rest of us might try out to possibly improve the world.

CHAPTER 20

An Apology for the 1950s (1982)

$\mathcal{P}$eriodically over the past decade, many teachers of my generation have found it necessary to explain to their students why we think the way we do.[1] The earliest version of this talk dates from the end of the Vietnam War. The latest version is prompted by the resurgence of the preppie and the alarming wave of nostalgia for the 1950s. Needless to say, it does not speak for everyone who came of age in those strange years.

This is a report from one generation to another about what it was like to be young in the 1950s. In the 1960s the concept of the generation gap became a well-worn cliché. The generation gap lay wide and deep across that decade, connecting the missile gap of the Kennedy years with the credibility gap of the Johnson-Nixon years, presumably leading beyond toward peak experience and point reconciliation in the 1970s. But like most overworked concepts it had a core of truth to it, and its constant use reflected an important contemporary reality. The 1960s are history now, and one doesn't hear the phrase "generation gap" very often anymore, but the validity of the term may well outlast its currency. No perceptive person over forty (it used to be thirty) could be blind to the radical contrast between assumptions about the way to a good life in a good society that governed the conventional thinking of the young in the 1950s and those that flowered in the years thereafter.

Actually the use of decades as signposts to generational change is a shorthand simplification. My recollection is that the 1960s got under way in earnest around 1964, sometime between the murder of President Kennedy, the end of the integrationist phase of the civil rights movement, and the military buildup in Vietnam. In any event, no one like myself, who spent four years on the Oberlin campus in the early 1950s and returned to teach here in the early 1960s, will deny that the mores and values of college students underwent a fundamental sea change in the next few years, at Oberlin as elsewhere. And despite the supposed quietism of the 1970s, the change endures to the present. There is no going back; there never is.

What follows does not attempt an explanation for the change. It is only a set of hunches about what disappeared in the process of change. Nor are any normative judgments implied, except that my hunches are more an apology for the 1950s than they are a hymn to the years that followed. To note that the condition of being young in the 1950s was different from what it is now is neither to flatter nor condemn, nor is it intended to suggest either descent from earlier standards or liberation from them. Every generation should remain free to write its own epitaph.

Generation gaps are nothing new.

> The sources of civic virtue and public spirit were beginning to run low. Men were less honest, women less modest, than of old. . . . The new generation was growing up less hardy, more passionate and lustful, than the old had been. The laws became ineffectual to restrain men who no longer reverenced justice.

That was the Harvard scholar Charles Eliot Norton writing in 1880 about fourteenth-century Sienna.

> The difference is that these young people take it for granted that they're going to get what they want, and that we almost always took it for granted that we shouldn't.

That was from the lips of one of Edith Wharton's nineteenth-century New Yorkers in *The Age of Innocence,* written in 1920.

Next here is the Progressive literary historian Vernon Parrington on the generation gap of the 1920s:

> Liberals whose hair is growing thin and the lines of whose figures are no longer what they were, are likely to find themselves in the unhappy predicament of being treated as mourners at their own funerals. . . . It is hard to be dispossessed by one's heirs, and especially hard when those heirs, in the cheerful ignorance of youth, forget to acknowledge any obligations to a hard-working generation that laid by a very substantial body of intellectual wealth, the income from which the heirs are spending without even a "Thank you."

Finally, reaching back almost a century behind Parrington, we find Henry Thoreau anticipating a central slogan of the young in the 1960s:

> Practically, the old have no very important advice to give the young, their own experience has been so partial, and their lives have been such miserable failures. . . . I have lived some thirty years on this planet, and I have yet to hear the first syllable of valuable or even earnest advice from my seniors.

Obviously no nation or generation is exempt from the tensions of youth against age. But midcentury America, lurching through history at a break-neck pace, certainly had more trouble than most societies maintaining a fund of perceived reality shared by its whole population regardless of age, binding them to common memories, norms, and wants.

In retrospect the 1950s seem to have provided an illusion of pause in the terrific pace of things—an interlude between catastrophes, a momentary calm between storms recently past and a future we thought we could postpone. World War II and the Great Depression were the two towering memories for those years, and they cast long shadows. The war's outcome was ambiguous. Nazi Germany was destroyed, but only because Stalin's communism had survived. This ambiguity robbed the victory of its full satisfactions, and streaked our thoughts with anxiety over new, unanticipated kinds of wars, nuclear or cold. And yet our country (we called it "our country") had survived the disasters of the 1930s and 1940s, and the knowledge of survival enforced a distinctive value system among those of us in the 1950s who were growing up to find places in the society that had made it through. Collective survival was the crucial memory, and acceptance (however grudging) of the terms of survival was the crucial value. When we disagreed with one or another of the terms, the word we used to describe our disagreement was "gripe." We understood that gripes required no answers or adjustments. We never learned to register demands.

Thus the Silent Generation. A writer for *Time* coined that term as early as 1951. Again I think the cliché has meaning. But the quality of the silence needs explaining. The term sometimes bears the connotation of repressed thoughts, as if some edict against rebellion and deep dissent was imposed coercively on a timid, frightened, and confused generation. The name of Joe McCarthy is commonly invoked in this connection, the assumption being that McCarthyism was the cause and the silence was the result. This is too simple. Certainly there were those, young and old, who were scared by McCarthy, or scared of McCarthy. There were of course a good many people (even at Oberlin) who believed McCarthy. But it credits him with too much to suggest that he was the coercive agent shaping the mind of the decade. McCarthy and the pervasive "ism" he and others exploited were rather the noisy symptoms of an age informed by deeper-running anxieties that antedated him and endured beyond his headline years.

McCarthyism was just one clue among many to the trouble Americans had adjusting to the cold war and to the ambiguities of America's primary response to the cold war—the foreign policy of containment, first articulated by the scholar-diplomat George Kennan. Over the thirty-five years since its inception, the containment policy for meeting the perceived threat of communist expansionism provoked a constant succession of protest from critics of its aims. The outcries came from both the left and the right over the years—from the Henry Wallace Progressives in the late 1940s; from the McCarthyites in the early 1950s; from the John Birch Society in the late 1950s; from the opponents of the Vietnam War in the 1960s (whose protest was joined early on, incidentally, by George Kennan); and most recently from the critics of President Reagan's cold war revivalism. Each succeeding protest brought a new focus and a new vocabulary to public controversy over the wisdom of containment as the primary theme of our foreign policy.

But in the meantime, back at the beginning, while debate flared and sputtered over containments as foreign policy, the idea of containment seems to have sifted down into private consciousness to shape the domestic living style of the post–World War II years. The containment ethic emerged in the 1950s, perhaps especially among the young and malleable, as a way of ordering personal behavior at home. It became an implicit domestic social corollary of cold war existence.

The argument is speculative, and the evidence will be impressionistic, even autobiographical. When I arrived in Oberlin as a freshman in the fall of 1949, the campus was still reverberating a little from the excitement of the Wallace campaign the year before. But political passions were waning, and the radicals of the day (the Progressives) had clearly entered one of their periodic postmortems on introspection and recrimination. The death of Arch Seven—those rousing after-dinner political rallies across the street from Peters Hall—was much on people's minds. The Carnegie Library stacks and seminar rooms filled quickly after dark. Later in the night people danced close and slow in Wilder's Rec Hall to the soft beat of Vaughan Monroe tone poems. Couples necked a lot in the old car barn behind May Cottage on Elm Street. (The car barn, May Cottage, and the constraints of necking have all long since disappeared.) So many men went out for football that autumn, there weren't enough game jerseys to go around.

Oberlin was suddenly a quiet, apolitical place. I remember people asking where Paul was that year. Paul was a campus rebel leader of the year before, a regular speaker at Arch Seven, and someone said that Paul was up in his new room in Burton listening to Beethoven. I also recall, a year or two later, my favorite history professor, Robert Fletcher, telling me he thought the biggest single difference between his college days and mine was the long-playing record, which came on the market in 1948. The LP not only opened the world of classical music to a huge new audience, it had also gotten us all into the habit of sitting around with our ears open and our mouths shut. We tended to absorb experience by listening rather than talking. It may not only be tidy, but also accurate, to say that sometime in 1950 a youthful quietism set in, at Oberlin and elsewhere across the country.

The silence may have meant a premature political wariness in some cases. (Harry Truman was not the stuff of youthful dreams when he was president.) In others it may have meant momentary alienation with no agenda or a separate peace with no timetable. It was hard to tell. Small groups, couples, and individuals began to go their own way, privately, quietly, unruffled and uncomplaining. Those who claimed to have a finger on the common pulse could only report that things had really calmed down. The rebels had disappeared. Soon we heard the charge that our acquiescence in our lot had made us hopelessly conformist. While the suggestion that we were the first or last student generation to follow the herd instinct was a bum rap, once again the charge touched a behavioral reality. Surface evidence abounded to prove our urge for common, almost regimented styles of expression. Barbershop quartets suddenly became popular. They toured the dining halls, appealing to a taste for tight harmony in a static format. For party breaks from close, slow-motion dancing, the conga line and the bunny hop were useful. They were as near as we came to group exhibitionism: quick jerks, single file, en masse, around the dance floor in a big circle. Close-cropped crew-cut hair came into favor among men, and thin rep ties

The 1950 Senior Prom in Hales Gym. Courtesy of Oberlin College Archives

with regimental stripes, and white bucks—although a brand-new, too-white pair of bucks attracted undesired attention. You tried to scuff them to a dull gray as soon as possible. It was in 1952 that three-button gray-flannel suits, the uniform of William H. Whyte's Organization Man, swept westward across the country from Brooks Brothers, replacing the padded shoulders and broad lapels of the 1940s. On campus we preferred khaki chinos and army surplus windbreakers—the fabrics of World War II.

In 1953 the Republicans returned to power, and Adlai Stevenson fans could now chuckle ruefully about the Eisenhower waltz—one step forward, two steps back, and a quick side step. The wisecracks multiplied: under FDR, the halt had led the blind; now with Ike in office, the bland led the bland. We were the generation with braces on our brains. Alternatively, we were recovering from a national prefrontal lobotomy. Soon the most influential sociological analysis of the decade announced the existence of the lonely crowd, its members all searching for each other with their private radar antenna. We read David Riesman's *The Lonely Crowd* with a shock of self-recognition.

Our professors may have grumbled about our ways, but many of the big lessons we carried away from lectures and reading lists enforced the idea that life was an activity to be carried on within fixed limits, and that there was danger in lunging past the limits in search of glowing absolutes and total solutions. This message emerged repeatedly in the books we read at other people's urging: Erich Fromm's *Escape from Freedom,* Reinhold Niebuhr's *The Children of Light and the Children of Darkness,* George Orwell's *1984,* H. Stuart Hughes's *An Essay for Our Time,* and Eric Hoffer's *The True Believer.*

In courses in American history and foreign policy we began to absorb the new realist concepts of national self-interest and controlled conflict that underwrote the cold war containment policy and displaced older Wilsonian concepts of international law and moral idealism as proper guides to foreign affairs. When George Kennan published his little classic, *American Diplomacy,* in 1950, it promptly appeared on college reading lists as a splendid introduction to realist assumptions about what was possible and what was not possible in the conduct of a national foreign policy. (It's still on some reading lists, including mine.) Meanwhile, in the arena of domestic American history, "consensus" gradually replaced "conflict" as the key phrase for explaining how Americans normally thought and behaved toward one another. As we learned to locate the terms of American consensus in the past, more often than not we also learned to identify those terms as values of our own.

From political science we absorbed comparable lessons. We discovered the intricacies of the peculiar American party system, traced for us in avid detail. We learned how the system worked for all its idiosyncrasies to master the tensions of a pluralistic society. Implicitly (and sometimes explicitly) we received the message that it was better to join a part and work within it for improvement than to stand on the periphery, wringing our hands in dismay over bosses, deals, and shady compromise. Bosses, deals, and compromise made the system work. We learned to our surprise that most professors of political science frowned on political independents as soft-minded, idealistic troublemakers. The independents' notion that party politics spelled a degradation of pure representative democracy was, we were told, a self-fulfilling prophecy, because it removed them from effective involvement in the system they disliked.

We learned the crisp new code words "decision-making process," which were used to track the intricate sequence of choices by which men of power made up their minds, and we fell into the habit of assuming that once we understood *how* decisions were made we would automatically know *why* they were made, and even why they *had* to be made. Decision-making analysis acquired a certain aura of determinism, even fatalism, that was somehow grimly comforting in a world where scary decisions by men in power seemed to happen rather often.

Sociology was also deeply concerned (or so it seemed to many of us taking our first course in it) with showing why things worked the way they did. One studied the location of groups within structures, the way structures shaped groups and the way groups shaped the behavior of individuals. And although the sociologists were on balance more reform-minded than other social scientists, still they shared the general social science concern for illuminating the operations of a system. The main lesson was the domination of the parts by the whole.

In the nature of things the humanities were less closely geared to contemporary national preoccupations, but here again the lessons obliquely fortified the containment ethic. In religion, the kingdom of God had receded beyond history; the social gospel had diminished to a set of personal Christian ethics that told us not to lean too hard on our neighbors, and the problem of original sin and how to control and contain it had reemerged as a major theological controversy. In American literature classes, the passionate, barbaric yawp, from Walt Whitman to Norman Mailer, was out. The tight, controlled habits of human behavior, from the characters of Henry James to the prose style and stoic code of Ernest Hemingway, were in. (Warren Taylor's boundless passion for large ideas was an exception here.) Philosophy classes seemed largely devoted to curbing loose thoughts about the meaning of words.

Meanwhile, late at night or on vacation, we read the popular war novels of World War II: *The Caine Mutiny, Bridge Over the River Kwai, From Here to Eternity,* and other best sellers, like Martin Russ's autobiographical account of the Korean War, *The Last Parallel,* and James Gould Cozzens' *By Love Possessed.* One way or another, the lesson was always the same: the rebel does not rebel, but *survives* by proving himself in terms of private goals that collide only secretly with formal, official structures and commands. Prewitt, the main character in *From Here to Eternity,* was a boxer who refused to box on the regimental boxing team and was persecuted by his superiors for his refusal. He was also a bugler, and one of the ways he rebelled was to blow taps differently from the way anyone else blew taps. This was his private protest. More organized forms of protest against the system and the people who ran it were not only dangerous but also somehow illegitimate. As one of the participants in the Caine mutiny against Captain Queeg put it after the trial of the mutineers: "I see that we were in the wrong. The idea is, once you get an incompetent ass of a skipper—and that's the chance of war—there's nothing to do but serve him as though he were the wisest and the best, cover his mistakes, keep the ship going, and bear up." And the hero of *By Love Possessed* (his name is Arthur Winner) says: "In this life we cannot have everything for ourselves we might like to have. . . . Victory is not in reaching certainties or solving mysteries; victory is making do with uncertainties and in supporting mysteries." Such were the limits of individual self-expression.

We did not find all this oppressive. We were not oppressed. The terms of our enclosure were by and large moderate and reasonable. They made sense to us. One reason for this was that we had the enormous good luck to believe that we possessed a desirable future. The society we were getting ready to enter seemed on balance to be a good society. Most of us were eager to find our places in its structure and fulfill ourselves in ways expected of us. We were remarkably career-oriented and achievement-oriented. We thought we were needed by society, and by the professions we wanted to pursue. The jobs were out there waiting for us, slots to be filled. We accepted the ethic of apprenticeship in order to get ready for them. We entered the training programs and graduate schools to find out what was expected of us, required of us, and we did it. Our drive for careers within the system can be caricatured, and has been, in the popular images of gray-suited young organization drones selling themselves to corporate America. The urge to achievement cut across occupations and was shared by those of us who wanted to be scholars and teachers as well as the incipient businessmen, lawyers, and doctors among us. It was a symptom of the age: alienation from the system was not yet in style.

Nor was alienation from our elders. Rebellion from parental indulgence and rejection of middle-class trappings of affluence somehow did not occur to us. Most of us vaguely remembered something about the Depression as it touched our families, and the memory gave us a durable connection with our own parents, the shared experience of hard times. Thus we could also share the little postdepression, postwar family triumphs—the new car, the bigger house, the first TV set—which we might otherwise have loftily scorned. They were the small rewards of collective survival.

There seemed to be so much more within the structure to reach for and achieve that only an ungrateful fool, ignorant of the history of the past twenty years, would try to reach for things that could *not* be achieved, according to what we had been taught. So we were not so much silent as contained.

Then came the future we did not expect. At first, for many of us, it was better than we had bargained for, or at least more exciting. John Kennedy replaced Adlai Stevenson as our hero, and that seemed like an important advance, because the Kennedy mystique mixed intelligence and wit with success. Our need for his success was so urgent that we simply filtered out his failures and clung to the mystique. Moreover, because he was still young, we used him to mirror and magnify our own youthful aspirations to success.

He encouraged us to savor the dream that we were all still young together, whether we were twenty or thirty or forty, and that the young could move the country beyond survival toward improvement. (I remember the day I awoke from that dream, when in class I was talking about the hopes of "our generation" and a student interrupted to ask, "What generation are you talking about?")

The early civil rights movement also momentarily held us all together in a mood of common virtue, mainly owing to its color-blind appeal, the exulting guidance of Martin Luther King, and its songs. The anthems of Pete Seeger and Joan Baez, and Peter, Paul & Mary were the last musical messages to uplift us in the 1960s. We not only listened to them but we sang them, though I suppose the fact that some of us needed mimeograph sheets to follow all the verses was a quiet sign of age.

Each of us might remember the last time we celebrated a desirable future that we thought we shared with everyone around us, before the killing and shouting started, and the music and the smells changed, and the American flag appeared on blue jeans upside down. The time I remember was when Joan Baez came to Finney Chapel in the early 1960s and stood up there on the stage barefoot with her peasant skirt and acoustical guitar and led two thousand of us with our arms interlocked, swaying to her throbbing beat—black and white, young and old, male and female—singing "We Shall Overcome." Sometime after that, group by group, one after the other, Americans discovered they each had different obstacles to clear. The working assumptions of the 1950s turned out to be one of the main obstacles. Suddenly we were part of the problem; we had to be solved. In the search for solutions, the tight, taut world of our youth began to come apart. There was no containing it, except in the scrapbooks of our private memories.

CHAPTER 21

Memorial Minute for
William E. Stevenson (1986)

William Edwards Stevenson, eighth president of Oberlin College, died last spring at age eighty-four.[1] He led a life of uncommon energy and versatility spanning several important careers, most of them global in scope. His nonacademic professional background made him unique among Oberlin presidents. Together with his wife Eleanor Bumstead Stevenson (known universally as Bumpy), he brought a fresh breeze to this campus, a mood of brisk, realistic confidence. His leadership from 1946 through 1959 exposed the college to the cosmopolitan culture he came from and left Oberlin a more open, heterogeneous, and resilient place.

Born in Chicago in 1900 into the home of a Presbyterian minister who later became dean of the Princeton Theological Seminary, Stevenson grew up in the early twentieth-century Protestant establishment of the Atlantic seaboard. He sailed through the educational structure of this establishment and gathered all sorts of prizes along the way. After prepping at Andover Academy, he graduated from Princeton in 1922. His scholastic, social, and athletic talent won him a Rhodes scholarship, and he proceeded to read law for three years at Balliol College, Oxford. Meanwhile he earned distinction as a transatlantic track star, winning the American quarter-mile championship in 1921, the English championship in 1923, and an Olympic gold medal in the 1600-meter relay at Paris in 1924.

Stevenson's first professional career was the practice of law. On his return to the United States, he entered the U.S. District Attorney's office in New York City and spent two years prosecuting violators of Prohibition, including the Mafia gangster Frank Costello. Then he joined the New York law firm headed by John W. Davis, the leading constitutional lawyer of his generation. In 1931, in partnership with Ely Deveboise, Stevenson organized his own law firm, "the best little law firm on Wall Street," as he later described it. By the time the United States entered World War II ten years later, he was ready for a new challenge.

Joined by Mrs. Stevenson, he took on the task of organizing American Red Cross services in Great Britain. This brought him into sometimes tense relations with the American military high command, including General Eisenhower—the main tension turning on job descriptions for Red Cross nurses in time of war.

In November 1942 the Stevensons followed the American invasion force into North Africa, and thereafter he had charge of organizing the Red Cross first in North Africa and later in Sicily and Italy. After suffering a leg injury while coming ashore in Salerno harbor, Stevenson came home with his wife in 1944 and resumed the practice of law. Mrs. Stevenson's book about her Red Cross adventures, *I Knew Your Soldier,* became a widely read paperback in 1945.

The Stevensons enjoyed their wartime teamwork, and when the war was over the word got out that they might be interested in continuing as a team somewhere in academia. In 1946 this word reached the trustees of Oberlin College, who, in alliance with the retiring president, Ernest Hatch Wilkins, were engaged in intense unarmed warfare with the faculty over the governance of the college. The upshot of this combat was the passage of new bylaws that a faculty majority believed jeopardized the Finney Compact [see Chapter 18]. Simultaneously with their passage in May 1946 the trustees announced the election of Stevenson to the presidency, and a month later they rejected a faculty petition calling for a rescission of the new bylaws. These were the grim circumstances in which the Stevenson presidency began.

His honeymoon was brief. Soon faculty members were calling at his home and stopping him on the street to test his convictions on the Finney Compact, which he had never heard of before his arrival. Diplomacy finally prevailed, and in 1949 all parties to the quarrel agreed to a resolution that created the modern council system of faculty governance and gave the president more clear control over the college budget. Stevenson never quite swallowed his lawyer's impatience with the hours consumed by council and committee meetings, but governance was not again a major issue for the balance of his tenure.

Early on, he focused much of his executive energy on the renovation of the college's antiquated physical facilities. In the wake of the depression and world war, biology was being taught in an old church; the humanities were housed in an abandoned high school; several other departments and a majority of students lived in converted wooden houses; college dramatic productions were homeless; and buildings-and-grounds personnel worked out of wooden shacks along Main Street. Stevenson took decisive steps to correct each of these situations and to create new facilities for the conservatory as well.

No doubt his major achievement along this line was to break the deadlock over the design and construction of Hall Auditorium, which had been blocked for twenty years by the stubbornness of Homer Johnson, executor of the Hall bequest. Solving this problem brought all of Stevenson's diplomatic savvy into play, and included, for example, the tactic of mollifying Homer Johnson at a crucial stage of the negotiations by hiring his son Philip as a design consultant. Years later, when asked why the college did not give the son the Hall Auditorium commission outright, Stevenson replied with a wry smile, "Well, you see, back in [1948] his son hadn't become the greatest architect in the world. His father had thought he was going to be, and maybe he was right. But on the face of it, I had never heard of Philip Johnson."

Modernization of the college's physical plant was accompanied by Stevenson's modernization of administrative arrangements. He created the office of business manager to aim the college toward more expansive, growth-oriented policies, and he organized almost from scratch Oberlin's fund-raising activities, which had languished for long decades since the Hall bequest. Stevenson's own tireless efforts to raise money on the alumni and foundation circuit consumed more and more of his time as his presidency evolved.

He also had a hand in what he regarded as a modernization of the Oberlin faculty. In his first annual report in 1947, in a none-too-subtle critique of the local academic atmosphere, he wrote that he regretted the failure in some quarters to realize that the college "is no longer the small community enterprise conducted by a group of homogeneous kindred spirits that it once was." In succeeding years Oberlin reached out repeatedly to attract scholars of established merit from other institutions, including among others George Simpson, Milton Yinger, Wade Ellis, Charles Murphy (for whose course on the Legacy of Greece and Rome Stevenson subsequently gave an annual lecture on Roman law), and Clyde Holbrook, who was brought in on Stevenson's personal initiative to fill a newly endowed chair and begin the teaching of religion as a humanistic discipline.

Meanwhile Stevenson supported the efforts of conservatory director David Robertson to create a modern full-time resident faculty of performing musicians. Stevenson came to value the social companionship of conservatory faculty members because—in contrast with their colleagues in the college—they were less interested in reminding him that he was not a practicing scholar, and because they had a more cosmopolitan taste for good food and drink. One conservatory teacher whom the Stevensons befriended was the young pianist Emil Danenberg, who in his bachelor days lived next door to them on Forest Street. Danenberg remembered Stevenson as a warm, multidimensional human being who was among other things an amateur musician. He played the cello, badly, Danenberg recalled, and he added that he used to wince at the sound, carried across the air of a summer's evening from the president's back terrace, of the cello version of "Loch Lomond."

Stevenson's role in diversifying the faculty was matched by his efforts to broaden the range of the student body to international dimensions. More foreign students attended Oberlin across the 1950s than ever in the past, and meanwhile five Oberlin students were named Rhodes Scholars over the same decade. Because of Oberlin's reputation for racial enlightenment, the Stevensons had been startled on arrival by patterns of racial segregation and discrimination in the town, and by the absence of blacks on the faculty and board of trustees. The appointment of Wade Ellis to the faculty and of

Ralph Bunche as a trustee, both on Stevenson's initiative, set important precedents in this regard. Mrs. Stevenson meanwhile tried hard to integrate some of the town's recreational facilities. She served on the Ohio Fair Employment Practices Commission for a time, and her husband was appointed to President Truman's Committee on Equality of Treatment and Opportunity in the Armed Forces, the committee that spurred the integration of the American military in 1950.

Several of the educational innovations launched at Oberlin during the Stevenson years turned out not to work. He suffered his sharpest defeat by the faculty when his proposal for a campus ROTC unit, an attempt to meet Oberlin's age-old male admissions problem, was voted down in 1949. A year later, after the outbreak of the Korean War, the faculty approved an ROTC unit, but the unit did not take to the Oberlin environment, and it was phased out in 1956. In 1950 an experiment sponsored by the Ford Foundation was launched to enroll a select group of fourteen- to sixteen-year-old high school students at the college. This project, which brought a future Oberlin president, Robert Fuller, to the campus, was phased out three years later, and an alternative arrangement, Advanced Placement, took its place. The Salzburg Plan, promoted by Stevenson and Robertson, to send conservatory students abroad for their junior year of training, was begun in 1957 but lasted only six years, owing to reservations among conservatory faculty. Finally Stevenson managed to disconcert some Oberlinians by proposing, tongue in cheek, that the long-standing problem of student privacy might be solved by lining the football field with abandoned automobiles for coed bonding after dark. Alternatives to this arrangement awaited the 1960s.

As the 1950s drew to a close, Stevenson was restless for a wider orbit than Oberlin allowed. A new career in public service of some kind seemed more and more alluring to him, as college fund-raising chores and endless campus committee meetings began to chafe. Having given public support to Adlai Stevenson in the 1952 and 1956 presidential campaigns, he was approached by Ohio Democratic party leaders about a U.S. Senate race in 1958. Although success in such a race would have fulfilled a lifetime ambition, he turned down the idea on the ground that a probable primary fight would be inappropriate for a college president. A year later, at age fifty-nine, he submitted his resignation as president and left Oberlin for Aspen, Colorado. In 1961 President Kennedy appointed him U.S. ambassador to the

Philippines, a post he held with distinction until 1964. After that he became president of the Aspen Institute for Humanistic Studies, and he served on the teaching staff of the Institute for many years after his formal retirement in 1970.

In retrospect, his years at Oberlin were a long and not always tranquil passage in a remarkably useful life. But together with Bumpy he carried an affection for this place that if anything deepened as his time here receded into the past. A few years before his death, he concluded a lengthy reminiscence of his Oberlin experience this way: "My wife and I came joyously, naively I guess in some ways, in light of . . . things we didn't know very much about. And we gave everything we had to it. We loved the college, loved the people, and tried to do the things that needed to be done."

CHAPTER 22

Student Opinion at Oberlin, 1936–1976: A Report for the Bicentennial (1976)

*I*n the summer of 1960 Mary Elizabeth Fletcher, widow of Professor Robert Fletcher '20, gave me a large batch of papers, offprints, and old magazines that had accumulated in their attic.[1] Among them I found the records of a student opinion poll that Fletcher had taken in his classes in American history at Oberlin, beginning in 1936. Returns for 1936, 1946, and 1956 were included. Students had been asked to respond to each of several dozen words by marking those to which they had a strong favorable or unfavorable reaction. The words were the names of prominent people, organizations, groups, and ideas of the day—"atheism," "American Legion," "Franklin Roosevelt," "pacifism," "Wall Street," and so on. Glancing over the results with their intriguing changes and continuities, I decided that the poll was a device worth perpetuating and used it in my own survey class in American history beginning in 1960.

With the returns for 1976 now in, forty years of student reactions can be compared. (In the accompanying chart, the returns for "1966" are actually a composite of the results for 1965 and 1967; I was away on sabbatical in 1966.) What the data prove, if anything, the reader may decide. The poll is somewhat lacking in scholarly elegance. The words on the list have changed over time—several added and a few dropped each year—and the total number has more than doubled since 1936. I imagine that Professor Fletcher compiled his lists with little more forethought and calculation than I have. The aim has simply been to see what happens to certain familiar or controversial terms when they are subjected to the quick reactions of undergraduates, mostly sophomores and juniors. Students often note that the poll fails to record the intensity or ambivalence of their attitudes. The size of the sample varies with enrollments. The rules of thumb I have followed in determining rank order may fairly be questioned.

Some of my best friends are social scientists. Those to whom I have confided the returns from the poll have managed to control their enthusiasm for the methodology involved. One colleague politely intimated that less scientific polling instruments may possibly have been devised in recent times, but none had yet come to his attention. The poll lacks everything but longevity and elemental interest.

Some of the more striking items of interest may be worth pointing out. Certain words have been blue-ribbon winners (or losers) over the full forty years. "Individualism" shows remarkable staying power, as I suppose any number of unlisted words, such as "equality" or "free speech," might have also. "Evolution" has performed with steady if less spectacular success over the decades. The consistently high losers—"Ku Klux Klan," "Hitler," "Mussolini," and "fascism"—reflect a keen and durable distaste for the more brutal enemies of individual freedom.

The careers of most other words have varied widely over four decades. "Christianity," after eliciting decisively favorable response from 1936 to 1956, fell rapidly across the 1960s. It ranked eleventh in 1960, twenty-fourth in 1963, and twenty-eighth in 1967. Meanwhile, "agnosticism" and "atheism," poorly received at the outset, have attracted a growing number of favorable responses over the past fifteen years. "United Nations," after strong friendly notice from 1946 to 1967, declined thereafter and became a mildly controversial item in 1976 (thirty-one favorable, ten unfavorable responses). "Supreme Court" has also dropped recently in the favorable rankings (twenty-first in 1976) but aroused only two negative responses. Meanwhile the changing temper of the years, from Depression to world war and cold war through the turbulence of the 1960s, has caused "pacifism" and "socialism" to bounce with some resilience. Both concepts dropped out of sight in the cold war years but had reemerged as strong attractions by 1976. "Capitalism" peaked in the 1950s and slipped badly over the 1960s. When the more euphemistic term "free enterprise" was added for comparative purposes, it fared better, but more recently it has also slumped.

Scanning the names of politicians, one notes the relentless ascent of Richard Nixon's unfavorable reputation since his first appearance on the charts in 1956, as well as the brief glory of John F. Kennedy, the brightest shooting star of our time, in the mid-1960s. All of the more prominent presidents had been added to the list by 1964. They ranked as follows in 1964 and 1976:

1964	1976
1. Abraham Lincoln	1. Abraham Lincoln
2. John F. Kennedy	2. Thomas Jefferson
3. Franklin Roosevelt	3. Franklin Roosevelt
4. Thomas Jefferson	4. George Washington
5. Woodrow Wilson	5. John F. Kennedy
6. Lyndon Johnson	6. Harry Truman
7. George Washington	7. Woodrow Wilson
8. Harry Truman	8. Andrew Jackson
9. Andrew Jackson	9. Theodore Roosevelt
10. Theodore Roosevelt	10. Dwight Eisenhower
11. Herbert Hoover	11. Lyndon Johnson
12. Dwight Eisenhower	12. Herbert Hoover
	13. Gerald Ford
	14. Richard Nixon

A final observation: since 1936 the divisions of opinion over words attracting a heavy response have grown ever more lopsided. The charts for 1936 and 1946 show an abundance of sharply contested items. More recently the big responses, whether pro or con, have become almost monolithic. The only double-digit controversy to make the top forty chart over the past decade is the historical reputation of Dwight Eisenhower. For whatever reasons—the emergence of a youth culture with its own special cluster of attitudes, or the growing homogeneity of the Oberlin student body—it has gotten harder to find words that will divide undergraduates in large numbers. In 1976 the hottest items in this regard were "law and order," "rugged individualism," "William F. Buckley," "Indira Gandhi," and "Fidel Castro." One wonders which of these will seem as puzzling by the year 2016 as the "Rotary" and "Martin Davey" of 1936 seem today. Martin Davey? Alumni who remember taking part in the 1936 survey will surely recall that at that time he was governor of Ohio. He studied at the Oberlin Academy in 1904–06 and in the College in 1906–1907.

Opinion Poll

History 104-February 1976

Do not sign your name.

Mark (−) after words to which you have a strong unfavorable reaction.

Mark (+) after words to which you have a strong favorable reaction.

If your response is neutral or mild either way, do not mark.

atheism	Democrats	Robert F. Kennedy
evolution	Nasser	socialism
Richard Nixon	pacifism	Andrew Jackson
Fidel Castro	Catholics	TVA
non-violence	Eugene McCarthy	rugged individualism
Wall Street	capitalism	Adlai Stevenson
Billy Graham	George Wallace	abortion
New Deal	collectivism	Che Guevera
elitism	Adolf Hitler	Black Panthers
Russians	American Legion	militarism
Woodrow Wilson	Lyndon Johnson	DAR
agnosticism	communism	Hollywood
Thomas Jefferson	Edmund Muskie	fascism
social security	Jews	United Nations
Malcolm X	Herbert Hoover	Ronald Reagan
bourgeois	socialized medicine	Theodore Roosevelt
Madison Avenue	John F. Kennedy	AMA
Benito Mussolini	A. D. A.	Weathermen

Republican
individualism
sit-ins
Joseph Stalin
heroin
Dwight Eisenhower
New Left
Barry Goldwater
imperialism
Negroes
John Lindsay
containment
S. D. S.
marijuana
Blacks
Hubert Humphrey
Gay Liberation
détente
Bella Abzug

Pete Seeger
Supreme Court
Joseph McCarthy
Christianity
Franklin Roosevelt
Free Enterprise
Wasps
Nelson Rockefeller
Ku Klux Klan
Abraham Lincoln
civil disobedience
Spiro Agnew
Mao Tse Tung
hard hats
Eldridge Cleaver
Mayor Daley
Gloria Steinem
Black Muslims
Gerald Ford

Ralph Nader
Women's Liberation
law and order
Harry Truman
NAACP
George Washington
John Birch Society
William F. Buckley
welfare state
communes
Black Power
Edward M. Kennedy
big business
Martin Luther King
Israel
George McGovern
capital punishment
Karl Marx
Indira Gandhi
revolution

Student Opinion at Oberlin College, 1936–1976, as polled in survey course in American History

1936 (74 polled)			1946 (121 polled)			1956 (81 polled)		
Favorable			**Favorable**			**Favorable**		
1.	Christianity	61-1	1.	United Nations	81-3	1.	United Nations	61-1
2.	individualism	50-4	2.	Christianity	70-2	2.	individualism	56-0
3.	British	49-0	3.	F. D. Roosevelt	60-7	3.	Supreme Court	55-0
4.	Supreme Court	48-3	4.	individualism	59-8	4.	Christianity	49-6
5.	pacifism	47-9	5.	Woodrow Wilson	55-2	5.	Woodrow Wilson	47-5
6.	evolution	44-5	6.	TVA	54-1	6.	UNESCO	47-1
7.	League of Nations	42-12	7.	Supreme Court	51-3	7.	British	44-5
8.	Woodrow Wilson	37-6	8.	evolution	50-4	8.	Dwight Eisenhower	40-6
9.	Alf Landon	32-8	9.	OPA	50-16	9.	Adlai Stevenson	39-7
10.	Republican	32-11	10.	League of Nations	43-10	10.	F. D. Roosevelt	38-6
11.	TVA	26-9	11.	British	42-16	11.	evolution	37-7
12.	F. D. Roosevelt	26-16	12.	New Deal	42-20	12.	Negroes	33-0
13.	Herbert Hoover	25-14	13.	Henry A. Wallace	38-25	13.	capitalism	32-4
14.	Prohibition	25-19	14.	MacArthur	30-19	14.	New Deal	32-10
15.	capitalism	23-17	15.	Negroes	28-1	15.	TVA	28-7
16.	Rotary	21-8	16.	Republican	24-18	16.	Democrat	27-11
17.	higher criticism	20-8	17.	socialism	23-7	17.	immigrants	26-3
18.	Norman Thomas	20-19	18.	capitalism	23-15	18.	Republican	24-14
19.	Wm Jennings Bryan	19-3	19.	Democrat	19-5	19.	ADA	22-6
20.	socialism	18-19	20.	Jews	18-6	20.	Deism	22-10
Unfavorable			**Unfavorable**			**Unfavorable**		
1.	Ku Klux Klan	55-5	1.	Ku Klux Klan	106-0	1.	Ku Klux Klan	73-1
2.	Mussolini	53-2	2.	Hitler	100-1	2.	Joseph McCarthy	67-1
3.	Hearst	52-3	3.	Mussolini	86-1	3.	Mussolini	62-1
4.	Hitler	52-5	4.	Coughlin	85-1	4.	fascism	59-2
5.	militarism	49-5	5.	fascism	83-0	5.	Hitler	58-2
6.	Coughlin	48-3	6.	Bilbo	83-1	6	communism	44-1
7.	strikes	45-4	7.	Hearst	76-0	7.	Prohibition	43-3
8.	atheism	44-3	8.	DAR	69-0	8.	militarism	39-3
9.	fascism	41-3	9.	Chicago Tribune	57-3	9.	DAR	38-7
10.	communism	40-4	10.	Prohibition	55-7	10.	Hearst	36-5
11.	teachers' oath	34-6	11.	militarism	54-4	11.	American Legion	36-7
12.	Martin Davey	33-2	12.	strikes	54-16	12.	Krushchev	34-3
13.	New Deal	29-18	13.	American Legion	46-6	13.	Truman	34-13
14.	American Legion	28-16	14.	communism	42-3	14.	J. F. Dulles	33-13
15.	Kaiser Wilhelm	27-1	15.	Catholicism	40-11	15.	atheism	32-11
16.	agnosticism	24-6	16.	Japan	39-2	16.	Chicago Tribune	27-6
17.	Liberty League	24-6	17.	atheism	38-4	17.	Catholicism	26-8
18.	Wall Street	24-16	18.	Truman	36-5	18.	Warren G. Harding	23-1
19.	immigrants	23-10	19.	pacifism	32-8	19.	Hollywood	23-11
20.	Brain Trust	22-10	20.	Kaiser Wilhelm	28-1	20.	Richard Nixon	23-14

1965-67 (110 polled		1976 (76 polled)	
Favorable		**Favorable**	
1. John F. Kennedy	78-2	1. individualism	59-2
2. Abraham Lincoln	74-1	2. Martin Luther King	58-1
3. United Nations	74-2	3. non-violence	58-1
4. Adlai Stevenson	72-1	4. socialized medicine	53-3
5. individualism	71-3	5. Ralph Nader	52-3
6. Martin Luther King	66-7	6. Women's Liberation	50-8
7. F. D. Roosevelt	60-5	7. Abraham Lincoln	48-2
8. Thomas Jefferson	56-1	8. Thomas Jefferson	47-3
9. NAACP	56-6	9. pacifism	45-5
10. social security	55-5	10. NAACP	38-1
11. New Deal	55-7	11. Israel	38-3
12. Supreme Court	53-2	12. F. D. Roosevelt	38-6
13. evolution	51-1	13. evolution	37-2
14. Pete Seeger	38-1	14. Pete Seeger	37-2
15. free enterprise	38-6	15. abortion	37-9
16. TVA	36-3	16. New Deal	36-1
17. Woodrow Wilson	36-5	17. George McGovern	36-5
18. CORE	36-12	18. social security	36-5
19. George Washington	35-3	19. civil disobedience	36-6
20. John Lindsay	34-2	20. socialism	35-2
Unfavorable		**Unfavorable**	
1. Ku Klux Klan	100-0	1. Hitler	69-0
2. John Birch Society	91-0	2. Ku Klux Klan	67-0
3. Hitler	91-1	3. Richard Nixon	66-2
4. DAR	81-0	4. George Wallace	64-0
5. Joseph McCarthy	80-1	5. John Birch Society	64-0
6. Barry Goldwater	80-3	6. Spiro Agnew	63-0
7. fascism	75-0	7. Mussolini	63-0
8. Mussolini	69-1	8. fascism	62-0
9. militarism	62-1	9. imperialism	60-0
10. Richard Nixon	62-4	10. Billy Graham	58-2
11. Fidel Castro	61-8	11. Joseph McCarthy	57-0
12. American Legion	60-1	12. Ronald Reagan	55-0
13. Black Muslims	60-4	13. heroin	55-4
14. Billy Graham	57-4	14. capital punishment	52-6
15. Stalin	50-3	15. militarism	50-0
16. Nasser	49-2	16. elitism	47-0
17. imperialism	46-3	17. Stalin	45-4
18. Dwight Eisenhower	42-11	18. Mayor Daley	44-3
19. Hollywood	38-4	19. big business	43-4
20. communism	35-3	20. Barry Goldwater	42-2

CHAPTER 23

Spreading the Calm (1984)

$\mathcal{T}$here is an old story about the man who found himself neck-high in a swamp full of alligators. His solution was to drain the swamp. That story always reminds me of Bob Longsworth. Ten years ago this place was filled with alligators and the water stank. Faculty members who weren't here then tend not to believe it all when they hear about it. They listen politely, but their mood is patient and their eyes glaze over, like youngsters learning about the Great Depression and World War II. Those grayhairs who were around in the early 1970s would just as soon forget the close details, and many of us have. It has been a kind of long amnesia.

The years 1973–74 witnessed the biggest exodus in modern Oberlin history—president, vice president, dean, physical education director, theater director, dean of women, and a host of others more obscure. The arrival of many of them made noisy headlines. Their departure was celebrated in quiet relief. Ten years ago the faculty came within six votes of unionizing, even after the exodus was mostly over. Oberlin had so many acting administrators they needed name tags.

But one of them required no introduction. Bob Longsworth moved quietly from the basement of Rice to the first floor of Cox that summer, and imperceptibly the calm began to spread. In one of the smartest of many smart moves, Emil Danenberg named Bog Longsworth the Real Dean in the spring of 1975. In the months and years that followed, Bob taught us slowly how to trust one another once again. He restored civility and comity to the faculty, and a measure of levity. Among the happiest sounds on the campus over the past decade have been the mellow roars of laughter rolling through his office door. Time and again he showed a knack for soothing raw nerves and stroking bruised egos with a deft phrase and a puckish smile. When that didn't work, when the people of a whole department or program were at each others' throats, and his as well, the faculty councils of the 1970s resorted more than once to a winning tactic. They made Bob acting chairman of the department or program in question. Sooner or later people would decide to emulate his tact and patience, and the calm would spread a little farther. Along the way, he came to know us all better than anyone else—our foibles and soft spots, our talents and our knots of pride. He has been right about us far more often than not. We learned that we could disagree with him on basics, and say so out loud, and come back another day to talk it through some more. He has been a man of friendly persuasion, and either party could be persuaded. All this has been more important for us than we sometimes remember to acknowledge.

Bob Longsworth has been a bracing model in other ways as well. In an era of academic austerity and hard choices, his personal style has served as a beacon in the gloom—his transparent-taped hornrims, his antique, broken-pedaled bicycles, his home-made haircuts, his fondness for ancestral clothing handed down across the generations among his Carroll County relatives. Some of us have learned to organize our lives around his odd sartorial habits. At the end of the week he liked to come to work in his best blue jeans, and we could calculate: if that's the dean, this must be Saturday. His other indulgences also have a certain low-budget flair about them—his lust for butterscotch milk shakes, for example, and machine-stamped Albanian neckties. Even the lowest-paid untenured English instructor could look at him and say, "There but for the grace of God go I."

Lyndon Johnson, another country boy who relished a well-turned phrase, enjoyed explaining back in the 1960s why he kept his quarrelling companions with him inside the tent rather than kicking them out. The explanation is probably too raw for mixed company, though I know Bob would like it. It has to do with whether it's better to get wet inside or outside. Let's just say to him, "Thanks to you, the flap is open and the ground is dry: welcome back to the tent."

CHAPTER 24

College and Commitment:
A Glance at the Past (1969)

The full history of Oberlin's institutional involvement in political and social issues affecting the world beyond the campus remains to be written.[1]
What follow are my impressions gained from a search for the crucial landmarks in that history. I want to stress how tentative these impressions are.
Both their adequacy and their relevance to the questions confronting
Oberlin today may be fairly questioned. At least they emerge from an effort
to read the record clearly and to get the facts straight—that is, to understand
the past on its terms as well as on our own. If the results seem clouded with
ambiguity, perhaps that is history's fault.[2] In the early Oberlin, college,
colony, and cause were organically connected. The original purposes of the
founders—to glorify God, train Christian missionaries, and elevate the status
of women—were consciously reformist, placing the institution at odds with
conventional American society from the outset. In 1835, just two years after
its founding, the institution's range of purposes decisively expanded to embrace the concept of intellectual freedom, with the arrival of the Lane
Seminary rebels, who left Cincinnati in protest over the squelching of their
antislavery views. From that day to this, the college has lived with internal tension among its component parts—students, faculty, president, and trustees—
between the claims of particular reformist causes on the one hand and the
concept of intellectual freedom on the other.

The great choices of 1835—the warm reception of the Lane rebels, the decision to open the college to black students, and the establishment of the principle of faculty control over the internal management of its concerns without trustee interference—fixed the reputation of the college as an outpost of radical moral education for the next three decades. Oberlin's identification with the abolitionist movement (among a multitude of other causes) was a national fact before and after the passage of the Fugitive Slave Law of 1850. Despite Charles G. Finney's reservations ("[W]e do not wish the trustees to hold out an Abolition or an Anti-abolition flag," he wrote in 1835), antislavery enthusiasm, expressed through economic boycotts, fundraising, and aid to fugitives, enforced a community consensus that at times made local dissent hazardous even among abolitionists. In 1846, for instance, the faculty attempted to bar disciples of William Lloyd Garrison's brand of antislavery from the campus. The college relented the following year when Garrison himself, in the company of Frederick Douglass, arrived in town to debate outstanding issues of goals and tactics.[3]

With the birth of the Republican party in the mid-1850s, disagreement emerged between advocates of political action to contain slavery and champions of civil disobedience and direct action to destroy it. It is impossible to determine with precision what role if any the college, as an institution distinct from the local antislavery majority, played in the more militant agitations of those years. For example, the actual participants in the Wellington Rescue of 1858 included more townsmen than college students and faculty, though the rescuers' cordial treatment by the whole community blurs the distinction. There is no evidence that the college was directly involved in the episode of March 1860, when a U.S. deputy marshal was run out of town by a band of angry black residents, but again the environment nurtured by the college was doubtless crucial to the act. A year later the community greeted the outbreak of the Civil War with a strong sense of vindication. And in 1866 a gathering of prominent community leaders, including Finney's successor as college president, James H. Fairchild, anticipated Andrew Johnson's impeachment by condemning his pro-southern reconstruction policies.[4]

The time between the Civil War and the turn of the century is traditionally regarded as the dark age in Oberlin's history, years when the college descended from its past commitments to the more orderly pursuit of conventional learning and fell into conformity with the goals of the larger society.[5] But local agitation for a better world did not cease. The major cause of these years—the prohibition of alcoholic beverages—was informed by many of the values that had inspired abolitionists in earlier years, including the dream of creating a more moral society of men for the greater glorification of God. The disparity in present reputation between abolitionism and prohibition need not obscure the ideological continuity between the two movements. President Fairchild was far more energetic in the cause of temperance than President Finney had been in the cause of antislavery. Beginning with the creation of the Oberlin Temperance Alliance in 1874, Fairchild's twenty-year agitation to wipe out the saloon won massive support from faculty and students.[6]

The college community's passion for temperance ultimately generated the birth in Oberlin of the organization that more than any other propelled the prohibition movement toward national success. This was the Anti-Saloon League, organized in First Church in 1893.[7] While the college never formally affiliated itself with the purposes of the league, the connection was indelible in the public mind. It remained for a college trustee, James Troup, to register the most emphatic protest against this identification. Oberlin College "depends for its success and usefulness upon the sympathy and support of men of all shades of political belief," Troup asserted in 1905. "As an alumnus and trustee of the college I object to 'the support of Oberlin College' being extended to the Anti-Saloon League, or to any other organization engaged in a political campagn."[8] The connection nevertheless remained intimate enough for the college faculty in 1918 to vote an invitation to the League to celebrate its twenty-fifth anniversary in the home of its birth.[9]

Only Oberlin's devotion to the Republican party surpassed its loyalty to the cause of prohibition. Succeeding straw votes indicate that the student body, like the town, was preponderantly Republican from the 1860s to the 1950s. The GOP's reputation as the Negro's friend helped to sustain Republican loyalty in the early twentieth century. At times rifts in this tight fabric of assumptions proved embarrassing. Thus when the black leader W. E. B. DuBois brought his Niagara Movement to Oberlin for its third annual meeting in 1908, and the movement, meeting in Council Hall, used the occasion to attack Republican race policies, indignant Oberlinians held a mass meeting under the Historic Elm to protest the Niagara heresy with a ringing counter-resolution: "Oberlin is not the place to utter such sentiments, Council Hall, the home of theologians, too sacred a place for colored Democrats to preach the doctrine of political infidelity to orthodox colored Republicans of the country."[10]

Oberlin did not escape complicity with the national drive toward racial segregation that gathered momentum after 1890. Recent researches of college archivist William Bigglestone suggest that the main impulse for segregation on campus came from the student body, and with the grudging acquiescence of faculty and administration, and over the protest of older alumni from Oberlin's antislavery days. In 1910, when blacks made up 4 percent of the student body, only one black student could be found among the 154 members of student literary societies. A student spokesman for one of the societies explained: "Phi Delta is not a reformer's club, it is an association of men for literary and social purposes. . . . The presence of a colored man in our ranks would for many of us spoil utterly the social side of society life." When black athletes protested at being forced into segregated facilities when traveling with college teams to nearby cities, Professor Azariah Root (in charge of college affairs in the temporary absence of President King) informed them that the college could not be held responsible for their treatment away from the campus, and they must therefore fend for themselves.[11] (A few years later, by way of contrast, the faculty indicated its wish that students conform to common rules of conduct while off campus, by voting the following resolution: "The college requests students to refrain from smoking in public when away from Oberlin on trips as members of representative teams or clubs, spectators at athletic contests, or in other distinctively college groups.")[12]

President King himself was constantly buffeted by contention on the race issue and bent repeatedly to the pressure for separation. Responding to the fierce criticism of Mary Church Terrell, a black alumna of the class of 1884 who waged a life-long fight against discrimination, King wrote plaintively:

> You do not seem to me to make a proper distinction between
> the official attitude of the college, and the attitude of individual
> students, or individual members of the community . . . I shall do
> everything I can to make sentiment for fairness and justice both
> in the college and the community; at the same time I cannot
> guarantee that, with large numbers coming to us without any spe-
> cial training on this subject, there will not be examples of lack of
> consideration.[13]

The issue plagued King to the end of his presidency, as various alumni
clubs across the country insisted on maintaining the lily-white ethic at college fund-raising dinners in the 1920s.[14] Only after the arrival of William E.
Stevenson and Eleanor Stevenson in 1946 did the Oberlin presidency become a force for racial equity.

Doubtless the most familiar example of Oberlin's institutional commitment to an educational cause beyond the campus was the creation in 1908
of the Shansi Memorial Association to commemorate the Oberlin-trained
missionaries who died in the Boxer Rebellion of 1900. Oberlinians had engaged in missionary activity in China since 1882, and to perpetuate their
work the association renewed the educational facilities in Shansi Province
destroyed by the rebellion. The commitment was subsequently underwrit-
ten (among other ways) by funds collected from undergraduates through
the student activity fee. Oberlin student representatives have been dispatched since 1918 to serve Shansi's purposes in the Far East. The association has ever since survived adversity both at Oberlin and in China to give
the college its most durable link to the nonwestern world.[15]

With the entry of the United States into World War I, the college embarked upon the first of its twentieth-century ventures in cooperation with
the federal government in the name of military necessity. The effort of
1917–18 was by all odds the college's most emphatic, and in many ways the
most disastrous. It set grim precedents that the college tried to avoid in later
wars by ever more cautious negotiations with Washington. As an educational institution interested in its own survival as well as the nation's,
Oberlin has set increasingly stringent terms on its cooperation in order to
maintain wartime control over its own affairs while simultaneously tapping

an adequate supply of male students. Meanwhile it has remained reasonably free of the hysteria that locked the campus into the cause of war in 1918.

On April 2, 1917, President King telegraphed the college's support for Woodrow Wilson's war message to Congress. Three days later the Oberlin faculty voted to "offer to the federal government the use of the science laboratories of the college and any other college property of which the government could make use; also the services of college teachers, especially the teachers of science, for any possible use by the government." At the same meeting the faculty authorized the prompt creation of a practical course in military training. By noon the following day 176 men had signed up, and before the semester was out 75 percent of the men's campus was enrolled in the course. "We have brought in this improvised training for the rest of the year," President King explained privately, "to guard against too many of the men being swept off their feet suddenly and prematurely enlisting." When Ohio Governor James Cox urged that colleges close that spring to allow men to help plant crops, the faculty declined to close Oberlin but agreed to ease departure for those who wanted to leave.[16]

In September 1918 the faculty approved plans for a government-sponsored Student Army Training Corps as an autonomous military school within the college that controlled its own policies of admission, academic standing, and student conduct. This abdication of control by the college over the lives of the SATC students (who were defined as members of the regular army) led to miserable results. Not only did the unit remain segregated; academic standards plummeted and classroom conduct deteriorated radically. At the end of the year the college was relieved to be rid of its "Sad Attempt to Cooperate."[17]

The war came to Oberlin in other ways, to make an extraordinary case study in tightening conformity to national purpose. Instructional units in the German department fell from 2,616 in 1916–17 to 159 in 1918–19. The college catalog for 1916–17 referred to the college's namesake as the "German pastor and philanthropist, Johann Friedrich Oberlin." The next year he became the "Alsatian pastor and philanthropist John Frederick Oberlin." In the spring of 1918 a new event—the grenade toss—was introduced at college track meets. A campus pacifist paper, *The Rational Patriot*, launched three weeks before the declaration of war, struggled through the next year against mounting animosity. When its following had dwindled to a dozen lonely supporters the

Oberlin Review (which had earlier pleaded for tolerance of pacifist activity) pontificated, "the time for the appearance of such a paper as *The Rational Patriot* has passed." In May 1918 the sheet disappeared.[18]

The reigning mood touched teachers as well as students. The great majority of the faculty sympathized with the efforts of President King and Dean Bosworth of the Graduate School of Theology to translate the lessons of liberal Christianity into support for a just war. A college faculty committee on patriotic education published a series of pamphlets designed to illuminate the meaning of the nation's effort. Dissenters were quickly identified—among them the aging Eugene Lyman, professor of systematic theology, whose strong pacifism was regarded as an embarrassment to the college. President King quietly expressed his hope that Lyman's replacement, even if he too were a pacifist, might be a man who could adapt his convictions to the present crisis.[19] But by all odds the most troublesome heretic was the strong-willed one-man political science department, Professor Karl Geiser. His cool intellectual approach to the war antagonized many for whom the issues were not intellectual but moral (see Chapter 15). The treatment he experienced during the war was not peculiar to him or to Oberlin. It was a footnote to one of the bleakest hours in the history of American dissent.[20]

The war apparently left the college with a certain lingering appetite for involvement in public affairs. Shortly after the war, in the fall of 1920, the college produced a brief spate of quasi-official pronouncements on particular national political issues. In response to a formal query from the American Council on Education, the faculty endorsed the proposed creation of a federal department of education with cabinet status, as well as the principle of federal match grants to states for educational purposes. Shortly thereafter the faculty declared its opposition to "any change by Congress of its long continued policy of complete conservation of our national parks and monuments" and urged the defeat of certain bills that seemed to jeopardize such policy.[21]

Most significantly, in response to student appeals, President King enlisted campus support for a national amnesty drive in behalf of radicals imprisoned during the war and red scare of 1919. In December 1920 King suggested in chapel that the following petition to President Wilson be circulated among the students and faculty:

> As teachers and students of Oberlin College may we unite
> with many others in expressing the earnest hope that, as a step
> toward the restoration of full liberty of speech, press and assem-
> blage you may find it wise on Christmas Day to grant amnesty to
> all federal political prisoners held under the Espionage act only
> for political opinions, or for words spoken or written, as distin-
> guished from direct incitement to violence, acts of violence or
> overt acts against the Government.[22]

The petition circulated and King dispatched it to the White House. He received no immediate reply, and it was not until 1923 that the last of the wartime prisoners were released from federal jails.[23] After one further faculty resolution, a 1922 protest against the execution in Bulgaria of former government ministers, the college appeared to lapse into the mood of quiescent normalcy shared by the nation at large.[24]

Ernest Hatch Wilkins replaced Henry Churchill King as president in 1927. A liberal and a pacifist, Wilkins brought a fresh atmosphere of political involvement with him to the campus. He rode the college through a turbulent era of Depression, peace agitation, minority radicalism, and finally World War II. Neither students nor faculty acquiesced easily with his leadership. Among both groups he found vocal critics of his stands on controversial issues. From the outset he thrust himself forward as an activist, presiding over political rallies, sponsoring student petitions for political rights in the state of Ohio, helping to organize the Public Affairs Club for the airing of domestic issues on all sides, leading in the creation of the Oberlin Peace Society (a body that claimed over seven hundred campus members at its peak), and signing innumerable telegrams and petitions in behalf of disarmament, neutrality legislation, and pacifist unity. He defined the presidency as an initiating agency and was undiscouraged by defeat.[25]

The early 1930s were heady years for Oberlin radicals of every stripe. Bewildered housemothers struggled to comprehend the outbreak of clenched fists, Nazi salutes, and angry harangues among their flock.[26] Socialists, communists, fascists, labor organizers, and technocrats came to deliver their rival messages. In the presidential campaign of 1932, left-wing students foraged the county for the socialist ticket, convinced by Chicago professor Paul

Douglas that the major parties offered a meaningless choice. (Six Norman Thomas campaigners were arrested in Lorain for rallying without a permit on the eve of the election.)[27] For the moderate majority the ferment seemed at times too much. In 1933 the faculty terminated permission for the Radical Club to publish its magazine *Progress,* in apparent disgust with its strident tone. *Progress* had combined demands for an end to compulsory chapel and a beginning for rational campus sex ethics with a charge that the college bore complicity with the imperialistic activities of the Aluminum Company of America. Driven underground by the faculty action, the magazine denounced the faculty as bourgeois reactionaries, and its editors exchanged blows with President Wilkins in the letter columns of *The Nation.* Passions calmed the following year, and at the urging of Wilkins, compromise with student radicals was achieved.[28] Thereafter radicalism slowly withered at Oberlin. As the decade wore on, campus attention focused ever more sharply on the dying cause of world peace.

In December 1938, at the end of a year that witnessed Germany's occupation of Austria, the Munich appeasement, Nazi assaults on Jewish synagogues, and, in Oberlin, growing faculty restlessness with Wilkins's pacifism, a special meeting of the general faculty passed this resolution:

> In view of the increasingly clear evidence that minority groups as well as institutions of higher learning in Germany are suffering from systematic mistreatment at the hands of the present German government, and believing as we do in the inalienable right of the individual to freedom of thought and speech, in the obligation of government to serve all its members, and in the value of an all-inclusive ideal of brotherhood, we, the faculty of Oberlin College, wish hereby to put ourselves on record as deploring racial and religious persecution and the curbing of freedom of speech and as being utterly opposed on moral and conscientious grounds to all such violation of personal, human rights, wherever such violation may occur.[29]

Three days later, the day after Pearl Harbor, President Wilkins himself presented a special faculty meeting with the following resolution:

The faculty of Oberlin College offers to the President of the
United States the assurance of its complete support in the now
tragically intensified effort of national defense and the assurance
of its profound desire that the college may serve the country as
effectively as possible in such ways as may be for the common
good of the nation.

An impatient faculty substituted for Wilkins's pacifist euphemism "now tragically intensified effort of national defense" the words "nation's effort to win
this war" and passed the resolution with a single negative vote.[30] Even as
amended, the language was notably less specific in its commitments than the
words used twenty-four years before, when buildings, equipment, and professors were offered up to the nation. Over the next year and a half, Wilkins
carried on strenuous negotiations with Washington over the precise terms of
the college's cooperation. He was aided by the work of the American
Council on Education, which served as intermediary between colleges and
the government in formulating plans for the use of college men in wartime.

Of the several federal programs devised for campuses, the Navy's V-12
program seemed the most attractive in that it promised a better caliber of
trainees and an academically oriented schedule of classroom work. Hopes
for such a unit were clouded momentarily in early 1943 when War Department officers arrived to survey the campus for use as a housing facility for
one thousand military police guarding the strategic industry of northern
Ohio. Wilkins wanted no part of this, told the army so, and intensified his
efforts to acquire an educational unit for the college. Finally he was able to
announce the promise of a seven-hundred-man Oberlin V-12 unit, and in
July 1943 the unit arrived. The college was not able to protect its own supply of men—only one hundred current undergraduates were able to join the
unit—but it had assured itself of a continuing educational function in the
context of a total national war effort. The extraordinary wartime mobility of
trainees from campus to campus caused problems. Academic standards suffered, and the honor system was temporarily scrapped. Nevertheless the academic environment fostered by the military presence was a distinct improvement over that of World War I. Moreover, the campus experienced no
sequel to the conformist hysteria of 1918.

One by-product of World War II was the growth of campus sentiment
in favor of a more equitable draft system for the postwar years, whether in

the form of universal military service or nonmilitary alternative service. As the country had now assumed a global role in world affairs, the assumption seemed safe that the draft issue would not soon disappear. Some feared it would compound the college's problem of attracting an adequate supply of good male students in the years ahead.

President William Stevenson's proposed solution was the ROTC. With the support of the trustees Stevenson broached this possibility to the faculty early in 1949. A reserve unit on campus, he hoped, would not only meet the draft problem for some Oberlin men; it might widen the range of the college's appeal for male applicants in general. While faculty sentiment was divided on the probable benefits to the ROTC, Stevenson was authorized to explore the possibility further. The voice of student opinion was then heard from. The student council opposed the plan on the ground that "the military method is inconsistent with the academic freedom present in Oberlin," and 821 students petitioned for a campus referendum. Thereupon the faculty, to Stevenson's dismay, voted down the ROTC idea, 59 to 63.[31]

In the summer of 1950 the Korean War broke out. Early the next fall Stevenson introduced the issue once again. The specter of the draft loomed larger now, as did the problem of male admissions. Depression babies were a meager crop, and the college found itself in the unhappy position of admitting virtually every male who met the formal entry requirements. Confronted with these facts, the faculty now authorized application for an ROTC unit, by a margin of 105 to 31, but only after satisfying itself that the college would control the criteria for selection, and the honor system would remain intact. "It is understood," the faculty voted, "that the presence of the unit will not alter the traditional interest of the college in academic freedom and freedom of speech; in this connection, attention is specifically called to the existence of some pacifist sentiment among faculty and students."[32] A formal poll taken in February 1951 at the request of the military indicated once again how the Korean War had altered the terms of the debate. Students were now found to favor a unit by a ratio of 5:1.[33] The unit, an Air Force ROTC, had scarcely settled itself on campus before the war ended, and Air Force training officers struggled through a hectic Oberlin existence until their departure in 1956.

Meanwhile in these years the activities of Joseph McCarthy and his friends were inspiring new efforts to define the meaning of academic freedom and intellectual freedom. As early as 1950 the Oberlin faculty began to dispatch formal expressions of appreciation and concern to various storm centers of the new red scare across the country.[34] (In varying contexts such resolutions have been voted, by both faculty and students, over the years down to the present.) A landmark document emerging from the McCarthy era was the Oberlin College Statement on Academic Freedom, voted unanimously by the faculty in February 1952. Two passages in the statement seem particularly relevant to the issues dividing the campus in the late 1960s:

> . . . fallible men can serve truth and knowledge best by ceaseless questioning and free exchange of ideas. Our hope of transcending our present and partial insights depends in large measure upon maintaining in these communities of scholars the freedom to pursue their studies wherever the truth, as they see it, may lead them.
>
> . . . The Oberlin College faculty regards all forms of interference with intellectual freedom, discriminatory loyalty oaths, censorship, and other restrictions on free speech and thought as inimical to the democratic way of life.[35]

Fourteen months later the student body approved a student council endorsement of the faculty statement by a ratio of over 30:1.[36] That the campus stand against McCarthyism was not purely academic was suggested in spring 1953 when one of McCarthy's aides (a one-time pro-communist who had, incidentally, visited the campus back in 1934 under the auspices of the Radical Club) slandered two distinguished members of the Oberlin faculty, Walter Horton and Warren Taylor, for supposed collaboration with the red menace, in the pages of the *American Mercury*.[37]

In the late 1950s congressional decisions to subsidize higher education for purposes associated with national defense posed a more subtle problem in political intervention for colleges and universities to confront. In 1959 Oberlin reasserted its commitment to academic freedom against outside intervention when it refused to participate in the student loan program of the National Defense Education Act because of the communist disclaimer affidavit required of loan recipients by the act. When Congress removed this relic of the McCarthy era in 1962, the board of trustees, supported by students and faculty, authorized college participation in the program.[38]

The decade of the 1960s witnessed a wave of student activism that, in its range and intensity, is unmatched in the history of American higher education. At Oberlin as elsewhere, the civil rights movement of the early 1960s and the Vietnam War protest of the later 1960s focused protest actions on and off campus. Demand for change in educational and social arrangements within the college itself sharpened the atmosphere of campus dissent. At Oberlin the onset of the presidency of Robert Carr, an established student of constitutional government, coincided roughly with the beginnings of the new student movement. This conjunction of circumstances, together with faculty involvement on both sides of most issues, resulted in a steadily escalating dialectic over the nature of the academic community, its role in national affairs, and the ethics of campus protest.

The debate on these issues developed a degree of refinement and elaboration surpassing all past local precedents. Against the moral imperatives of student activists (supported by a substantial minority of the faculty) urging direct action by the college community against the Vietnam War, President Carr posed the libertarian concepts of rational discourse, institutional neutrality, and the open campus. Perhaps the most succinct statement of Carr's position appeared in his annual report for 1965–66, when he addressed himself to the issues posed by the student demonstration against the draft deferment test at Finney Chapel. While stressing that separate groups and individuals within the college community should not refrain from speaking out on pressing national concerns, the president urged that the college itself should avoid taking institutional stands on controversial public issues not directly related to the academic process.[39] Efforts to create arrangements that accommodate the thrust of both the president's convictions and those of student activities remain in progress.

The Oberlin record, then, suggests a multitude of partial and proximate precedents for college involvement in public social issues. It also suggests that no clear analogy to the present situation ever existed in the past. In that sense we are on our own to make our choices and run our risks. The record further suggests that in the complex workings of the institution no segment of the college community enjoyed a monopoly over the desire for change from past norms. A kaleidoscopic sequence of change emerged, as students, faculty, president, and trustees competed to define the stance of the college in the public eye. On several occasions these various components of the college achieved a degree of mutual consensus on vexed issues sufficient to produce what might be called an "institutional commitment," whether or not it was formalized by written resolutions, voted, sealed, and delivered. Thus the freedom of the slave was a goal pursued by all segments of the community in the 1850s, though Oberlinians divided over tactics to achieve that goal. Thus prohibition was similarly valued by all elements in the late nineteenth century. Again all elements shared, in varying degree, the Shansi commitment to missionary education. And the campus achieved a nearly unanimous response to the challenge to academic freedom in the 1950s.

Presumably in each of these instances the resulting image and atmosphere of the college discouraged individuals who did not share the value in question from joining and participating in the Oberlin community. From the reformist or goal-oriented point of view, this may have been an acceptable price for advancing the goal. From the viewpoint of the friend of intellectual pluralism, the community may at times have suffered from its stand. Over the long pull, diversity of purpose inevitably generated both reprisals against nonconformists in the name of consensus and impatience with community neutrality among those moved by moral indignation. Yet, with the exception of the disastrous World War I experience, the community generally fell short of enforcing monolithic conformance to a single ideal. In situations where specific expressions of opinion among the several components was desired, the device of the referendum or the petition was usefully employed, as during the ROTC controversy and—earlier—when President King organized the protest over political prisoners. In each of these cases, the prevailing attitude of the community was asserted, with room left for dissent among those with different views.

Rival conceptions of Oberlin's obligations to the world have always flourished here, nourished by rival conceptions of the college's academic and moral integrity. Oberlinians of all persuasions have always pointed to the past history of their college to vindicate their special dreams. The past has rarely failed them. History works that way.

Afterword

In the spring of 1970, fifteen months after this essay first appeared, the American invasion of Cambodia provoked a fresh surge of campus protest across the country against the war in Southeast Asia. On May 1, 1970, a referendum among 1,442 Oberlin students found 95 percent of them favoring an immediate end to American fighting in the war. On May 2, the faculty gathered in King 306 for a tense special Saturday afternoon meeting to debate its response, as several hundred students packed the hall outside the meeting. After long and heated debate, including complaints that the faculty had been barricaded, a motion passed by a vote of 88 to 56 demanding "the immediate withdrawal of American troops from Vietnam and the rest of Indochina." The votes on this motion and several others were communicated to President Nixon, along with a letter of protest prepared by the general faculty council for signature by individual faculty members. President Carr subsequently announced that he had joined some thirty other college and university presidents in signing a telegram to President Nixon protesting the Cambodian invasion.

On May 23, 1970, shortly before Carr's retirement as Oberlin's president, the *Oberlin Review* published some of his reflections on his tenure. They included the following observation:

> What we've proved in the last few weeks is that there can, in the face of great external crisis, be a drawing together of people who discover that they react in much the same way, and insomuch as the students, faculty, and administration may be taking much the same position, you could say that this amounts to an institutional stand. I wouldn't quarrel with you, but if by institutional stand it is meant that somehow a legal corporate being, Oberlin College, has committed itself to do this and not do that, I don't think we've taken an institutional stand, and I wouldn't want to see the College in its corporate sense take very many institutional stands.

In the mid-1970s, as American military involvement in Vietnam finally ended, student demands for an institutional stand against South African apartheid began to mount. These demands were aimed at the board of trustees rather than the faculty, since they had to do with college divestment of companies doing business in South Africa. As of 1979, 20 percent of the college endowment was invested in such companies. That year the trustees rejected motions calling for immediate or phased divestment, but pressures for divestment continued. Finally in 1987, at President Starr's recommendation, a phased divestment got under way and was completed by September 1988.

Meanwhile over the years since the early 1970s, changes had occurred in the membership and temper of Oberlin faculty meetings. Veterans of the 1960s student protest movement began to seed the faculty in growing numbers, and over a dozen current student leaders now enjoyed membership with voice and vote in faculty meetings. For both of these groups, the concept of institutional neutrality on morally charged social issues—a concept that had provoked such fierce and agonized debate across the 1960s—now seemed quaint and bankrupt. Many older faculty members shared this attitude. As a result, when a student-sponsored motion calling for comprehensive federal sanctions against South Africa came to the faculty in May 1988, the motion was approved by voice vote with scattered dissent. Debate on the motion was relatively brief, attention having been diverted by on-campus racial hostilities that erupted that spring.

CHAPTER 25

The Oberlin Mock-Convention Tradition (1992)

"What has happened to the Oberlin mock-convention tradition? I was a minor participant in 1940," Orville Willard Bidwell '40, of Manhattan, Kansas, asked in 1992.[1]

What happened was the Twenty-sixth Constitutional Amendment, which lowered the voting age to eighteen in 1971. After that, mock politics gave way to real politics, or—in too many young minds—no politics at all, as far as parties and presidents were concerned. Legend has it that Abraham Lincoln received Oberlin's first mock nomination in 1860. I share college historian Robert Fletcher's skepticism about that claim. Lincoln was too soft on slavery for Oberlin abolitionists. But in later years Lincoln made a nice mythical beginning to a rarely interrupted string of Republican mock-convention selections, from Salmon P. Chase in 1864 to Nelson Rockefeller in 1968.

From the 1860s to the 1960s, Oberlin—college and town—sustained a local Republican majority and applauded the student habit of holding Republican conventions. Only three deviations from the GOP occurred. In 1932, spurning the Depression-dogged Republican incumbent but unable to stomach the Democratic challenger Franklin Roosevelt, Oberlin chose Owen D. Young, head of the General Electric Company. In 1956 Democrat

Adlai Stevenson was tapped, with young John Kennedy as his running mate. In 1960 Kennedy himself was the Oberlin nominee, but won only 37 percent of the Oberlin town vote on his way to victory in the fall election. It took Barry Goldwater to inspire the town's first Democratic majority four years later.

The students' mock choices meshed with national choices nine times: Ulysses Grant (twice), Benjamin Harrison, William McKinley (twice), Theodore Roosevelt, William Howard Taft, Herbert Hoover, and Kennedy. Some other picks have faded gently into historical obscurity: George Edmunds, Walter Gresham, John Winant, Charles McNary, and William Scranton.

Only once did the Oberlin faculty block a mock convention—in the spring of 1912. Two Republican rivals, Theodore Roosevelt and William Howard Taft, both whistle-stopped in Oberlin that spring. But earlier, in a straw poll run by the *Oberlin Review*, Democratic hopeful Woodrow Wilson won an alarming 62 percent of student votes compared with the 14 percent for Taft and 4 percent for Rossevelt. When the faculty intervened to cancel the campus nominating process, citing the prospect of "ridiculous, rowdy elements" upsetting its tone, students contented themselves with a mock burial of the convention, and added the faculty to the grave for good measure.

College women were barred from participation in mock conventions until 1916, when they held their own convention to promote women's suffrage and protective legislation for female and child labor. In 1930 they joined the men on equal terms.

The most radical mock convention choice in Oberlin's history came four years later, in the midst of Coolidge prosperity, when the progressive isolationist William Borah was picked to run on the platform calling for recognition of the Soviet Union and a compulsory national referendum on declarations of war.

Over the years the mock conventions acquired more and more of the balloons and ballyhoo of the national party conventions—costumes, banners, parades complete with state floats, brass bands, and Cadillac motorcades for visiting dignitaries. The first elephant was hired in 1936. Radio, then television coverage arrived next. Endless hours went into delegation organizing and platform debate in the weeks beforehand. Role-playing was

Ohio senator Harold Burton at the 1940 Mock Convention.
Courtesy of Oberlin College Archives.

in deadly earnest. One of my cherished college mementos is a 1952 photo that caught me carrying an Eisenhower banner for the Texas delegation. Earlier I had solemnly addressed the convention on behalf of Texas offshore oil rights. What pleases me about the photo is that in it my eyes are closed tight. I liked Ike all right that night, but I liked the convention's choice much more: Earl Warren.

Well before college students finally got the vote in 1971, the political activism of the 1960s began to jeopardize the mock-convention ritual. By the spring of 1968, hundreds of Oberlin undergraduates were passionately involved in the real-world primary fight for the Democratic nomination between Eugene McCarthy and Robert Kennedy, the fight that ended in Kennedy's murder. The Republican mock convention that year was by comparison a campus sideshow. When Rockefeller beat Richard Nixon for its nomination, the *Oberlin Review* accurately dismissed it as a "game," and the lights went out on a once vibrant Oberlin tradition.

CHAPTER 26

Recollection of the 1960s—
and Beyond (1992)

*A*mong today's college students, most of whom were born in the 1970s, there floats a fascination with the 1960s almost as reverent as the strange nostalgia that my generation, born in the 1930s, lavished on the 1920s. On the other hand, I read somewhere recently that after the 1980s, the 1990s are going to make the 1960s seem like the 1950s. I am not looking forward to this prospect with any special enthusiasm, but if it happens my sense that recent American history oscillates and recycles itself by decades will certainly be confirmed.

For the twenty-fifth reunion of the Oberlin class of 1965, a forum was organized around the theme "Staying awake through the great revolution"— a phrase borrowed from Martin Luther King's commencement address to that class. I went to the forum hoping to get a fix on the changing temper of the sixties generation. But the forum was quickly broken up into small discussion groups. I complained about this to the forum organizer, Peter Anderson (now a judge in Boston), saying that discussion groups never yielded total answers. Peter replied with a wry smile, "We're not interested in total answers anymore." That suggested possible grounds for intergenerational reconciliation between his cohort and mine.

What follows is a loose sequence of memories about teaching at Oberlin in the 1960s, and living with the consequences of that decade ever since. I will string these memories along a time line like this:

Oberlin Time Line for 1960s

November 1958	College installs six IBM data processing machines for student records.
March 1959	Dean of Men bans coed parties in men's dorms. Students ask: "Don't you trust us?"
September 1960	President Carr in first assembly talk says: "It is not for you to make your peace with IBM and settle down to split-level security."
May 1961	Student group raises money for black tenant farmers in Fayette County, Tennessee, who lost land for voting in 1960 election.
May 1961	College announces plans to build North, South, and East Halls. *Review* opposes big-dorm policy. A junior Phi Beta Kappa denounces Dascomb as "a symbol of triviality and intellectual sterility."
June 1961	Lipstick reported disappearing among Oberlin women. Beards, uncut hair, T-shirts, and jeans spreading among men. "One theory is that students dress like groups they want to help," says town editorial.
August 1961	Oberlin town chapter of John Birch Society organized.
September 1961	President Carr in opening assembly talk says: "Sloppy dress, stringy hair, dirty faces or bare feet, or for that matter, public demonstrations of affection, are a meaningless flaunting of inconsequential freedoms."
October 1961	1600 students sign petition protesting lack of student voice in long-range campus dorm planning, and demand direct access to the board of trustees. President Carr says petition is prompted by "delusions of grandeur."

November 1961	President Carr tells student forum on building program: "You are undergraduates. I suggest that you ponder the meaning of that word."
May 1962	Faculty votes down Saturday night women's visiting hours in men's dorms.
April 1963	Faculty approves Saturday night and Sunday afternoon visiting hours, stipulating that room doors must be "visibly open."
April 1963	Students picket President Carr's assembly talk with signs that read: "End Creeping Ivyism."
October 1963	400 students picket local telephone company for discriminatory hiring practices.
November 1963	Martin Luther King appears at packed assembly in Finney, speaking only briefly because of illness.
November 1963	Appearance of Malcolm X canceled because of assassination of John Kennedy.
February 1964	Dick Gregory in interview before his appearance says: "The liberal says we're going to win the struggle, but he says we have to do it in the spirit of love. Man, we're not talking about love; we're talking about respect."
February 1964	*The Activist,* launched in 1960, now has nationwide circulation of 3000.
April 1964	*Review* poll reports that 20 percent of Oberlin students had sex during the past year.
May 1964	Use of marijuana and hallucinatory drugs is reported spreading on campus.
May 1964	Faculty suspends Saturday night calling hours.
July 1964	A dozen Oberlin students participate in Mississippi Summer.
July 1964	Bernie Adams, new dean of students, says: "Frankly, I like student demonstrations. I won't put up with any violence, mind you, but placard-carrying, speech-making student demonstrations: why, I think they're kind of fun."
October 1964	Martin Luther King speaks in Finney, warning against complacency in the drive for integration.

November 1964	Four Oberlin students arrested for civil rights activity in Meridian, Mississippi.
December 1964	Faculty recommends legalization of 3.2 beer on campus.
December 1964	Oberlin group, Carpenters for Christmas, rebuild burned black church in Ripley, Mississippi, helped by Oberlin contractor Burrell Scott.
March 1965	Student group holds forty-eight-hour hunger strike against Vietnam War.
March 1965	Navy recruiter is picketed in Peters Hall.
March 1965	In response to Martin Luther King's telegram from Selma, Alabama, to student council president, two hundred Oberlinians march in Cleveland's Public Square.
March 1965	As trustees weigh 3.2 beer legalization, a student says: "We'll riot if they pass it and we'll riot if they don't."
April 1965	1100 students march to President Carr's house to protest for co-op expansion and for community governance at the college. President Carr not home.
May 1965	3.2 beer legalized.
June 1965	Martin Luther King speaks at commencement. Secretary of State Dean Rusk also present. Students organize a teach-in on U.S. foreign policy. Obscene words are sprayed on King, Kettering, and Wright buildings.
February 1966	Two Oberlin student civil rights workers are wounded by gunshot fire in Kosciusko, Mississippi.
May 1966	Antiwar protesters block draft deferment tests in Finney Chapel.
February 1967	Air Force recruiters are held hostage in Wilder for three hours. Student leader says that the war has "so offended the principles of morality that in order to end the war it has become necessary to infringe on the rights of free speech and association." Six hundred students petition for access to recruiters. Faculty supports them.

June 1967	Senior class president at alumni commencement luncheon criticizes demolition of small dorms, misspent college money, faculty brain drain, and the "strange conservatism" of students.
June 1967	"Carr for Ex-President" buttons appear on student graduation gowns at commencement.
November 1967	Navy recruiter is trapped in car on North Main Street by student protesters who are hosed and booked by police.
February 1968	On President Carr's recommendation, faculty bans recruiters from campus in protest against draft delinquency notice sent to John Dove, student protester. Notice is rescinded a month later, and recruiters return.
March 1968	Faculty votes down an open dorm policy.
April 1968	The Oberlin Resistance buries a symbolic black coffin containing the senior class.
May 1968	President Carr declares the campus off-limits to all recruiters from all outside organizations.
May 1968	Faculty approves open dorm policy.
November 1968	Faculty re-opens campus to all outside recruiters.
November 1968	Students respond to open-campus policy with a hunger strike and torchlight parade to president's house.
November 1968	Fencing team protests no-beard policy for college athletes.
November 1968	Faculty approves student membership on college faculty committees.
February 1969	Poll of students shows 91 percent oppose the war, 48 percent favor open campus for military recruiters, 36 percent opposed, 15 percent unsure. Poll of faculty shows 72 percent favor open campus for military recruiters, and 79 percent oppose an institutional stand against the war.
February 1969	A student sit-in against Marine recruiters in Peters is followed by a two-hundred-person march on Cox building, marchers chanting "Work, Study, Get

Ahead, Kill," as a Vietcong flag is raised on Tappan Square.

March 1969   Student activist Bill Hedges tells interim judicial board on Peters sit-in: "I find you guilty of irrelevance and I sentence you to spending several years at Oberlin thinking what you do is important."

March 1969   SDS sponsors guerrilla theater disruption of college classes in King Building to protest Peace Corps recruiters on campus. With faculty support, President Carr suspends three participants. In response, students stage class boycott, lowering attendance by 50 percent.

April 1969   400 students occupy Cox all night.

May 1969   Assaults by black teenage townies against Oberlin students on Tappan Square and downtown streets are reported to be a growing problem.

November 1969   Jerry Rubin of the Chicago Seven advises Oberlin students to "drop out of the college or destroy it, or perhaps take it over and change it."

December 1969   President Carr announces termination of his presidency by trustees, effective June 30, 1970.

May 1970   Invasion of Cambodia and killings at Kent State force college to close down. One hundred students arrive from Kent State. An eighteen-person steering committee is appointed to run Liberation College activities as town race tension, charges of police brutality, and attempted arson in Carnegie Library break out.

July 1970   Bobby Fuller arrives to become president of Oberlin College.

President Robert Carr looms importantly in this time line as a lighting rod for the growing anger of the decade. He was a stubborn man, and not always diplomatic. He had the habit of saying in public exactly what he thought and where he stood. He fought a long, damaging battle to maintain an open campus in the teeth of the anger, which intensified when opponents of the war in Vietnam tried to close off the college from military and corporate recruiters. Carr won that battle, but in the process he lost his job. I think that as an academic and political liberal he was blindsided by the decade, which taught us all a harsh lesson about the difference between liberalism and radicalism.

Most liberals were blindsided by the 1960s. We didn't know ahead of time that they were going to happen. I remember how eagerly I started teaching American history here in 1960. I was not only a conventional liberal; I was a closet patriot. I thought I was going to teach the history of a good country and how it went about solving its big problems over time. Of course there was the residue of McCarthyism to reckon with, and fifties conformity, and Cadillac tailfins. Also Eisenhower was still president. But with alternatives like Adlai Stevenson, and now young John Kennedy, how could we go wrong?

John Kennedy. To paraphrase a popular song, we could fly higher than an eagle; he was the wind beneath our wings. Sentiment. But that's the point: we were sentimental optimists. His murder hurt us as badly as our parents would have been hurt if Charles Lindbergh had been shot in a homecoming parade after his flight. But the difference was that Kennedy's presidency had yielded no achievement psychologically comparable to Lindbergh's flight. The Kennedy flight was all ours. After his death, many of his admirers went into political free fall.

Before that, back in the summer of 1960 when I arrived in Oberlin to teach, I already knew how I was going to end my first lecture. I would quote from the last page of *The Great Gatsby*, where Nick Carroway stands on the shore in front of Gatsby's house and gradually becomes "aware of the old island here that flowered once for Dutch sailors' eyes—a fresh, green breast of the new world. . . . For a transitory enchanted moment man must have held his breath in the presence of this continent, compelled into an aesthetic contemplation he neither understood nor desired, face to face for the last time in history with something commensurate to his capacity to wonder." What the 1960s did to people with the sentimental temerity to start teaching that way was to turn the wonder from awe to puzzlement, and then confusion, and then dismay. What the teacher didn't know was what Gatsby didn't know, that the dream was "already behind him, somewhere back in that vast obscurity beyond the city, where the dark fields of the republic rolled on under the night." The teacher was ready to be blindsided.

But when did the sixties really begin for Oberlin? With the arrival of the IBM card (do not fold, spindle, or mutilate)? With the arrival of President Carr in February 1960? With Kennedy's murder? With the first whiff of marijuana in the snack bar? The first sight of an American flag sewn upside down on the seat of the jeans?

Early on in the decade, the college had young faculty couples host student cell groups to talk in their living rooms about sex, as a way of dealing with *that* problem. I had never talked about sex with students in front of my wife—in the 1950s men rarely talked about sex to anyone outside the locker room—and I felt a bit of stress waiting for the students to arrive. The last thing I did before the doorbell rang was to go to the bathroom. When the bell rang and I answered the door, a young man walked in and without saying his name asked if *he* could go to the bathroom. I knew then that the intergenerational bond was still intact, and the 1950s were not entirely over.

That aspect of the new decade finally set in definitively for me one fine spring Saturday when I took my six-year-old daughter to a folk dance festival in front of Hales Gym. We sat on the grass, and I was feeling very fatherly and virtuous about stretching my daughter's cultural horizons. Then one of the dancers in a peasant skirt began doing cartwheels in front of us. I suddenly realized she had on no underwear. The counterculture had arrived.

Architecture seems to have been the main medium through which the anger of the sixties came to Oberlin. The trustees' "big dorm" building program—a campus version of urban renewal that obliterated a dozen popular small dormitories—brought students of all political persuasions together, triggered their interest in the college's "decision-making process," and got them into the rhythm of collective protest. This was new in its frequency and intensity. It startled Carr, who knew little about architecture, and his reactions betrayed his utter lack of sweet talk and soft soap. Meanwhile, as he became the beleaguered point man for the trustees' building policy, other issues simmered to a boil: *in loco parentis,* race relations, drugs, curricular rigidity, cultural radicalism (what history professor Ron Suny, the only authentic Marxist on the faculty in the late 1960s, scornfully called "radical pottery"), and finally, inexorably, the war.

Many of these contested issues would fade quickly in the 1970s, as Bobby Fuller replaced Carr and campus debate began to swirl around Fuller's educational and governance remedies for what he thought ailed the college. And architectural politics subsided with the end of the building program in 1975. But a decade later, in the mid-1980s, architecture would resurface as a catalyst for dissent.

In September 1983 a fire broke out in the attic of Tank Hall, a co-op dorm and the college's best example of the nineteenth-century shingle style. As a crowd gathered to watch, a top administrator rubbed his hands and joked, "Now we can tear it down." But President Starr, newly arrived, with more architectural savvy than any of his predecessors, decided otherwise. He figured that it would cost more to demolish and replace Tank than to reno-vate it, and that any replacement would not be nearly as interesting. So the college proceeded to pump well over a million dollars into a historically sym-pathetic modernization of Tank. Students and faculty critics predictably protested this lavish expenditure. Why not spend it instead on financial aid or more books for the library? Meanwhile, within a year, co-opers turned the renovated Tank into a comfortable, self-respecting student slum.

The Tank project was just the beginning of a large-scale, expensive campus building and renovation program, which included interior revivals of Talcott, Baldwin, Keep, and Allencroft; a recycling of Carnegie Library; a core addition to North Hall; a library addition for the Conservatory of Music; a neuroscience addition to Kettering; a new bandstand for Tappan Square; a big new dining and social facility named for President Stevenson; and a thoughtful decade-long landscape improvement program.

Each of these projects (and especially the last three listed) touched off strong student backlash. This reaction was not peculiar to Oberlin. Students everywhere in recent times have been quite conservative in response to sud-den changes in their spatial environment. Architects are well aware of this hazard and comment on it often in their professional journals and confer-ences. Theories abound to explain its causes. One cause is a rational and rea-sonable concern about how money is spent. Another is the difficulty in understanding the nuances of modern and postmodern architecture. Yet another may be the rising divorce rate, which disrupts the lives of so many college-bound teenagers and makes them want their campus to be an oasis of familiar calm and stability. To this speculation I would add the relative brevity of everybody's college years, which makes each visible campus change a sud-denly looming threat to a temporary student lifestyle. All this makes the so-cial history of contemporary architecture an absorbing subject. It made the work of the college architectural review committee the most interesting committee assignment I had across the 1980s. The college could have used such a committee, with student as well as faculty membership, back in the 1960s.

The main academic legacy of the sixties was the strong ripple effect it had on classroom teaching. Oberlin classrooms were at least as mind-bending a learning experience for the professors as for their students in those years. I remember talking after class one day early on with Rennie Davis, who was getting ready to help launch SDS (Students for a Democratic Society) and who would win notoriety later on as one of the Chicago Seven. I remember that our conversation had to do with democratic possibilities. The possibilities he was imagining stretched far beyond my own. I told him to go read Reinhold Niebuhr on democracy. Instead he went off to join Tom Hayden. He was only the first of many to disturb my image of myself as mentor. By the end of the decade I had learned more about Marxist theory and practice from classroom rebels in the back row than I had absorbed in five years of graduate work at Harvard in the 1950s, when Marx rarely came up.

Meanwhile, like many other professors young and old, I gradually softened my stance on all the rules governing student behavior in and out of the classroom. With others I was enormously relieved when the faculty finally extricated itself from its ancient responsibilities *in loco parentis* and liberated dormitory living arrangements from its wavering gaze. Classroom liberation came more slowly. The disappearance of distribution requirements in the early 1970s, the scrapping of course prerequisites in many departments (including history), the invention of credit/no entry to erase the ancient stigma of flunking, and the proliferation of new area studies programs to straddle established disciplines were all more or less grudging faculty responses to impressive student restlessness across the 1960s. They combined to impose a culture of choice on the learning experience without precedent since Charles W. Eliot's elective system broke out a century before.

One bracing consequence of these reforms was a decisive improvement in classroom morale. Most of us now had a voluntary audience in front of us when we began to talk. But the downside has been this: at the beginning of each semester, in each class, we don't know how much our students know already about what we propose to teach. The zones of shared prior knowledge among them are very patchy. English and art are not the only departments to have lost their canons.

Recently I flipped through my grade books for the early 1960s and noticed a pattern that no longer exists. In those days, students would take the relevant prerequisite survey course, then after that one of the advanced courses in the field, and next a research seminar, and maybe cap off the major with an honors thesis. A teacher got to know them, and to know what they knew—not just as individuals but as a group, foraging through the curriculum. The side effects were wonderful. They made each graduation day something akin to a harvest.

It's not that way so much anymore. There are plenty of individual flashes of brilliance and innovation, often quite breathtaking, in term papers, bluebooks, and theses. But the exposures of unexpected ignorance can be a tad discouraging: the misspelling of Eisenhower, confusing Joe McCarthy with Eugene McCarthy, confusing William Jennings Bryan with William Cullen Bryant, and, most recently, the beginnings of confusion about the difference between World War I and World War II. Here are two nuggets from last year's bluebooks: "The mood of the Gilded Age was a reaction to the turmoil and antebellum of the Civil War." "After the crash of 1929, the Democrats returned to power with two New Deals, the first under Herbert Hoover and the second under FDR." (Historians of the New Left, that lively and durable legacy of the 1960s, might find the latter nugget quite sparkling.)

Like most historians I had hard reservations about Allan Bloom's polemic of 1987, *The Closing of the American Mind.* But I confess to agreement with him when he says, "Today's select students know so much less, are so much more cut off from the tradition . . . that they make their predecessors look like prodigies of culture." Again one can cite many individual exceptions, but that sense of collective momentum, of a shared fund of knowledge and assumptions, has greatly contracted. This is as much the professors' fault as it is the students'. The student generation of the sixties put on the pressure for change, my generation of teachers slowly responded, and the latest student generation has paid the price. Of course the wheel is always turning. Today's Oberlin undergraduates meet new mandatory distribution requirements quite similar to those in place in 1960. And owing to a writing proficiency requirement installed in 1985, students are beginning to write again as well as their parents.

In 1990 the faculty mandated student course evaluations in all departments. Here is another legacy of the sixties that had been optional until then.

We have been using them in history since 1967. They work, but they some-times work in unexpected ways. In the early 1970s, as one contribution to the culture of choice, I began to offer the option of a second term paper in lieu of the final exam. A few years later a course evaluation reported that this meant you didn't have to do the reading for the last month of a Blodgett course. That ended the option. Final exams are now mandatory in all my courses.

Yet another legacy of the sixties was the change in student lifestyle (a term I once tried to avoid but which has the advantage of everybody's knowing what it means). To briefly belabor the obvious, what was alienated, rebellious, and often shocking in the 1960s entered the porous mainstream in the 1970s. Articles written about the twentieth anniversary of Woodstock in 1989 made this point repeatedly. The lifestyle signals defiantly celebrated as defining a "Woodstock nation"—an alternative culture of hair, love, drugs, hard rock, and hedonism—quickly lost their subversive connotations and blended to define the pop culture of the 1970s.

One clue to this process was the changing appearance of working-class men—the sons and younger brothers of the straight-laced hardhats of the 1960s. They soon took up beards, long hair, tight jeans, cowboy boots, and country rock and wound up looking like Willie Nelson and Waylon Jennings, the "outlaws" of the 1970s, who were themselves close-cropped and clean-shaven when they started singing in the 1950s.

You could see this process at work in the Oberlin classroom coming down across the years. I taught a colloquium on the 1960s a few years ago. One of our top history majors showed up for class one spring night unshaven and barefoot, wearing a message T-shirt and cutoff jeans. In the ensuing dis-cussion about the counterculture, slumped there in his chair, he said that the trouble with students in the 1960s was that they had no discipline; they were just a bunch of spoiled brats. (He graduated with honors, went on to gradu-ate school with a big fellowship, and today is completing his Ph.D.)

Another lifestyle anecdote along the same line: one of my advisees in the late 1980s filed a last-minute request for an academic incomplete. Her reason, written rather breathlessly, summed up so much that I saved it:

> Intentionally, due to personal relationship problems situated at home and then a phone call which kept me up late but could not be avoided due to another relationship crisis, compounded by an

average of 4 hours of sleep per night for the past week, I was
thinking of taking an incomplete for Black Studies 101. Then last
night, my housemate, who I am seeing, I had to accompany to
the Emergency Room from midnight to 3 A.M. At this point in
order to pass the exam today I need more time.

The sequel to her story is that she graduated on schedule (she burst into
my office the day before commencement to announce, "I'm going to walk!")
and today she is a fund-raiser in the field of historic preservation, recently
promoted.

Generalizations from a white professor about persons of color are always
hazardous. For one thing, you have to watch the labels and the code words,
and the message they convey. Back in the late 1960s many whites, myself included, tended to assume that all black students, for instance, thought pretty
much alike on race issues. This assumption was reinforced by the constant
use by everyone of terms like "Black Power," "Black Community," "Black is
beautiful" and by the popularity of Afro haircuts. Sometimes professors didn't
pay enough attention. I remember sheepishly that when the 1968 Olympic
sprinter Tommie Smith arrived to become Oberlin's basketball coach, we
were all conscious of his clenched fist at Mexico City. When I met him in
the locker room at Philips Gym he was wearing a T-shirt that said "Adidas,"
and I thought it was a Black Power slogan.

I like to think that today I am much more alert to the variety and sub-
tlety of thinking among black students about race and race relations than I
was twenty-five years ago. I vividly recall the confused shock I shared in the
spring of 1968 when Martin Luther King was killed. Whites in Oberlin lit
up their neighborhoods that night with candles along the sidewalks as a
gesture of prudent respect. The next night we filled Finney Chapel for a
memorial service. A black student leader was on the program, and her statement compounded our shock. She began: "In my opinion King was a Tom.
He was a friend of the white man preaching shit that was not relevant to
black people in this country. Martin Luther King preached non-violence."
She went on to say that blacks would meet violence with violence even
though it meant their extermination. She concluded with this warning: "You
have no weapon powerful enough to stop us, for the thought of genocide
will not deter us."

We had no idea, of course, how many people shared her bitterness, or how long it would last. But I would hazard the guess that among many African-American students today the legacy of Malcolm X remains more meaningful than that of King—the Malcolm X who asked, if your goal is integration, what comes after that; the Malcolm X who said to whites in December 1964, "If you have a contribution to make to our development, do it. But that doesn't mean we're with you or against you. We're neutral. We're for ourselves. Whatever is good for us, that's what we're interested in." If that sounded arrogant and a little scary to white ears in 1964, it seems quite reasonable today, almost mainstream.

I don't know as many black students as I did before the arrival of the black studies program. But among those in my classes recently, I sense a nice cool irony, an autonomy, and a quiet bite in their conversation. I was talking with a black student from Youngstown about the genealogical essay he wrote for my survey course. When I expressed admiration for his mother, who was the first black woman to become a CIO official in that city, he replied, "Yes, but they always need at least one." And when another black student came by to borrow a stapler, he had on a crimson running suit with yellow piping that spelled Oberlin up one leg. I asked him if he was on the track team. He said, "No, I'm a Con student. I spend too much time practicing the piano to develop my natural athletic ability." I was in a negotiation session in 1988 with a group of minority students concerned with affirmative action in faculty hiring practices. A colleague of my vintage expressed the hope that ideally some day we would reach the point where we could be more or less colorblind in our hiring. To this a black woman sitting next to me quietly replied, "Oh come off it. This isn't the 1960s!"

Affirmative action may be the most important institutional legacy left over from the sixties drive for racial justice. Most of its consequences have been positive, but more for gender than for race. Women faculty members pressed for its systematic implementation at Oberlin in the early 1970s to change old-boy faculty hiring practices. And they have benefited more than blacks from the results because they constitute a larger pool of new Ph.D.s. For a long time now we have been encouraging our top black students to go on for the Ph.D., with not much to show for it. A grand total of two blacks among my former students have acquired a Ph.D. in history—both women, both graduates of the mid-1970s. The problem is a hard mix of motivation and money.

Oberlin College treasures two proud traditions. One is our nineteenth-century record of admitting black students in more numbers than any other predominantly white college or university. The other is a twentieth-century record of being the largest undergraduate source of future Ph.D.s among American colleges. These two traditions need to be fused. Back in 1971 Oberlin launched a concerted program to increase black enrollments. If we had at the same time launched a comparable program to encourage and subsidize graduate training for the Ph.D. among black students, we would be in much better shape than we are today. The college now has in place a variety of such programs, funded by the Mellon, Ford, and Pew Foundations. We will not know until next century how successful they will prove to be in improving Oberlin's share of the country's black Ph.D.s.

The young political liberal who arrived to teach American history at Oberlin in 1960 is much less disenchanted with this country's liberal tradition than many of his fellow historians and current students seem to be. The decline of interest in national politics since the 1960s is surely one of the most unexpected and deflating trends of the last twenty years. Here again Oberlin has fed off a national mood, nicely captured by Russell Baker back in 1983 when he noted that the difference between Republicans and Democrats has all the ideological excitement of a confrontation between a plate of cold spaghetti and a bag of dead mice. To one who cut his teeth on boyhood memories of Franklin Roosevelt, and later on was moved by the rhetoric of Adlai Stevenson, the elegance of John Kennedy, the passion of Robert Kennedy, the false promise of Gary Hart, and the disappointment of "waiting for Mario," the prospects have not been all that brightening. The gloom cannot be blamed on the 1960s, but certainly its origins can be located in that decade, and especially in the dark melodrama of election year 1968. The titles of the best books on the subject, *The Unraveling of America, Coming Apart, The End of Liberalism,* and more recently *Why Americans Hate Politics* combine to provide a thumbnail guide to what has happened. And as always, snack bar conversations overheard at lunchtime provide telling comment. On February 23, 1990, I listened to this exchange: First Student: "What we're learning is, Gorbachev is a true anarchist. He's the most powerful leader in the world, and he's just letting the system come apart so people can do what they want—and it's working!" Second Student: "My course is more philosophical. We spend a lot of time on liberalism and why it's so disgusting."

When I hear things like that, and come back to my office and scribble them down, I am consoled by another message I copied long ago. Back in 1913 Justice Holmes, the liberal's favorite conservative, said to some friends: "If I am right it will be a slow business for our people to reach rational views, assuming that we are allowed to work peaceably to that end. But as I grow old I grow calm." And then he went on to offer his famous butterfly metaphor: 'I think it not improbable that man, like the grub that prepared a chamber for the winged thing it never has seen but is to be—that man may have cosmic destinies that he does not understand. And so beyond the vision of battling races and an impoverished earth I catch a dreaming glimpse of peace." Holmes was seventy-two when he said that. A year later world war broke out. But he lived twenty-two more active years alert for the next glimpse. If he could be that tough and tender-minded, I want to think, why can't we?

CHAPTER 27

Oberlin and the Kent State Murders (1998)

$\mathcal{W}$hile roaming recently through five decades of campus memories, I had no trouble choosing the most searing of them—the day the Kent State murder report arrived in Oberlin on May 4, 1970.[1] There had been plenty of angry local moments in the Vietnam War protest before Kent State. The Finney Chapel draft test blockade in May 1966. The capture of the Navy recruiter in his car on North Main Street in October 1967. The Peters sit-in against Marine recruiters while a Vietcong flag flapped on Tappan Square in February 1969. The guerrilla theater classroom disruptions protesting a campus visit by Peace Corps recruiters in March 1969. But Kent State was different. Psychologically it brought the possibility of official violence against war protesters to every campus in America.

A few years ago I sat on the floor of a Seattle living room with a batch of Oberlin alumni from the late sixties and early seventies. Their testimony was that Kent State was the turning point. Until then everything seemed possible. The protests had been working, and the hopeful idealism of the mid-sixties was intact.

Oberlin political scientist Jere Bruner, who joined the faculty in 1967, captured the mood in a brilliant talk for the twenty-fifth reunion of the class of 1963. Here is a bit of what he said: "Many of us were caught up in revolutionary enthusiasm. We lived in expectation that what before had not been possible was somehow now about to happen. The incantatory words! Peace would come. Change. Relevance. America would be greening. The age of Aquarius was before us. . . . We would make love, not war. Classical structure would fall before the assaults of moralistic militance, which would give way to romantic self-actualization. Training from without would yield to unfolding from within. The kingdom would come."

Then students began to be killed, at Kent and elsewhere, and the movement snapped.

I was a little older than Jere. I never thought I knew what was going to happen next in the 1960s. I was blindsided by the likes of Rennie Davis [see Chapter 26] and by the war and by all the protest. I did learn a lot from my fellow historian Ron Suny, the main faculty mentor to Oberlin protesters after his arrival in 1968. Ron's guidance of the campus left through the Kent State crisis was crucial in curbing a disruptive local backlash against the murders. In contrast to Ron and Jere, I was mostly a puzzled observer.

On the night of the murders Finney Chapel filled for an angry protest. Since I wondered what was going to happen next, I went to the chapel and stood by the back wall to listen. The rhetoric was as passionately revolutionary as any I had ever heard, and the shouted responses were loud and hot. Then an eyewitness from Kent State was brought to the stage to tell what he had seen. I remember his concluding words exactly: "If you want to make a revolution, you've got to be prepared to die." After that you could have heard a pin drop.

The war and various student protests against it, increasingly stylized and media-tuned, continued. But I think that for Oberlin at least, something ended that night in Finney. Talk of revolution was still on the tongue, but it seemed less firm in its conviction.

Meanwhile the faculty debated whether to take an "institutional stand" against the war. Campus polls showed that an overwhelming majority of faculty and students opposed the war, but many professors, along with President Carr, mistrusted a formal stand as a cramp on freedom of inquiry. Others felt such a stand would be merely symbolic. To this latter objection a student spokesman, freshman Lee Fisher, made an apt reply. While a resolution against the war might well be symbolic, he said, the faculty should not reject one symbol in favor of another—the ivory tower—but should decide which was more important. In the end an antiwar resolution passed with the understanding that each faculty member could sign on or not as he or she decided.

The day after the shootings Oberlin suspended its normal academic year. A "Liberation College" of lectures, debates, and organizing committees used the time before commencement to condemn the war and study its origins. Meanwhile 250 students led by the conservatory's Robert Fountain went to Washington to perform Mozart's Requiem in Washington Cathedral. Graduating seniors voted not to wear caps and gowns to their commencement, which was a brief and solemn ceremony addressed by Jesse Jackson. It was Bob Carr's last public appearance as college president. At the end of the summer Bobby Fuller succeeded him. A new era in Oberlin history began, and we all wondered what was going to happen next.

CHAPTER 28

He Held His Ground: Memorial
Minute for Robert K. Carr (1979)

*T*he death of Robert Kenneth Carr, the ninth president of Oberlin College, on February 21 closed a remarkably vigorous career as teacher, scholar, public advocate, and college executive. Few academic lives had more sustained momentum or touched more dimensions of higher education as a force in modern American life.

Educated in the public schools of East Cleveland, Carr entered Dartmouth College in 1925 as a scholarship student, majored in political science, was elected to Phi Beta Kappa, and graduated in 1929. From Dartmouth he moved to Harvard University, where he received the master's degree in political science in 1930. A year later he joined the faculty of the University of Oklahoma.

There, in addition to his teaching, he served as director of the university's Bureau of Municipal Research and completed the research and writing of his Harvard doctoral thesis. In 1935 he received from Harvard the Tappan Prize for the best Ph.D. thesis in political science. Within another year he had turned the thesis into a book, *State Control of Local Finance in Oklahoma*. From the outset of his scholarly career, Carr not only established a high personal standard of quality, but he also showed a knack for aiming his talents directly at the eye of complex public controversies just as they emerged from the interplay of political change with the ambiguities of the federal Constitution. His study of Oklahoma finance addressed a problem of national urgency, compounded by depression and the haphazard growth of state bureaucracies—the need for rational planning to preserve the fiscal base of local self-government.

Meanwhile the growing quarrel over the constitutionality of Franklin Roosevelt's anti-depression measures drew Carr's attention. In 1936 he joined the quarrel with a book-length essay, *Democracy and the Supreme Court*, which was a spirited critique of the Supreme Court's obstruction of the New Deal.

The issues swirling in this controversy were resolved a year later, in the great court fight of 1937. In 1942 Carr returned to the problem in a longer book, *The Supreme Court and Judicial Review*. Here he argued for an acceptance of the reality that the Court is a political agency, sharing with the president and Congress the power to govern. His perception that judicial behavior involved a quasi-legislative function forecasted the powerful role the Court would play in future years as a trigger for social and political change.

Carr had returned to his alma mater in 1937 to join the government department. A decade later, at age forty, he became the Joel Parker professor of law and political science at Dartmouth. During the World War II, his interest turned to the issue that would bring him national prominence, the oppression of racial and cultural minorities by both majoritarian governments and established interest groups in the private sector. His next major book, *Federal Protection of Civil Rights* (1947), was a study of the new and as yet obscure civil rights section of the Justice Department. His conclusion called for the forging of an aggressive federal program to protect minorities and enhance their life chances. A decade later the civil rights section became the main public agency of support for the civil rights movement, which got under way in the late 1950s.

In 1947 Carr became the executive secretary of the president's committee on civil rights, created by Harry Truman, and was the principal author of the committee's landmark report, *To Secure These Rights* (1947). This was a broad, searching review of public and private patterns of discrimination in American life. In retrospect, its findings and recommendations anticipated with vivid clarity the agenda of unsolved problems with which the country would cope over the next three decades. President Truman's response to the issues raised by the report promptly divided liberals and conservatives in the Democratic party and remains to this day a central item of historical debate about the Truman presidency.

In the late forties and early fifties, as the anticommunist Congressional witch-hunts of Richard Nixon, Joseph McCarthy, and others began to poison the well of public confidence, Carr once again swung his talents as scholar and critic to the constitutional issues raised. In his book *The House Committee on Un-American Activities* (1952) and in several pamphlets and articles, he explored the use and misuse of the congressional investigating committee as a political weapon and called on Congress to bring this weapon under control. He calmly ignored the inevitable countercharge of being soft on communism directed at him by spokesmen for the radical right. But the McCarthy era's general assault on academic freedom quickened his concern, and in 1957 he once again left Dartmouth for Washington to become general secretary of the American Association of University Professors and chairman of the AAUP committee on academic freedom and tenure.

On January 1, 1960, Robert Carr replaced William Stevenson as Oberlin's president. His splendid academic record and his liberal credentials as a civil libertarian, together with the college's own peculiar traditions and concerns, seemed to promise a happy mix. Yet Carr himself characteristically anticipated sooner than anyone else the troubles and challenges he would confront in the decade ahead. In his first assembly address, two weeks after his arrival, he cheerfully described himself as a college teacher whose bluff had been called. He indicated that he was not interested in a long honeymoon and said, "It may be that never again will so many Oberlin people be so uncritical in thinking well of me. . . . I promise you that I will not hesitate to begin expending whatever good will I may enjoy as soon as I am reasonably convinced that the cause is important." He kept that promise. Even before his formal inauguration, he plunged into campus controversies over curricular calendar reform and other vexed matters.

He defined himself as *primus inter pares* in his faculty relations and rarely hesitated to join in open faculty debate over educational policy or the privacy of the councils about the caliber of individual teachers. He was candid, tenacious, and utterly lacking in protective guile in pressing his views in these forums.

If his scholarly standards of judgment were demanding, so was his determination to raise the status of the faculty through frequent general salary increases and special awards for merit and research. Early on he accepted the constraints and frustrations imposed on the Oberlin presidency by the tradition of faculty self-governance. Within these boundaries he worked and talked hard for what he believed was right, whether he thought he had a majority behind him or not. He was not a chummy, easygoing man, and his patience for idle small talk was limited. He developed only a few intimate friendships among the faculty. We never called him Bobby. Yet he earned the respect of his fellow academics, if not always their love, and as the years went by, that respect became more deeply mutual. Toward the end of his career at Oberlin he regarded himself, in his own phrase, as "a faculty man."

Although he brought no special fund of expertise in money-raising and business management to the presidency, he presided over a decade of impressive growth in the size of the college, its endowment, and capital gift funds for the modernization of its physical plant. One-third of the buildings on the campus today were built or planned during the Carr years. His fund-raising efforts in behalf of the college outlasted his presidency, and he played an important part in bringing to fruition the McCandless bequest, the second largest gift in the history of the college.

It was in his relations with Oberlin undergraduates that Carr's reputation as a liberal leader received its sternest test. His presidency coincided exactly with a decade of fundamental and ever deeper cleavage between the values of American youth and the established arrangements of the world in which they came of age. He met this challenge head-on. He used his assembly addresses and commencement talks to open a blunt dialogue with students—a dialogue that exposed important differences between the liberal assumptions of his generation and the more freewheeling impulses of the young. He was skeptical of students' complaints about "academic pressure," lectured them about the discipline of old-fashioned fact-grubbing hard work, and suggested that more creative research-oriented learning be built into their lives.

Never very sympathetic with the emerging youth culture of the sixties, he regarded the external symbols of this culture—long hair, bizarre clothing, and rude talk—as "a meaningless flaunting of inconsequential freedoms." The civil libertarian in him increasingly dwelt on what he called "the

other side of freedom," the liberty that is achieved in the context of authority, and the need for self-restraint to ensure that in the pursuit of one's own
right to free expression the rights of others are not abused and thus the fabric of freedom is not unraveled.

The Vietnam War and mounting protests against its wisdom and
morality brought these issues into sharp focus on every important college
campus in the country. Oberlin sustained its fair share of the resulting turmoil. The recurring appearance of military recruiters on campus seemed to
many to bind the college in complicity with the war. Against these demands
President Carr asserted the principle of institutional neutrality, the concept
of the open campus, and the value of rational discourse to maintain the college as a civil sanctuary for intellectual disagreement. Under relentless pressure, he remained inflexible in these convictions and stubborn in the tactics
he used to assert them. Often at great cost to his personal popularity, time
and again he used the governing machinery of the college to rally a majority of faculty support for his stance. And despite his stubbornness, or perhaps in some important measure because of it, the campus was spared the
harsher forms of disruption experienced elsewhere. The community survived, and in the summer of the last year of his presidency, he dared to hope
that he had also survived.

The trustee decision in November 1969 to seek a new president startled
and dismayed him. But he accepted the judgment with grace and with a
sense that he had been true to himself and true to the best interests of
Oberlin College.

His career was not over. He left Oberlin in 1970 to become an associ-
ate of the American Council on Education and to pursue research and consultation on the future of the academic profession. The subject of his last
book, *Collective Bargaining Comes to the Campus,* showed that unerring instinct, present from the beginning in his scholarship, for the new, the puzzling, and the controversial. The book arrived in Oberlin in the spring of
1973, just as its faculty began pondering the wisdom of unionization.

Carr himself returned to Oberlin in 1975 as distinguished visiting professor to teach courses in his favorite field, topics in constitutional law, and
to renew old friendships in a more mellow hour. With his wife, Olive
Grabill Carr (his devoted companion over forty-five years and a spirited
practitioner of free speech in her own right), he came home to this village

for good in 1976 and promptly assumed citizenship in the affairs of the city and his church.

Back in October 1960, in his inaugural address in Finney Chapel, President Carr remarked that "when the going gets really rough, the free market in ideas is likely to find its staunchest defenders in the students, faculties, administrative officers and trustees of our independent institutions." In the decade that followed, when the going got rough at Oberlin, and the free market of ideas became a stormy place, the president of the college proved to be its staunchest defender. He held his ground and kept the market open. For that service, and for many others, the rest of the college is free now to say that we are grateful.

CHAPTER 29

The Grand March of Oberlin Campus Plans (1995)

$\mathcal{M}$aster planning at Oberlin has been a growth industry from the outset, but master plans that build on earlier master plans are not as common as they might be.[1] Sometimes the record shows an awareness of what has gone before, but too often it shows ignorance and a failure to mesh. My aim here is to introduce Oberlin's present campus planners to our predecessors.

The Founders' Plan, launched in 1833, was to clear a thirteen-acre square north and west of Peter Pindar Pease's log house at the corner of College and Main and build a campus on it. That is why Tappan Square (known as The Campus as late as the 1940s) is so much larger than your average village green. Some half-dozen college buildings of brick and stone once stood on the square, until the last of them was leveled in 1927. Meanwhile temporary wood-frame buildings, beginning in 1833 with Oberlin Hall on the present site of the Java Zone, went up along West College Street. Professors were expected to live in little wooden houses facing the square along Professor Street between the red brick homes of President Asa Mahan (where King Building now is) and Charles G. Finney (where Finney Chapel stands). This was the first master plan, modeled after an idealized eighteenth-century New England village.

Wars have a way of killing master plans. After the Civil War, affluence hit the college for the first time, and Oberlin's Stone Age got under way. Massive, seemingly indestructible sandstone buildings now rose along Professor Street, from Baldwin Cottage to the south northward to Severance Chemistry Lab, with Talcott, (old) Warner Concert Hall, Warner Gym, and Peters in between, all of them facing east. The campus now had a domineering new western edge, the makings of an academic grand avenue.

At the outset of his long presidency in 1902, Henry Churchill King asked the Olmsted brothers of Boston, sons of the great landscape architect Frederick Law Olmsted and distinguished campus designers in their own right, to provide the college with a master plan for the new century. The Olmsted Plan of 1903, the most far-sighted in Oberlin's history, charted a design whose main elements would endure to the present day. It called for clearing Tappan Square of all buildings to create a large green open space accessible to both town and gown. It urged the college to buy up available land fronting the square on all four sides for future buildings, including a library and art museum. Science facilities should cluster along Lorain west of Professor, with new men's dormitories and athletic grounds stretching to the north. New women's dorms should be located to the south of West College. A new academic quadrangle west of Tappan Square could then fill gradually with classroom and social facilities, with heating plant and hospital still further west.

Critics of the Olmsted Plan called it grandiose, expensive, and impractical, especially its call for turning Tappan Square into an open pleasure ground—"a serious mistake," said architect J. L. Silsbee, who wanted his freshly built Memorial Arch (1903) to serve as portal to a new generation of college buildings on the square, all designed by him. But Silsbee's architectural rival Cass Gilbert, who became campus architect on the strength of his Finney Chapel (1908), soon developed his own plan, which meshed nicely with the Olmsted vision.

The Gilbert Plan [see Chapter 10] was far from finished when Gilbert died in 1934. Meanwhile in the late 1920s trustees launched an ambitious plan to build a new men's campus in the quadrangle north of West Lorain between Professor and Woodland. This was the Bosworth Plan, named for the dean who chaired the committee that hatched it. The Bosworth Plan

marked one of Oberlin's rare efforts to grapple directly with the chronic im-
balance, obvious since the 1880s, in the college's relative appeal to men and
women. The Bosworth Plan called for ten new men's dormitories, all in red
brick neo-Georgian styling, to bring an air of self-contained eighteenth-
century male dignity to the campus—comparable to the then-new house
system at Harvard and the new colleges at Yale.

The Great Depression, followed by World War II, did in the Bosworth
Plan. Only Noah Hall (1934) went up before the war intervened. Burton
Hall (1946) followed right after the war—the last local Georgian statement
before architectural Modernism reached Oberlin.

Just before World War II broke out, art professor William Hoskins
Brown came up with a plan for a new science quadrangle that won almost
unanimous support from Oberlin's scientists. To be located just north of
West Lorain and anchored at its southeast corner by Severance Chemistry
Lab, the science quad promised to nudge the unfinished new men's campus
pretty intimately, but the onset of war postponed that problem until the
mid-1980s. At that point the new north campus dining facility (now named
Stevenson Hall) threatened to intrude itself between the dorms on the
north campus and the still-unrealized science quad—a tight squeeze indeed. Led by Danforth Professor of Biology David Benzing, the scientists
mobilized against this prospect, and Stevenson migrated to its present site
on North Professor, where it remains among the college's least-loved monuments. Meanwhile the Sperry Neuroscience addition to Kettering was
consciously designed by its architect, Reed Axelrod, to provide a western leg
for the anticipated science quadrangle of the early twenty-first century.

Architectural Modernism hit Oberlin full force in the late 1950s, its flat
roofs and no-nonsense cinderblock economies heavy in appeal to trustees
and administrators as they eyed baby-boom expansion. Bulldozer development, a campus version of urban renewal, commanded a rapt audience.
Douglas Orr, a planner with a Modern vengeance, answered Oberlin's call
with a breathtaking program of demolition. If the Orr Plan, published in
1959, had been implemented in full, the following buildings would have
been blown away and replaced by mutants of the Oberlin Inn and Dascomb
Hall: Johnson House (1885), Allencroft (1861), Baldwin (1887), Talcott (1887),
Rice (1910), Warner Gym (1900), Peters (1885), Wilder (1911), Severance
(1900), and Keep (1913). Apologists explained that the honored names of

many of these buildings could be used again for their replacements, as was the case with Dascomb—after all, it is the names that count. As things worked out, the main casualty of the Orr Plan was old Warner Concert Hall, leveled to make way for Minoru Yamasaki's pretty if somewhat brittle King Building (1964), while his new conservatory complex rose diagonally across the way. The conservatory would become an overnight bonanza for contractors in the business of renovation and repair.

Just fourteen years later consultant Richard Dober came in with a plan that swung 180 degrees away from Douglas Orr's. The Dober Plan of 1973 identified eighteen college buildings, most of them on Orr's hit list, in need of careful preservation and recycling. What had happened in the interim to provoke this sharp reversal? The short answer is accurate: the sixties. The record shows that modern campus architecture was the main medium through which the student anger and alienation of the 1960s arrived in Oberlin—in protest against the big new slabs of sleeping and feeding space that went by the fetching names East, North, and South. The new mood, in reaction against the predictable rectangular regularities of cereal-box Modernism, had yet to acquire the label Postmodern, but the value it placed on idiosyncrasy, irregularity, and the quirks of history meshed with the surging ethic of historic preservation to create an attitude that has governed most architectural choices on this campus ever since.

When landscape designer Edward Thompson, grounds manager, arrived in 1980, he brought with him a concept that many Oberlinians regarded with surly mistrust: outdoor beauty. The Thompson Plan, implemented across the following decade, wove a fabric of trees, shrubbery, grassy mounds, rock gardens, and perennial beds that lent pleasant continuity to an otherwise highly eclectic campus. Alumni old-timers agreed with Ed Thompson's local fans that after his ten years here he left the campus more agreeable in appearance than it had ever been before.

Where do we go from here? *Architecture,* the journal of the American Institute of Architects, devoted its February 1995 issue to campus planning. Its lead editorial acknowledged that communication and computer technologies are merging to create an academic environment that collapses global distance and brings virtual learning to every wired room. The editorial argues that while "technology will deliver the learning tools of the twenty-first century, it cannot provide the setting for students to develop skills of interaction and empathy." The challenge for campus planners, it concludes, will be to demonstrate "how the built environment can fit appropriately with the climate, the landscape, and the culture of the region." Planners must urgently search for ways to pull people from their screens and bring them together. In other words, campus planning must provide an antidote to the technological revolution, not a surrender to it.

I think that the campus landscape handed on to us by the Olmsted brothers, Cass Gilbert, and Ed Thompson can be improved upon in ways that will accomplish this and in ways they would surely endorse. Their priorities—the need for well-designed shared spaces, for amenities of color and brightness to help us through the winter, for more places where indoor space flows to meet the outdoors—can be reasserted endlessly: sheltered porches and atriums, striped awnings on tall windows, green ivy over gray stone, more red brick underfoot, and less concrete. And, oh yes, tougher spring grasses for the Frisbee games in Wilder Bowl.

Of course we can improve this place. And to protect our investment against the Ohio Turnpike's new interchange on Route 58 we should start right now to do to Route 58 what Oberlin did to Route 20 back in 1937— arrange for a bypass around the town. Otherwise the automobile, the finest American masterpiece of modern technology, will crowd us out and do us in.

CHAPTER 30

Memorial Minute for
Robert E. Neil (1991)

$\mathcal{B}$ob Neil died on February 13.[1] In the days that followed, many people in this room said they had a sense that a phase of Oberlin history had ended. They were right. Bob's three decades on the faculty gave this college the most remarkable record of classroom teaching in anybody's memory. The list of Oberlin's fine teachers is long, and all of us hope we are on it. The list of its great teachers is short: Fairchild, Fullerton, Wager, Fletcher, Taylor, Holbrook—the names could be extended, but not far. Bob Neil joins the short list.

The things we remember most easily about him—the elegant German blazers and bow ties, the ever-present lit cigar, the zest for language, the husky laughter and the bear-trap punch lines, his love of music and musical lore, his George Szell stories, what a piano-playing friend calls his special keyboard taste for the "florid Teutonic"—all this is lively among us. But it can obscure what was closer to his core—a driving urge for perfection in everything he turned his talent to. He knew he was gifted with uncommon intelligence, and his unassuming candor about it was his form of modesty. Beyond that, the gift carried an obligation. The obligation was to share the gift by teaching, or as he might prefer to put it, to spread it around among the kids. To do that required not self-indulgence or self-display, but

Robert Neil, AB Oberlin (1953), PhD Harvard (1963), taught European history from 1969 to 1988. Courtesy of Oberlin College Archives.

discipline. And it was a lifetime devotion to the discipline of teaching history that comes through most clearly in the record that he left. That, and an affection for his alma mater.

Robert Elgy Neil was born in 1931 in Findlay, Ohio. His application to Oberlin seventeen years later included the following statement about the home he came from:

> My father, ever since I was a very small child, has made a practice of reading to me from the world's greatest books. He has also encouraged and helped me in the study of the German language with the result that, although I have never taken a formal course in it, I have been corresponding in their native language with several young Germans. It was largely through the efforts of my mother that I began studying the clarinet and later the piano. She has been a constant source of help to me in all my musical activities ever since.

He went on to say that at age fourteen he spent his first summer at the National Music Camp in Interlochen, Michigan. "Here amidst the great north woods," he said, "my feeling for the beautiful—not only music, but nature, drama, the dance, and painting—was greatly increased and my tastes were broadened." He came home from Interlochen to be concertmaster of his high school band, and he organized a little German band to play for public entertainment on the side.

Meanwhile he started taking tests. In 1946, in the Ohio State Scholarship Test in Latin, he placed second in the state. In 1947, in biology, he placed first in the state. In 1948, in chemistry, he placed sixteenth. There is no explanation for this slump. According to his Oberlin application statement, at this point he began reading self-improvement books to remedy the situation by increasing his skill in planning and scheduling his daily activities. "I hope with the passage of time," he added, "to become more adept at this so as to increase my personal efficiency." As for his long-range career plans, he said he wanted to become a college teacher. "It would satisfy my perfectionist tendencies to be able to devote my entire life to the study of one particular subject," he wrote. "Then too, I love a quiet, contemplative sort of life and feel that it can best be found in the atmosphere of a small college town."

In 1949 Oberlin decided to admit him. For the next eight semesters he placed first in his class every semester but one, when his performance failed to please his physical education instructor. If memory serves, his preferred form of exercise was trotting to class loaded down with a large green book bag; that, and playing in the symphonic band. He was a junior Phi Beta Kappa, and he graduated at the head of his class in 1953.

If I may indulge in a personal anecdote as one of his classmates, Bob and I were history majors. In our senior year we took a class together with Freddie Artz, European Intellectual History. Neil was Artz's prize student and everybody knew it. I got a B on my first bluebook. I worked hard to improve my grade, and finally by the end of the year I managed to push it up to A minus. Several years later, when I recounted that struggle to Neil, he grinned at me and said, "I was the grader."

From Oberlin he headed for Harvard with a Woodrow Wilson Fellowship. After one year of graduate study he was drafted into the army and wound up at the new guided missile center in Fort Bliss, Texas, where he studied antiaircraft radar electronics. Upon completing the course he became an instructor in it for the next batch of trainees. When his service was up he returned to Harvard, where in 1957 he was elected to the Harvard Society of Fellows, a group of two dozen young scholars chosen to pursue their studies with no further academic restrictions or financial worries. Bob was the first Oberlinian to be elected to this society.

Three years later he was offered a position on the Harvard faculty. In February 1960 he turned down that offer to accept a job at Oberlin at lower pay, since, as he wrote to Oberlin, "It has always been my hope to return there to teach some day." When he was told by the chairman of the Oberlin history department that he would teach one survey section at 8:00 A.M. on Tuesday, Thursday, and Saturday and another at 1:30 P.M. Monday, Wednesday, and Friday, he replied that he wanted to teach both classes at 8:00. "Having an 8 o'clock class every day," he explained, "will establish a greater regularity in my daily schedule." Eleven students tentatively signed up to take his new course in modern German history.

The numbers rose thereafter. By the time he completed his doctoral thesis in 1963 on the Nazi revolution, and wrote his first scholarly article, on the Reichstag fire, for a festschrift for Freddie Artz, he was drawing crowds at Oberlin and attention elsewhere. That same year he received an offer from Northwestern to take charge of the large European survey course there, with the promise of five course assistants and an ample salary. His response was to request tenure at Oberlin. "The musical chairs approach to the academic profession does not appeal to me," he said. "I would much prefer to establish myself permanently in a congenial school where I can work free from distraction. Frankly, I would like this school to be Oberlin." Oberlin agreed.

His teaching and scholarship did not remain free from distraction for long. As the 1960s arrived in earnest at Oberlin, his service on important campus committees began to be greatly prized. When an antiwar protest in Peters Hall got out of control in 1968, he spent endless weeks on the ad hoc judicial board created to hear the cases. He chaired the student life committee in 1970–71. The next year he chaired the special committee to salvage faculty children's tuition benefits. Election to standing committees began to crowd his life. He served on the educational plans and policies committee once, the general faculty council twice, and the college faculty council four times. He assumed the chair of the history department in 1974, and again in 1981, carrying that burden longer than any other person since 1960. The trust he enjoyed among faculty colleagues brought him the chairmanship of the search committee for a new dean in 1983.

Meanwhile his first love remained the classroom. He was a stunning teacher. He began his history earlier than most, by locating human origins in what he liked to call the "primal ooze." From there he brought his introductory students on a vivid panoramic year-long journey toward the present. He supplemented his lectures with wonderfully eclectic chronology handouts, which covered events for every century from 2000 B.C., every decade from the first century A.D., and every year since 1209. Here it is for the year 1539:

Reformation spreads to Brandenburg and Lower Saxony
Spanish conquest of Cuba
Holbein, *Henry VIII*
Titian, *Sleeping Venus*
First lead pipes

Discovery of the chemical process of making ether
Earliest documented appearance of the Christmas tree

The lectures themselves, by all accounts, were constantly compelling. Bob had the ability to use language to make the past quiver in the imagination of his listeners. And he could make his students quiver. As one of his colleagues recently put it, he tried to destabilize their assumptions about the way the world worked. Another colleague, who took three Neil courses as an undergraduate, called him an "iconoclastic conservative." Original sin, in secularized form, was central to his history. Most people in the past were not lucky. Poverty, disease, religious animosities, ethnic rivalries, racial hatreds, and stupid human arrogance competed on pretty even terms with intelligence, civility, and enterprise to determine human outcomes. The rise and fall of Nazi Germany, his career specialty, provided climactic evidence for the tale he told. Year after year students testified that his lectures were unlike anything else they'd ever heard.

Numbers bear them out. Across the 1960s Bob taught an average of 265 students per year, well over twice the normal load. In the 1970s, his average rose to 342 students per year. And amazingly, in his last five years in the classroom, the number reached 412. Year after year his enrollments equaled 20 to 25 percent of his department's total—a department of ten or more historians. His Saturday morning lectures in King 106 became part of the Oberlin tour for prospective students, their parents, visiting guests, and nostalgic alumni. He gave them everything he had. In return, Oberlin's seniors chose him on five separate occasions between 1965 and 1984 to deliver senior assembly talks in Finney Chapel, an honor unmatched by any colleague.

The earliest of these assembly talks, an analysis of the twentieth-century population explosion titled "The Mushroom Crowd," was published and anthologized repeatedly over the next few years. Its conclusion is worth quoting for its vintage Neil:

> I think it is going to take lots of plain, old-fashioned guts for us to get through the rest of this century. It is going to be a world where, seemingly, a man can't step into the same river even once, and where there are no certitudes. Under these circumstances, I

can only urge you to cultivate the most useful social grace in such a world: the ability to live with permanent crisis without panic.

A century ago, when one of Oberlin's luminaries, John Keep, died at age 89, President Fairchild wrote of him: "When others were depressed he sustained them and bore them on by his cheerful courage, and thus he held on to the end of his days. He died not from disease, but because life was completed."

We live in a more clinical and fractured time. Bob Neil's life was incomplete. In the 1980s, a decade when he should have been entering his prime, instead an alien fatigue set in. He lived with leukemia for the last eleven years of his life. He faced those years with cheerful courage. For the first time he decided to cut back on his committee assignments, so that he could focus more sharply on his teaching, savor the joy of his young marriage to Marie-Thérèse, and perhaps complete the book on modern Germany he had been working on for twenty years. "A terminal disease causes one to reflect on priorities," he wrote. "I owe my time and energy to my wife and to my work as a professional historian of Modern Germany." In August 1988 a stroke disabled and silenced him just when Oberlin needed most his wisdom about the sudden transformations awaiting Germany and Central Europe.

One bright October afternoon last fall, Bob took a leisurely automobile tour of the Oberlin campus to see what was going on in the sunshine. The campus was busy with Frisbee games in Wilder Bowl, books being read under trees on Tappan Square, a discussion section at the Arch, and lots of traffic in and out of Kettering and the Con. Bob came out of his silence to say, "The old place looks pretty lively." Perhaps we can best remember him, and honor his memory, by keeping it that way.

CHAPTER 31

Memorial Minute for
Barry McGill (1997)

*B*arry McGill died in Oberlin on September 7 last fall after thirty-eight years as an active member of the Oberlin College faculty.[1] Barry spent his boyhood in the city where he was born in 1924, New Rochelle, New York. Early on, he showed a bent for tracking what was going on in the larger world outside New Rochelle, and a desire to understand it. Aspects of that world in the 1930s were ugly and scary, but he wanted the facts in order to calculate the outcomes. Thus the following letter to Benito Mussolini in the spring of 1935:

> Dear Mr. Mussolini:
>
> I know you are very busy now but I hope you are able to answer this letter. A boy at the school I go to bet me that your troops in Africa would lose against the Abyssinians in the war between Italy and Abyssinia. I would like you to send me an account of all the battles that have been fought and the side that won. I am only ten years old and you already have my address. [15 Park Avenue, New Rochelle, NY United States of America.]
>
> Yours truly,
> Barry McGill

P.S. I would like a reply before school closes. School closes June
28, 1935.

In other words, no extensions, no incompletes. For Barry, those were lifetime expectations. Mussolini evidently did not measure up.

Barry's undergraduate career at Williams College was interrupted by
World War II and three years in the U.S. army. He returned from the war
to graduate from Williams in 1947—Summa Cum Laude, Phi Beta Kappa,
class valedictorian. A master's degree from Oxford followed that, and then
a Harvard Ph.D. in 1953. His thesis was a study of British parliamentary
politics from 1865 through the 1880s, the years of the Disraeli–Gladstone
rivalry.

Barry began his long career at Oberlin as a teacher of British and
European history in 1952. Two years later he married another faculty newcomer, Barbara Bunce, a sparkling young chemistry instructor. Meanwhile
the atmosphere of his classroom became legendary. Tall, lean, austere, mixing Edwardian elegance with lightning intellect and lashing wit, he gathered a surprised audience of quiet, awestruck students who later testified
that his impress on them was deep and permanent. After ten years a colleague wrote about Barry this way: "When he first came to Oberlin, students were afraid to get near him. He has definitely mellowed. . . . He [still]
terrorizes some students, but he also helps them, and he gets results." The
results showed, among other ways, in the growing number of honors students he mentored and in the several assembly addresses that the senior
class voted to ask him to deliver across the 1960s.

Barry used his early sabbatical leaves, including a research status appointment in 1965–66, to pursue work in London on what turned out to be
his lifelong specialty, British parliamentary history from the 1860s through
the 1920s. His published writing was modest in quantity, deeply quarried,
appearing in journals of impeccable address. A fellow researcher commented this way about Barry's scholarship: "He is more of an historian than
a social scientist. He is likely to get rather thoroughly acquainted with his
material before he decides what questions it can be used to answer." His answers, when they came, were very hard to quarrel with.

Barry believed fervently in what he and the rest of the faculty were
doing here. As baby-boomers began to hit the campuses around 1960, and

state university systems, community colleges, and advanced-placement programs expanded to meet the boomers' needs, many wondered how schools like Oberlin would fare in the new academic environment. Barry confessed no doubts. "Our task," he wrote for the *Oberlin Review,* "is imparting an education of high quality to a comparatively small number. Obviously this is expensive. The question is whether it is worth it. My answer is 'Yes. Now more than ever.'"

Barry was not always sure that the people in Cox administration building toed the line with the faculty in this ongoing educational crisis. Like most faculty members of his vintage, he was a stern defender of the Finney Compact, and when he thought that presidents and trustees were not living up to the compact, he said so. From the back bench in open faculty meeting he once instructed President Carr to reflect on the words of political philosopher Edmund Burke: "It is not what a lawyer tells me I may do, but what justice tells me I ought to do." As one of the youngsters on the faculty at the time, I recall that thrusts like that intimidated even some of us.

Barry served as history department chair from 1966 to 1969 and again in 1986, and for years he was a regular on the educational plans and policies committee, always precise, generally diplomatic. But this sort of work did not arouse him very much. What he enjoyed most, I believe, was explaining to students what they did not yet know about the past, and making sure the explanations stuck. His teaching was rigorous and demanding. It was also very traditional. It had to do mostly with the politics of nations—prime ministers and chancellors, elections, legislation, diplomacy and war. Midway through his career, the new social history arrived in force, and Barry discovered, along with many other teachers in the field, that what he thought were the most important questions to answer about the past were no longer being widely asked. One of Barry's students acknowledged in a course evaluation that his lectures about Britain and the nations of the European continent were arresting and provocative, but added, "I'd like to know more about those countries not busy initiating wars or being conquered. What was everybody else doing?"

"What was everybody else doing?" Barry and fellow historians of his vintage everywhere were destined to spend the rest of their careers doctoring their lectures to answer that question. But he never lost the stubborn belief that what people like the great wartime leader Winston Churchill did mattered more than what most other folks in the world were doing. Churchill's life was the subject of the last new course that Barry put together and taught across the 1980s.

I suspect that no one on the Oberlin faculty today handles the classroom and its occupants quite the way he did. That way might not be possible anymore. In any event, through no fault of their own, today's college students, including the history majors, are unlikely to have heard very much about Barry McGill. For a long generation of Oberlin alumni, he remains unforgettable.

CHAPTER 32

A Liberal Education:
How It Can Work (1999)

*A*t the risk of juggling an old chestnut, I want to consider what a liberal education might be about.[1] In most discussions of the educational process that I've read or heard, the stress lies on teaching and teaching methodology—team teaching, computerized teaching, lecture versus discussion, circling chairs, the sage on the stage giving way to guide on the side. (At Oberlin we don't have to worry about the hack in the back.)

I think that in searching for the essence of a first-rate college education, we should pay more attention to how people learn rather than how they are taught. The tactics of the teacher may be less controlling than we sometimes like to think. Opinions vary as to whether our initial aim should be to shake up or to stroke the preconceptions that our students bring to class. Since I teach American history, a subject that American schoolchildren absorb repeatedly from about third grade on, I am inclined to believe that by the time they enter college most of them are ready to be shaken up. Year after year after year, they have, for example, watched victory in the American Revolution lead inexorably to flaws in the Articles of Confederation which send the Founding Fathers packing for Philadelphia to write the Federal Constitution. You can't change the chronology, but you can raise some fresh doubts about the reasons why.

What is crucial is to somehow ignite (or reignite) in a student's mind the passion of curiosity—to convey a belief in the integrity and urgency of your subject, whatever it may be, and try to inspire a hungry love for it that will never be completely satisfied.

After that, the best part of the learning process comes when you realize as a teacher that you are losing control. In the end a liberal education is an unplanned experience. It is what happens when a curious young mind gathers the messy flux of three or four rival subjects taught in rival classrooms each semester and begins to make connections, connections often unknown to any of the student's teachers. We remain unaware of these connections unless the student tells us about them, because the student has been there, listened to those other teachers, and we have not. We know these other teachers as friends and colleagues, but we really don't know what they teach because with rare exceptions we have never been there. For each of us it is a different configuration of colleagues, depending on our specialty. In my case, to offer an arbitrary short list, it might be Harlan Wilson in political theory, Norm Care in philosophy, Pat Mathews in art history, and Dewey Ganzel or Scott McMillin in American literature. Unknown to us all, our students are mixing our particular ideas with their own priorities and patching together new designs, designs that are, again, uncontrolled and unpredictable, because they are the student's personal creation. This is interdisciplinary learning at its most rewarding.

Every spring a number of students will tell me over the water cooler after class or in the Mudd stacks or during office hours that it's happening to them, and that it is a kick. Their personal paradigm is coming into focus. And it is a kick for me as well, because I can still remember when it first happened to me at Oberlin, and again in graduate school several years running. These were temporary paradigms, victories of momentary intellectual assurance about the way the world really worked, before the next flux, the next wave of learning poured in. But they were wonderful while they lasted. And since my professors had no idea what they were all about—we did not chat so much with them over water coolers in those days—pondering them brought a valuable sense of academic autonomy and personal control. I imagine that every student here today has been moved by this experience in one form or another. It may be the best thing that can happen to you in this place.

A lot of you have just finished senior honors projects. I was recently the second reader on a thesis in American political history, in which the author—senior Jason Sokol—summed up the meaning of the honors experience this way:

> Admittedly, I am still very much drawn by visions, by ideals, by dreams of a better tomorrow. . . . Most likely, my work will not be read by more than a handful of people. But it has importance for me as I begin my career, a journey that I am sure will be filled by more time in the academy. I see myself as no great altruist, but the way that I have written is very much linked with what I believe about the world, and where my place in it may be.

Each of you could write your own version of this statement. It is a very personal statement, but it also speaks for this college in its peculiar mix of driving scholarly ambition and stubborn moral idealism—testimony to the survival of the two Oberlins, the college of reformist activism and the college of academic excellence. As teachers we can admire this evidence and respectfully applaud it, sometimes wondering exactly what we had to do with it.

CHAPTER 33

Reflections upon Retirement (2000)

*T*his has been a long and wonderful evening—long for you, wonderful for me.[1] I will make it a little longer by saying something about two topics: one, what it's been like to do history at Oberlin, and two, what it's been like just to *be* at Oberlin.

After forty years of it, I've concluded that teaching history is pretty complex, and doing history is pretty simple. Teaching history, at Oberlin at least, is pretty complex because it involves saying a lot of unexpected things in class to combat the assumption that what students need to know is what they want to know ahead of time. You have to keep wedging in unwanted ideas and force people to try them out. That's complex business. On the other hand, I've come to think that *doing* history is pretty simple. At least the rules are simple. There are six of them. I learned the first rule from Robert Fletcher here at Oberlin back in the 1950s. It sounds like a cliché: history is storytelling. After forty years the art of writing narrative remains enjoyable, and it has even gained some respectability among university scholars in recent years. The second rule I learned from Samuel Eliot Morison at Harvard. It is that history is everywhere, in low places as well as high places, located centuries ago and also yesterday. Nothing is too mundane or too close for the historian's curiosity. The third rule comes from the

English historian Sir Lewis Namier. It is that the historian's most important task for starters is to find out who the guys were. Most important political history has to do with group analysis. The first job in group analysis
is to find out who the guys were. (Women included: "Are you guys ready to
order?") The fourth rule I learned from Sam Hays, who teaches history at
the University of Pittsburgh. Sam always said that to define a group, the
trick was not simply to discover what its members all believed in but also
who they opposed. The surest way to figure out a group's motivational cohesion is to identify its relevant enemies. The next rule I learned from my
younger colleague Clayton Koppes. It is that the job is never over until you
have found out which guys have the power, and why. Since Clayton isn't
here to defend himself, I'll simply say that he taught me to keep an eye
peeled for power, and the subtle ways that people set about acquiring it.
And the sixth and final rule I learned from another graduate-school mentor, Arthur Schlesinger, Jr. His rule, which he practices more by example
than exhortation, is that when you finally get it the way you want it, if you
have opinions about it all, feel free to express them. So those are the six simple rules for doing history: to tell a story, remember that the stories can be
found everywhere, that you need to find out who the guys were and who
their relevant enemies were, who had the power, how they got it and what
they did with it, and finally run the happy risk of saying what you think of
it all. Digging out the answers was a kick, and writing them up was enjoyable (though that part gets harder), and seeing it in print does wonders for
the ego. And best of all, doing it made you a better teacher, which is the really complex part. I believe that.

The main thing I wanted to say this evening is that I think I have been
very lucky—that my whole age group on the faculty has been lucky, right
from the beginning. And since we are retiring left and right these days, I
thought this would be a good chance to say something about us all, in defiance of rule four about relevant enemies. We were Depression kids who
remembered its lessons, and enjoyed glazing the eyes of our children—and
sometimes our students—by talking about them; we listened to World War II
on the radio; we grew up to become children of the fifties without worry-
ing about the stigma the fifties would bear; we went to the colleges of our
choice, more or less, after applying to maybe two or three of them; if we saw
military service, it was mostly nonviolent; we married young, which meant

our wives could work hard to get us through graduate school; we hit the job market at just the right time—the beginning of the baby boom—to meet a sudden big demand and so land jobs we really wanted; we came here to work at a college we believed was just about the best college in the country; and we had a great batch of senior colleagues who knew how to bring us along. Most of them are gone now: Ben Lewis and J. D. Lewis, Luke Steiner, Don Love, Andrew Bongiorno, Clyde Holbrook, George Simpson, Bob Tufts, David Anderson, Chester Shaver, Ells Carlson. The list could go on. As I rattle off their names, yet another old mentor comes to mind, the guy who as chair of the history department hired me, and hired my friend and classmate Bob Neil as well, back in 1960. He's pushing ninety now, and he's here tonight: Tom LeDuc. With the *possible* exception of Azariah Root, no one has made a more important contribution to the quality of the American history collection in Mudd Library than Tom LeDuc.

Back to the theme of our generational good luck back in the 1960s: our salaries were pretty good for starters and rose faster than we expected; we got to teach what we really wanted to teach sooner than expected; we got tenure in the mail after four years, which we took as a signal it was time to buy a house; we got to know each other and our wives very well, we knew each others' kids, we knew each others' favorite potluck dishes, and we knew which of us could play the piano or guitar, and which of us could carry a tune and remember the words. Meanwhile we thought we were doing the college a favor by helping to run this place; we thought that was an important part of our job, especially across the rough years of the late 1960s and early 1970s. More generally we thought we were *needed*, which was an extremely valuable thing to believe about yourself. So we stuck around, and we're glad we did. In all this I think we were lucky. As things begin to wind down, I feel very lucky. So thanks to everyone here. Every one of you has helped in some way to make it possible, and enjoyable. It's been great to spend time together, tonight and over the years.

$\mathcal{N}otes$

1. Myth and Reality in Oberlin History (1971)

1. Reprinted with changes from the *Oberlin Alumni Magazine*, May–June 1972. The *OAM* article is based on a talk Professor Blodgett gave at Baldwin Cottage residence hall in November 1971.

2. James Schouler, *History of the United States of America under the Constitution*, vol. 4 (Washington, DC: W. H. and O. H. Morrison, 1889), 313.

3. "The Joint Education of the Sexes," *Oberlin Evangelist*, June 7, 1854, p. 94.

4. Benjamin Woodbury to John J. Shipherd, March 24, 1835, Treasurer's Office files, Box 1, Oberlin College Archives.

5. William Bigglestone, "Oberlin College and the Negro Student, 1865–1940," *Journal of Negro History* 56 (July 1971): 198–210.

2. Asa Mahan at Oberlin: The Pitfalls of Perfection (1984)

1. Reprinted with changes from the *Oberlin Alumni Magazine*, spring 1984. The *OAM* article is excerpted from a talk Professor Blodgett gave at Adrian College in January 1984.

2. This portrait, now hanging in Mudd Library, was acquired for the college through the enterprise and generosity of historians Richard DuPuis and Marlene Merrill, college librarian William Moffett, and several anonymous donors.

3. Robert S. Fletcher, *A History of Oberlin College* (Oberlin, OH: Oberlin College, 1943), 110.

4. Silvan Tomkins, "The Psychology of Commitment: The Constructive Role of Violence and Suffering for the Individual and His Society," in Martin Duberman, ed., *The Antislavery Vanguard: New Essays on the Abolitionists* (Princeton, NJ: Princeton University Press, 1965), 270–98.

5. Nathaniel Hawthorne, *The Blithedale Romance* [1852], Norton Library Edition (New York: W. W. Norton, 1958), 92–93.

6. These issues are earnestly explored in Edward H. Madden and James E. Hamilton, *Freedom and Grace: The Life of Asa Mahan* (Metuchen, NJ: Scarecrow Press, 1982), Ch. 4.

7. Fletcher, *History of Oberlin College,* 234–35.

8. Prudential Committee Minutes, April 24, 1840, Oberlin College Archives.

3. Father Finney's Church (1997)

1. This article originally appeared in the January–February 1997 issue of *Timeline,* a publication of the Ohio Historical Society. It is reprinted, with changes, by permission of the Ohio Historical Society.

2. Joseph P. Thompson, *The Last Sabbath in the Broadway Tabernacle: A Historical Discourse* (New York: Calkins and Stiles, 1857), 13; L. Nelson Nichols, *History of the Broadway Tabernacle of New York City* (New Haven: Tuttle, Morehouse and Taylor, 1940), 58–61; Charles G. Finney, *Memoirs of Charles G. Finney* (New York: A. S. Barnes & Co., 1876), 326.

3. Delavan Leonard, "Early Annals of the Oberlin Church," reprint from *Ohio Church History Society Papers,* Vol. 8, 103.

4. Prudential Committee Minutes, April 24, 1840; Charles G. Finney to Henry Cowles, December 23, 1841, Cowles Papers, Oberlin College Archives. Bond's original plans for First Church are also in the Oberlin College Archives. Biographical information on Bond is sparse. See Henry F. Withey and Elsie Withey, *Biographical Dictionary of American Architects (Deceased)* (Los Angeles, 1970), 65. Fletcher, *History,* 573, unaccountably attributes the design of the church to "an architect named Lodge."

5. Oberlin Society Minutes, March 2, 1842, Oberlin College Archives.

6. *Lorain County News,* December 28, 1871.

7. Oberlin Society Minutes, October 21, 1842 and October 24, 1842, Oberlin College Archives; *Lorain County News,* June 19, 1873.

8. Mary Rudd Cochran to Geoffrey Blodgett, February 12, 1972; in Jane Blodgett's possession.

9. Oberlin Society Minutes, August 2 and August 12, 1842, Oberlin College Archives.

10. Oberlin Society Minutes, August 19 and September 9, 1842, Oberlin College Archives.

11. Leonard, "Early Annals," 106, n. 2.

12. Oberlin Society Minutes, March 13, 1848, September 10, 1850, and September 13, 1852, Oberlin College Archives.

13. *Lorain County News,* June 17, 1868, and *Oberlin News,* March 18, 1875; Alfred Vance Churchill, "Midwestern: Early Oberlin Personalities," *Northwest Ohio Quarterly,* 23, 4 (Autumn 1951): 214–16.

4. Finney's Oberlin (1975)

1. Reprinted with changes from the *Oberlin Alumni Magazine,* March–April 1976. The *OAM* article is based on an October 1975 lecture, part of the Mead-Swing series commemorating the hundredth anniversary of Finney's death.

2. Robert M. Pirsig, *Zen and the Art of Motorcycle Maintenance: An Inquiry into Values* (New York: HarperCollins, 1974), 146–54.

3. Arthur S. Link, ed., *The Papers of Woodrow Wilson* (Princeton, NJ: Princeton University Press, 1970), Vol. 9, 257.

4. Garth Rosell and Richard Depuis, eds., *The Memoirs of Charles G. Finney: The Complete Restored Text* (Grand Rapids, MI: Zondervan, 1989), 386.

5. John Kouwenhoven, *Made in America: The Arts in Modern Civilization* (Garden City, NY: Doubleday, 1962), 50; Sigfried Giedion, *Space, Time and Architecture,* 5th ed. (Cambridge, MA: Harvard University Press, 1967), 350; James Marston Fitch, *American Building: The Historical Forces that Shaped It,* 2nd ed. (New York: Schocken Books, 1966), 37–38, 50; Carl Condit, *American Building: Materials and Techniques from the First Colonial Settlements to the Present* (Chicago: University of Chicago Press, 1968), 41, 44.

6. Robert S. Fletcher, *A History of Oberlin College from Its Foundation Through the Civil War* (Oberlin, OH: Oberlin College, 1943), 81–84.

7. The full text of the covenant appears in James H. Fairchild, *Oberlin: The Colony and the College, 1833–1883* (Oberlin, OH: Goodrich, 1883), 25–27.

8. Delavan Leonard, *The Story of Oberlin* (Boston: Pilgrim Press, 1898), 89.

9. Leonard, *The Story of Oberlin,* 88; Fletcher, *A History of Oberlin College,* 115; Wilbur Phillips, *Oberlin Colony: The Story of a Century* (Oberlin, OH: author, 1933), 62–63.

10. Prudential Committee Minutes, June 13, 1840 and October 3, 1843, Oberlin College Archives.

11. Charles G. Finney to Henry Cowles, December 31, 1841. Cowles Papers, Oberlin College Archives.

12. Phillips, *Oberlin Colony,* 22.

13. Leonard, *The Story of Oberlin,* 27; *History of Lorain County, Ohio* (Philadelphia: Williams Brothers, 1879), 189; Albert Temple Swing, *James Harris Fairchild* (New York: Fleming H. Revell, 1907), 46.

14. Leonard, *The Story of Oberlin,* 434.

15. Leonard, *The Story of Oberlin,* 435–36. See also Prudential Committee Minutes, June 30, 1842, Oberlin College Archives.

16. Robert Fletcher, "The Meeting House," pamphlet published by the First Church in Oberlin [n.d.], 2.

17. John Mercer Langston, *From the Virginia Plantation to the National Capitol* (Hartford, CT: American Publishing Company, 1894), 157–59. For a thoroughly detailed survey of Oberlin's nineteenth-century African American population, see William Bigglestone, *They Stopped in Oberlin: Black Residents and Visitors of the Nineteenth Century* (Oberlin, OH: private printing, 1981).

18. The best discussions of balloon framing are in the works cited in note 5.

19. *Lorain County News,* May 9, 1866.

20. *Lorain County News,* December 12, 1866.

21. Kouwenhoven, *Made in America,* 51; Calvert Vaux, *Villas and Cottages* (New York: Harper Brothers, 1864), 48, 70.

22. Oberlin Society Minutes, 1841–1856, Oberlin College Archives. *Williams' Oberlin Directory for 1859–60* was the earliest village directory. The next one issued, *Camp's Oberlin Directory, 1873–74,* includes a useful summary of the town's business history.

23. Information about local personal incomes was published in the *Lorain County News,* September 13, 1865, and July 25, 1866.

24.　A clue to Straus's success as a clothier and dry-goods merchant may be found in the following notice, which he placed in the Oberlin newspaper: "Having relatives doing business in New York, who I have empowered to purchase goods for me when they can be bought cheap, I am enabled to sell a great many goods cheaper than they can be bought at wholesale in the season." *Lorain County News,* September 21, 1871.

25.　*Lorain County News,* December 26, 1866.

26.　*Oberlin Weekly News,* October 3, 1884. James H. Fairchild explained: "The early inhabitants of Oberlin, those who came as colonists, were New Englanders immediately or remotely, and hence were members of the Whig party. There was probably no exception to this rule. The Whig party, as they knew it, was the party of order and progress and intelligence, and they felt it almost as necessary to be Whigs as to be Christians." Fairchild went on to say that the Liberty party ticket of 1840 and 1844 and the Free Soil ticket of 1848 won Oberlin majorities, and that in 1856 the town became solidly Republican. Fairchild, *Oberlin,* 109–11.

27.　*Lorain County News,* August 31, 1871.

28.　*Lorain County News,* May 23, 1869 and August 29, 1866.

29.　*Lorain County News,* August 25, 1870.

30.　Delavan Leonard, "Early Annals of the Oberlin Church," reprint from *Ohio Church History Society Papers,* Vol. 8, 94.

31.　George Frederick Wright, *Charles Grandison Finney* (Boston: Houghton-Mifflin, 1891), 285.

32.　Mary Eleanor Barnes, *John Henry Barrows: A Memoir* (Chicago, 1904), 422. See the sketch of Finney in Alfred Vance Churchill, "Midwestern: Early Oberlin Personalities," *Northwest Ohio Quarterly,* 23, 4 (Autumn 1951): 224–37.

33.　Sermon outline, July 3, 1870, Finney Papers, Oberlin College Archives. See also the report of the sermon in *Lorain County News,* July 7, 1870.

34.　Churchill, "Midwestern," 234–35.

5. Oberlin and Harpers Ferry (1972)

1.　Remarks at the dedication in Martin Luther King Park, Pleasant and Vine Streets, of the monument to John Brown's Oberlin followers on October 15, 1972.

2.　Stephen B. Oates, *To Purge This Land with Blood: A Biography of John Brown* (New York: Harper & Row, 1970), 289.

3.　An original manuscript copy of this letter is in the Autograph File, Record Group 16, Oberlin College Archives. See Robert S. Fletcher, "John Brown and Oberlin," *Oberlin Alumni Magazine,* 28, 5 (February 1932): 135–41.

6. Oberlin Starts the Civil War (1990)

1.　Reprinted with changes from the *Oberlin Alumni Magazine,* Summer 1990.

2.　Nat Brandt, *The Town That Started the Civil War* (Syracuse, NY: Syracuse University Press, 1990)

3.　The Rescue Monument, designed by Oberlin art professor Paul Arnold and constructed by Oberlin brick mason Burrell Scott, was completed in the spring of 1990. The monument includes a reproduction of the photograph taken of the Rescuers standing in the jailyard of the Cuyahoga County Jail in Cleveland. The inscription, written by

Geoffrey Blodgett, reads, "In the spring of 1859 twenty Oberlinians went to jail for the crime of rescuing John Price from slavery. With their comrades in the abolition cause, they kindled hopes of freedom for us all."

7. Spiced Wine: An Oberlin Scandal of 1862 (1968)

1. Reprinted with changes from *Oberlin Alumni Magazine,* February 1970. An earlier version appeared in the *Journal of Negro History,* July 1968.

2. *The Athenaeum* (London, March 3, 1866), 302; *National Cyclopedia of American Biography* (New York: James T. White and Co., 1907), Vol. V, 173.

3. James H. Fairchild, "John Keep," *History of Lorain County, Ohio* (Philadelphia, 1879), 192–196.

4. Robert S. Fletcher, *A History of Oberlin College from Its Foundation Through the Civil War* (Oberlin, OH: Oberlin College, 1943), Vol. II, 523–536.

5. *Lorain County News,* September 25, 1860.

6. *Oberlin Evangelist,* February 12, 1862.

7. *Cleveland Plain Dealer,* February 11, 1862; *Cleveland Morning Leader,* March 3, 1862; John M. Langston, *From the Virginia Plantation to the National Capitol* (Hartford, CT: American Publishing Co., 1894), 171–74.

8. Langston, *From the Virginia Plantation,* 174–75.

9. *Lorain County News,* February 19, 1862; Langston, *From the Virginia Plantation,* 176–77; Diary of Fannie Maria White, entry for January 31, 1862, Oberlin College Archives.

10. James H. Fairchild, *Oberlin: Its Origins, Progress and Results: An Address Prepared for the Alumni of Oberlin College, Assembled August 22, 1860* (Oberlin, OH, 1869), 27; *Cleveland Plain Dealer,* January 29, 1862, February 1, 1862, February 10, 1862.

11. *Cleveland Plain Dealer,* February 11, 1862.

12. Fletcher, *History of Oberlin College,* Vol. I, 408, and Vol. II, 691–92; *History of Lorain County, Ohio,* 64–65.

13. *Lorain County News,* February 19, 1862.

14. Langston, *From the Virginia Plantation to Capitol,* 11–17, 77–125. See also the excellent recent biography, William and Aimee Lee Cheek, *John Mercer Langston and the Fight for Black Freedom, 1829–1865* (Urbana, IL: University of Illinois Press, 1989), *passim.*

15. Langston, *From the Virginia Plantation,* 157–63; Frank U. Quillin, *The Color Line in Ohio* (Ann Arbor, MI: George Wahr, 1913), 88.

16. *Lorain County News,* June 13, 1860; C. F. Cox to J. D. Cox, July 22, 1865, Jacob Dolson Cox Papers, Oberlin College Archives.

17. Langston, *From the Virginia Plantation,* 175–176.

18. *Cleveland Morning Leader,* March 3, 1862; *Elyria Independent Democrat,* March 5, 1962.

19. *Cleveland Morning Leader,* March 3, 1862.

20. E. L. Newcomb *et al.,* eds., *Kramer's Scientific and Applied Pharmacognosy,* 3rd edition (New York, 1928), 833; H. S. Denniger, "A History of Substances Known as Aphrodisiac," *Annals of Medical History* (New Series), II: 383–91.

21. Langston, *Plantation to Capitol,* 179.

22. Langston, *Plantation to Capitol,* 178–79; *Cleveland Morning Leader,* March 3, 1862.

23. *Cleveland Plain Dealer,* March 3, 1862.

24. *Lorain County News,* March 12, 1862.
25. *Lorain County News,* March 28, 1866 and April 4, 1866.
26. James A. Porter, *Modern Negro Art* (New York: Dryden Press, 1943), 57–63. Recent years have witnessed a revival of interest in Lewis's career. See Arna A. Bontemps, ed., *Forever Free: Art by African-American Women, 1862–1980* (Alexandria, VA: Stephenson, 1980), 13–15, 98, 190–92.
27. *Oberlin News,* November 26, 1897.
28. Fletcher, *History of Oberlin College,* 533; Porter, *Modern Negro Art,* 57–63, 171–72, 177.

8. Warfare between Science and Religion (1999)

1. Reprinted with changes from the *Oberlin Alumni Magazine,* March 1999.
2. Alfred Vance Churchill, "Midwestern: Professor Charles Henry Churchill of Oberlin," *Northwest Ohio Quarterly,* 24, 3 (Summer 1952): 150.

9. Oberlin College Architecture: A Short History (1992)

1. The *Oberlin Alumni Magazine* published "Oberlin College Architecture: A Historian's Assessment" in May/June 1978; the college published the article as a brochure in 1979 and as an updated, expanded booklet in 1992.

10. President King and Cass Gilbert: The Grand Collaboration (1982)

1. Reprinted with changes from the *Oberlin Alumni Magazine,* Winter 1983. The *OAM* article uses evidence mainly drawn from the Oberlin College Archives, Cass Gilbert's personal papers in the Library of Congress, and the Cass Gilbert office papers in the New York Historical Society. It first appeared in a slightly different form as two articles in the *Oberlin College Observer* (February 4 and 18, 1982).
2. Cass Gilbert to G. B. Rose, October 4, 1933, Cass Gilbert Papers, Manuscript Collections, Library of Congress.

11. Saving Peters Hall (1997)

1. Reprinted with changes from the *Oberlin Alumni Magazine,* Fall 1997. The *OAM* article, "The Meaning of Peters Hall," was taken from Professor Blodgett's talk at the rededication of Peters on October 11, 1997.

12. A Century of Football, 1891–1991 (1991)

1. Reprinted with changes from the *Oberlin Review,* October 4, 1991.

13. The Day Oberlin Beat Michigan—or Did We? (1999)

1. Reprinted with changes from the *Oberlin Alumni Magazine,* Winter 1999.

14. Tobacco at Oberlin: A Backward Glance at Moral Reform (1999)

1. Reprinted with changes from the *Oberlin Alumni Magazine,* May 1999.

15. Professor Geiser's Heresies (1992)

1. Talk given to the Lorain County Historical Society, April 23, 1992.

16. Campus Life at Oberlin, 1930–1945 (1998)

1. Reprinted with changes from the *Oberlin Alumni Magazine,* Winter 1998.

17. Oberlin and the G.I. Bill: Forty Years Later (1987)

1. Reprinted with changes from the *Oberlin Alumni Magazine,* Spring 1987.

18. Observations on Governance at Oberlin: Another Look at Its History (1992)

1. Reprinted with changes from the *Oberlin College Observer,* October 29, 1992, where the article appeared alongside a companion article by honorary trustee Erwin N. Griswold '25, hon. '82. Griswold (1904–1994) was an active trustee from 1936 to 1980. He was dean of the Harvard Law School from 1946 to 1967 and solicitor general of the United States from 1967 to 1973.

19. Memorial Minute for Ellsworth Carlson (2000)

1. Reprinted with changes from the *Oberlin Alumni Magazine,* Summer 2000. The memorial minute was adopted by the general faculty of Oberlin College March 21, 2000.

20. An Apology for the 1950s (1982)

1. Reprinted with changes from the *Oberlin Alumni Magazine,* Spring 1982.

21. Memorial Minute for William E. Stevenson (1986)

1. This memorial minute was adopted by the general faculty of Oberlin College February 25, 1986.

22. Student Opinion at Oberlin, 1936–1976: A Report for the Bicentennial (1976)

1. Reprinted with changes from the *Oberlin Alumni Magazine,* May–June 1976.

23. Spreading the Calm (1984)

1. Reprinted with changes from the *Oberlin Alumni Magazine,* Summer 1984. Professor Blodgett read this essay while Longsworth was chairing his last meeting of the College of Arts and Sciences faculty.

24. College and Commitment: A Glance at the Past (1969)

1. *Author's note, ca. 1988:* This essay first appeared as a prologue to a collection of statements and position papers published by the college in February 1969 titled *The*

College and the War. It was written in the stormy context of protest against the Vietnam War, which crested at Oberlin as elsewhere between 1968 and 1970. Many campus opponents of the war wanted the college to make an institutional commitment against the war. Others, while also opposing the war, believed that such an institutional stance might jeopardize the role of the college as a sanctuary for academic freedom and political dissent. My essay tries to provide a historical backdrop to inform this debate.

2. For an earlier overview of the issues involved, see Kemper Fullerton, "Oberlin, College or Cause?" in *Essays and Sketches* (New Haven, CT: Yale University Press, 1938), 143–65.

3. Charles C. Cole, Jr., *The Social Ideas of Northern Evangelists, 1826–1860* (New York: Columbia University Press, 1954), 206; Robert Fletcher, *A History of Oberlin College from Its Foundations through the Civil War* (Oberlin, OH: Oberlin College, 1943), Vol. I, 265–70; Edward Madden, *Civil Disobedience and the Moral Law in Nineteenth Century American Philosophy* (Seattle, WA: University of Washington Press, 1968), 70–82.

4. Fletcher, *History,* Vol. I, 401–13; Wilbur H. Phillips, *Oberlin Colony: The Story of a Century* (Oberlin, OH: author, 1933), 113.

5. This view is modified by John Barnard, *From Evangelicalism to Progressivism at Oberlin College, 1866–1917* (Columbus, OH: Ohio State University Press, 1969).

6. Peter Odegard, *Pressure Politics: The Story of the Anti-Saloon League* (New York: Columbia University Press, 1928), 1–4.

7. *Oberlin Review,* June 7, 1893.

8. *Oberlin Alumni Magazine,* 2, 2 (November 1905), 55–56.

9. College Faculty Meeting Minutes, April 2, 1918, Oberlin College Archives.

10. *Oberlin News,* September 2, 1908 and September 9, 1908.

11. William E. Bigglestone, "Oberlin College and the Negro, 1865–1940," *Journal of Negro History,* 56, 3 (July 1971): 203–205.

12. The President's Report, Oberlin College, 1919–1920, 41.

13. Henry Churchill King to Mary Church Terrell, February 4, 1914, King Papers; Oberlin College Archives.

14. Bigglestone, "Oberlin College and the Negro," 213–215.

15. Ellsworth Carlson, *Oberlin in Asia: The First Hundred Years, 1882–1982* (Oberlin, OH: Oberlin Shansi Memorial Association, 1982), is a fine concise history.

16. General Faculty Meeting Minutes, April 5, 1917 and April 17, 1917; Henry Churchill King to Dan Bradley, April 14, 1917, King Papers, Oberlin College Archives.

17. General Faculty Meeting Minutes, September 20, 1918; Todd Endo, "Oberlin College and World War I," History seminar paper, Oberlin College, 1963, 14.

18. Endo, "Oberlin College and World War I," 6, 8, 13, 18, 20–25.

19. Endo, "Oberlin College and World War I," 21.

20. General Council Minutes, June 10, 1919, Oberlin College Archives. Geiser's Oberlin career is discussed in closer detail in Chapter 15.

21. College Faculty Meeting Minutes, October 19, 1920 and December 7, 1920, Oberlin College Archives.

22. General Faculty Meeting Minutes, December 14, 1920, Oberlin College Archives; *Oberlin Review,* December 17, 1920.

23. General Faculty Meeting Minutes, January 11, 1921; Henry Churchill King to Joseph Tumulty, December 21, 1920, Oberlin College Archives; William Preston, *Aliens*

and Dissenters: Federal Suppression of Radicals, 1903–1933 (New York: Harper, 1966), 139–40, 258–266.

24. General Faculty Meeting Minutes, December 5, 1922, Oberlin College Archives.

25. Charles Sowerwine, "Oberlin Responds to the Depression," History seminar paper, Oberlin College, 1965, 4–6; Ann Richards, "Pacifism in Oberlin in the 1930s," History seminar paper, Oberlin College, 1965, *passim.*

26. Alice Stone Blackwell Diary, August 25, 1933 and August 26, 1934, Blackwell Papers, Manuscripts Division, Library of Congress.

27. Sowerwine, "Oberlin Responds to the Depression," 9–10.

28. General Faculty Meeting Minutes, March 6, 1934, April 17, 1934, and June 12, 1934, Oberlin College Archives; Sowerwine, "Oberlin Responds to the Depression," *Nation,* March 28, 1934 and April 11, 1934, 19

29. General Faculty Meetings Minutes, December 1, 1938, Oberlin College Archives.

30. General Faculty Meetings Minutes, December 8, 1941, Oberlin College Archives.

31. General Faculty Meetings Minutes, January 18, 1949 and January 25, 1949, Oberlin College Archives.

32. General Faculty Meetings Minutes, October 17, 1950 and November 7, 1950, Oberlin College Archives.

33. General Faculty Meetings Minutes, February 8, 1951 and February 13, 1951, Oberlin College Archives.

34. General Faculty Meetings Minutes, October 10, 1950, Oberlin College Archives.

35. General Faculty Meetings Minutes, February 12, 1952, Oberlin College Archives.

36. *Oberlin Review,* April 28, 1953.

37. J. B. Matthews, "Communism and the College," *American Mercury* (May 1953): 122, 124.

38. The President's Report, Oberlin College, 1962–1963, 18.

39. The President's Report, Oberlin College, 1965–1966, 16–18.

25. The Oberlin Mock-Convention Tradition (1992)

1. Reprinted with changes from the *Oberlin Alumni Magazine,* Fall 1992.

26. Recollection of the 1960s—and Beyond (1992)

1. This essay is published here for the first time.

27. Oberlin and the Kent State Murders (1998)

1. Reprinted with changes from the *Oberlin Alumni Magazine* (Fall 1998).

28. He Held His Ground: Memorial Minute for Robert K. Carr (1979)

1. Reprinted with changes from the *Oberlin Alumni Magazine,* Spring 1979. The memorial minute was adopted by the general faculty of Oberlin College on April 17, 1979.

29. The Grand March of Oberlin Campus Plans (1995)

1. Reprinted with changes from the *Oberlin College Observer,* May 11, 1995. Professor Blodgett adapted the *Observer* article from a presentation he made to a faculty planning subcommittee.

30. Memorial Minute for Robert E. Neil (1991)

1. This memorial minute was adopted by the general faculty of Oberlin College on March 19, 1991. A shortened version appeared in the *Oberlin Alumni Magazine,* Summer 1991.

31. Memorial Minute for Barry McGill (1997)

1. Reprinted with changes from the *Oberlin Alumni Magazine,* Spring 1997. The memorial minute was adopted by the general faculty of Oberlin College on February 18, 1997.

32. A Liberal Education: How It Can Work (1999)

1. Reprinted with changes from the *Oberlin Alumni Magazine,* August 1999. The *OAM* article was taken from Professor Blodgett's Honors Day talk given in May 1999.

33. Reflections upon Retirement (2000)

1. Professor Blodgett made these remarks at his retirement dinner on April 15, 2000.